The Cambridge Companion to
Public Law

The Cambridge Companion to Public Law examines key themes, debates
and issues in contemporary public law. The book identifies and
draws out five key themes: the notions of government and the state; the
place of the state and public law in the world at large; relationships
between institutions and officials within the state; the legitimacy of
institutions; and the identity and value of public law in relation to
politics. The book also presents a contemporary examination, taking
account of the substantial changes witnessed in this area in recent
decades and of the resulting need to reassess orthodox accounts of the
subject. Written by leading authorities in the common law world, their
approach is rigorous, engaging and highly accessible. This Companion
acts as both a thoughtful introduction and a collection that consciously
moves the discipline forward.

Mark Elliott is Professor of Public Law at the University of Cambridge
and a Fellow of St Catharine's College.

David Feldman is Rouse Ball Professor of English Law at the University
of Cambridge and a Fellow of Downing College, Cambridge.

Cambridge Companions to Law

Cambridge Companions to Law offers thought-provoking introductions to different legal disciplines, invaluable to both the student and the scholar. Edited by world-leading academics, each offers a collection of essays which both map out the subject and allow the reader to delve deeper. Critical and enlightening, the Companions library represents legal scholarship at its best.

The Cambridge Companion to European Private Law
Edited by Christian Twigg-Flesner

The Cambridge Companion to International Law
Edited by James Crawford and Martti Koskenniemi

The Cambridge Companion to Comparative Law
Edited by Mauro Bussani and Ugo Mattei

The Cambridge Companion to Human Rights Law
Edited by Conor Gearty and Costas Douzinas

The Cambridge Companion to Public Law
Edited by Mark Elliott and David Feldman

The Cambridge Companion to
Public Law

Edited by

Mark Elliott and David Feldman

CAMBRIDGE
UNIVERSITY PRESS

CAMBRIDGE
UNIVERSITY PRESS

University Printing House, Cambridge CB2 8BS, United Kingdom

Cambridge University Press is part of the University of Cambridge.

It furthers the University's mission by disseminating knowledge in the pursuit of education, learning and research at the highest international levels of excellence.

www.cambridge.org
Information on this title: www.cambridge.org/9781107655096

© Cambridge University Press 2015

First published 2015

Printing in the United Kingdom by TJ International Ltd. Padstow Cornwall

A catalogue record for this publication is available from the British Library

Library of Congress Cataloguing in Publication data
The Cambridge companion to public law / edited by Mark Elliott, David Feldman.
    pages   cm. –
(Cambridge companions to law)
ISBN 978-1-107-02975-0 (hardback)
1. Public law – England – History.   2. Civil rights – England – History.
3. Common law – England – History.   I. Elliott, Mark,
1975– editor.   II. Feldman, David, 1953– editor.
KD3930.C36   2015
342.42–dc23

                                                              2015005590

ISBN 978-1-107-02975-0 Hardback
ISBN 978-1-107-65509-6 Paperback

Cambridge University Press has no responsibility for the persistence or accuracy of URLs for external or third-party internet websites referred to in this publication, and does not guarantee that any content on such websites is, or will remain, accurate or appropriate.

Contents

Notes on contributors   *page* vii

Introduction   1
Mark Elliott and David Feldman

1 The distinctiveness of public law   17
David Feldman

2 The politics of public law   37
David Howarth

3 The rule of law in public law   56
Jeremy Waldron

4 Legislative supremacy in a multidimensional constitution   73
Mark Elliott

5 The politics of accountability   96
Tony Wright

6 Rights and democracy in UK public law   116
Aileen McHarg

7 Public law values in the common law   134
Mark Aronson

8 Public law and public laws   153
Paul Craig

9 Public law and privatisation   172
A.C.L. Davies

10 State architecture: subsidiarity, devolution, federalism
and independence   193
Christopher McCrudden

11   Soft law never dies   215
         Richard Rawlings

12   The impact of public law litigation   236
         Maurice Sunkin

13   Designing and operating constitutions in global context   256
         Cheryl Saunders

         Index   275

Notes on contributors

Mark Aronson is Emeritus Professor of Law, University of New South Wales, Australia. His publications have ranged over a number of areas, including civil and criminal procedure, the law of evidence, tort liability of public authorities, and administrative law.

Paul Craig is Professor of English Law at the University of Oxford and a Professorial Fellow of St. John's College, Oxford, a QC (hon.), and a Fellow of the British Academy. His research interests range widely across constitutional law, administrative law, human rights law and European Union law. He is the author of a number of leading works in these fields.

A.C.L. Davies is Professor of Law and Public Policy at the University of Oxford and the Garrick Fellow and Tutor in Law at Brasenose College. Her research is in the fields of public law and labour/employment law.

Mark Elliott is Reader in Public Law at the University of Cambridge and a Fellow of St Catharine's College, Cambridge. He has written widely in the field of public law.

David Feldman is the Rouse Ball Professor of English Law in the University of Cambridge and a Fellow of Downing College, Cambridge, a QC (hon), and a Fellow of the British Academy. He has been a Judge of the Constitutional Court of Bosnia and Herzegovina and Legal Adviser to the Joint Committee on Human Rights in the UK Parliament. His writing lies mainly in the fields of constitutional law, comparative public law, criminal procedure, civil liberties, and human rights, and he has a special interest in boundaries between legal categories.

David Howarth is Reader in Law and Director of the MPhil in Public Policy at the University of Cambridge, where he is also Co-Chair of the University's Strategic Research Initiative in Public Policy. He was previously a member of the UK House of Commons, in which capacity he served on the Constitutional Affairs and Justice Committees and as shadow Secretary of State for Justice.

Christopher McCrudden is Professor of Human Rights and Equality Law, Queen's University Belfast, William W Cook Global Professor of Law,

University of Michigan Law School, and a Fellow of the British Academy. He was a Fellow of the Straus Institute, New York University Law School (2013), and a Fellow of the *Wissenschaftskolleg zu Berlin* (2014–15).

Aileen McHarg is Professor of Public Law at the University of Strathclyde, having previously taught at the Universities of Bristol and Glasgow. Her research interests span many aspects of UK and Scottish public law. She is a member of the Law Society of Scotland's Constitutional Law Sub-Committee and a member of the Executive Committee of the UK Constitutional Law Association.

Richard Rawlings is Professor of Public Law, University College London. He is a former Legal Adviser to the House of Lords Constitution Committee.

Cheryl Saunders, AO, is a Laureate Professor at Melbourne Law School and the founding Director of its Centre for Comparative Constitutional Studies. She works generally in the fields of Australian and comparative public law and has specialist interests in constitution making, federalism and comparative method.

Maurice Sunkin is Professor of Public Law and Socio Legal Studies at the University of Essex and General Editor of *Public Law*. His research is concerned with the use and impact of judicial review in the United Kingdom and administrative justice. He is currently leading a Nuffield-funded project establishing the United Kingdom Administrative Justice Institute.

Jeremy Waldron is Professor of Law at New York University's School of Law. Until recently, he was also Chichele Professor of Social and Political Theory at the University of Oxford. He has delivered lectures in several prestigious series, including the 2011 Hamlyn Lectures (published as *The Rule of Law and the Measure of Property* (Cambridge University Press, 2012).

Tony Wright is Professor of Government and Public Policy at University College London and Professorial Fellow in Politics at Birkbeck College, University of London. Formerly a Member of Parliament, he chaired the Public Administration Select Committee and the Select Committee on Reform of the House of Commons.

Introduction

Mark Elliott and David Feldman

This collection of essays explores themes and controversies (legal, political and scholarly) in public law which are subjects of current debate in that area, while also (we hope) contributing to those debates from both practical and theoretical perspectives. The purposes of this Introduction are to set the scene by outlining the political context in which public law and its scholarship have developed over the past forty or so years, and to locate within that context and in relation to each other some of the themes which our contributors develop in the chapters which follow.

The context in which public law develops and operates

At the risk of pre-empting what follows, one can say that public law is concerned with the state – its structures, the actions and interactions of its institutions and people who operate them, the principles and mechanisms on which it runs – and its relationships with other entities and individuals inside and outside the state. These structures and relationships are not static. They change constantly in response to developments in ideas about the role of states in society and to changing political dynamics. Whilst many states are thought to be stable, they are at best maintaining an unstable equilibrium between competing forces, and can easily be tipped out of that equilibrium by unexpected changes. These may be economic or financial, as we saw in 2008 when shocks to the banking system of much of the western world reduced many states to dependency on other states and international organisations. As a result, Greece, Cyprus, Italy, Spain and Portugal, among other states, suffered a severe loss of control over their political as well as economic futures. This may prove to have been only a temporary phenomenon, but it is hard to believe that it will not have a long-term effect on states' assessments of their own relative independence and authority. Other challenges to states come in the form of political or economic ideologies. Over the last thirty-five years, there have been huge changes in ideas about the state in many countries. The idea that state institutions have, or even could have, obligations to provide services which advance social welfare among citizens, common in the mid-twentieth century among right-wing as well as left-wing politicians and political theorists, was attacked by neo-conservative, liberal economists whose critique became part of political orthodoxy among right-leaning political parties by the early 1980s. Republican government under President Reagan in the USA and Conservative government under Mrs Thatcher in the UK adopted radical policies of privatising the delivery of socially important services, and much of what had been the realm of state politics became a matter of individual choices to be exercised through the market.

In the UK, the Conservative governments of 1979 to 1997 significantly changed the functions and organisation of central and local government (altering the role and personnel of the civil service on the New Public Management model, hiving off many functions to semi-autonomous agencies, privatised bodies and the private sector, and imposing strict controls on spending by local government), the funding of public projects (through public–private partnerships and private finance initiatives of various kinds), and the balance of power between levels of government. In the process, they presented challenges to traditional, parliamentary methods of scrutinising government and securing accountability, despite the strengthening of the system of House of Commons Select Committees after 1979. Public law was largely reshaped in response. As ordinary politics concentrated more on defining the limits of state action than on delivering social goods, state institutions lost the ability to impose political solutions to competition for those goods. Their roles changed. Rather than allocating such goods, state institutions tended to become regulators of markets and managers of conflicts flowing from the process by which markets allocate goods. The institutions' main role was progressively limited to determining the outcome of such conflicts.

Under the Labour governments of 1997 to 2010 those trends continued apace. In addition, the reach of central government was limited: territorially in respect of certain matters by way of devolution of governmental powers to Scotland, Northern Ireland and Wales; in terms of institutions' competences by the introduction of justiciable human rights to the legal systems of the UK; and in relation to knowledge of government by legislation on freedom of information. Following the General Election in May

2010, the advent of the Conservative–Liberal Democrat coalition changed (at least temporarily) the nature of government, and put pressure on traditional conventions of collective responsibility, which have been adjusted either by agreement or by conduct.

Another structural change in states has been demographic. The make-up of societies has altered across much of the world, although the character and causes of those changes are many and varied. Age profiles have changed. In the UK, rising longevity and a falling birth rate are producing a society in which elderly people predominate. Across large parts of Africa, by contrast, the effect of disease has been to produce societies dominated by large numbers of orphaned children and widows. In some parts of the world, including the UK, migration has produced greater racial and cultural diversity in society. Elsewhere, war and displacement of civilian populations have made even pre-existing levels of diversity difficult to sustain, while inflicting on other states the problem of coping with the forced diversity which results from migration of refugees. Attempts to manage such problems often involve rebuilding the state and submitting to international intervention. This creates pressure on traditional structures and presents continuous challenges to public law.

Alongside these structural changes in the state, there has been a decline in public trust and confidence in politicians and, to a lesser extent, traditional ways of doing business. In recent decades political leaders have been content to follow public opinion rather than aiming to inform and shape it. This tendency, manifested in the growing influence of focus groups and opinion polls on parties' policies, is related to the idea that citizens are consumers of public goods rather than citizens sharing public burdens. If people are consumers, the role of political parties is seen to be to give them what they want, not what is good for them (or, more accurately, the political elite starts from a rebuttable but powerful presumption that what people want and what is good for them are the same). As a result, principle is less influential in politics than responsiveness to wants. In the short term, this seems to bolster the popular standing of politicians. Over time, however, it has sapped respect for politicians, whose role is increasingly seen as being to deliver what people want rather than provide good government in the public interest. Some politicians, already seen as glorified ice-cream vendors, have contributed to their own loss of dignity by manipulating public funds to their own benefit or using their positions of influence as a means of securing private gain, and being caught doing so.

Political and other public institutions more generally in the UK have begun to adapt to what some see as a crisis of confidence in politics in the context of growing concern about the challenges posed by a society characterised by increasing diversity and pressures imposed by group identities. In the UK, Parliament has to some extent reformed itself. Most recently, it has admitted independent, external scrutiny of some of its activities in the face of public outrage at the expenses claimed by some of its members. This creates a breach in the traditional claim of each House to autonomy. But other developments have also changed the character and, perhaps, the role of Parliament. They include reform of House of Commons procedure to make the lives of MPs more family-friendly, reassertion by the House of Commons of control over its own business and select committees at the expense of the power of the government's business managers, and changes to the composition of the House of Lords. But such structural changes are usually slow, because they have to negotiate legislative and political channels which are designed in such a way as to be resistant to hasty amendment. Indeed, it is a characteristic of good government to be resistant to change. When attempted at speed, change tends to be poorly planned, and even well thought out plans can have unexpected and unwanted consequences when ordinary people act in an economically rational way in response to new opportunities, instead of conducting themselves in accordance with the good intentions and optimistic expectations of the planners. (Reforms in systems of taxation and welfare benefits are particularly prone to these problems, but they arise everywhere and always.)

These developments set up stresses which public law has had to manage. But public law changes in ways which have little to do with the structural problems afflicting states, and such changes can have consequential effects on the structure of states and their ability to react to structural problems. In the UK, they include, for example, the growing impact of EEC/EC/EU law on domestic law, including the doctrine of the legislative sovereignty of the Queen in Parliament; the steady development of judicial review of administrative action (given a further fillip by the human rights legislation) which sometimes affects the ability of public bodies to pursue politically desired purposes; the various measures introduced in response to international terrorism since 2001, and the resulting increase in the effect of international influences on our constitutional system; and the recasting of the role of the Lord Chancellor and the replacement of the Appellate Committee of the House of Lords with a new Supreme Court, resulting from and in a heightened significance for the notion of the separation of powers in the constitution. Some of these problems, especially those flowing from the interaction of different levels or realms of governance within and outwith the state and from extrinsic threats such as regional or global economic meltdown or terrorism, affect all states to a greater or lesser extent, and require management by both their political systems and their systems of public law.

The contested nature and functions of public law

The contest over the nature and functions of public law has at least five dimensions. Each contribution to this volume addresses one or more of them. The five dimensions are: (1) the notions of government and the state; (2) the place of the state and public law in the world at large; (3) relationships between institutions and officials within the state; (4) the legitimacy of institutions; (5) the identity and worth of public law in relation to politics.

Government and the state

There are competing ideas about the proper function of government and state. In terms of ideals, there is a contest between those who think that the state's proper function is limited to peacekeeping internally and defence from external threats. Supporters of the minimal state, such as Robert Nozick, regard government's role as being to protect property and persons against attack.[1] They deny that governments have authority to interfere with property or persons themselves, except for those limited purposes. At the other extreme are supporters of state action to engineer social changes by limiting freedom of person and property, in order (for example) to diminish social or economic inequality, provide welfare services or enforce (non-libertarian) morality. Views about the place of public law reflect views of the proper role of the state. A libertarian idealist sees the role of public law as being to constrain state action, preventing it from exceeding

---

[1] R. Nozick, *Anarchy, State and Utopia* (Oxford: Basil Blackwell, 1974). See also F. A. Hayek, *The Constitution of Liberty* (London: Routledge, 1960).

its very narrow function. Social activists want public law to be able to establish and guide institutions devoted to the control of people, property and markets, and to provide services beyond the limits of peacekeeping and property protection. As Jeremy Waldron points out in his chapter on the rule of law, the economically liberal version of public law effectively sidelines democracy, because there are few policy choices to be made which might be settled by democratic processes apart from the choice of means for protecting people and property.

If one takes politics seriously as a means of settling contests over goals, not merely means, of state action, it entails a more than minimal state, and, as Waldron argues, the rule of law has to adapt to the more extensive role which this implies for public law: law as a method of giving effect to choices as to public, social goals of state action. Public law may still constrain government action by insisting on procedural values such as fairness in decision-making, a need for legal authorisation for action, and more generally a desire to avoid arbitrariness in government. It will have less scope, however, for entirely ruling out goals of state action than in the libertarian, minimal-state model.

Allowing governments to make a wider range of political choices raises a further question. Is government to be competent to change fundamental features of the structure of the state? In practice, it must have that competence, subject to constraints; but the nature of the constraints is itself likely to be politically and perhaps legally contested. One of the tasks of public law may be to set legal limits to that competence, as in India, where the Supreme Court has occasionally struck down formally valid amendments to the Constitution on the ground of inconsistency with a basic feature of the structure of the Constitution.[2] This use of law is controversial, because it limits the scope for political restructuring of the state so far as government desires legal support for resulting arrangements. It stems from fidelity to the Constitution where the Constitution is seen as having core features or values apart from the text of any constitutional document, and where law and courts are treated as the guardians of those higher-order features or values. It goes beyond the economic liberal's notion of the rule of law but restricts, or allows courts to restrict, what can be done by way of restructuring the state.

---

[2] *Kesavananda Bharati* v. *State of Kerala* (1973) 4 SCC 225. See S. Krishnaswamy, *Democracy and Constitutionalism in India: A Study of the Basic Structure Doctrine* (New Delhi: Oxford University Press, 2009).

In many states, by contrast, governmental power extends to restructuring the state in accordance with a government's vision of the Good. Politics (which may or may not be democratic) is a process by which a political elite secures that power for a definite or indefinite period. A government need not use the power. Some governments consider that it is in the public interest to act in a more managerial way. But even proponents of limited governmental intervention in people's lives may need to embark on fundamental changes to the state in order to bring about conditions in which they can then retreat to management. One sees this in the UK. When Harold Macmillan (unsuccessfully) and Edward Heath (successfully) negotiated for the UK to become a Member State of the European Economic Community, the effect of what is now called EU law on core constitutional and political ideas about the legislative supremacy of the UK's Parliament was, as later became clear, fundamental, as Mark Elliott discusses in his chapter on sovereignty. Margaret Thatcher set about changing the welfare state of the 1970s into a property- and share-owning democracy in the 1980s through selling state assets, and reined in the welfare functions of state institutions by requiring them to farm many functions out to the private and third sectors and fund activities wholly or partly with private capital. As a result, the state became more a contractor for public services than a provider of them. As A.C.L. Davies explains in her chapter on privatisation and public law, this created a need for a new sort of regulatory law; but it also, as Aileen McHarg shows in her chapter on democracy and rights, led to difficulty in giving effect through law to important principles of human rights, procedural fairness and non-arbitrariness where border disputes arose between public and private law. What justification is there for imposing public-law values on private providers of services and goods previously, but no longer, provided by the state? There is a direct connection between Margaret Thatcher's idea of the proper (fairly limited) role of the state and the procedural boundary disputes that arose between public and private law procedures investigated by Mark Aronson in his chapter on the scope and exclusivity of the judicial procedure for review of administrative or governmental action.

Margaret Thatcher's crusade to restructure the UK is just one example of governments attempting similar feats in other states under the influence of liberal economic theories. In the United States, President George Bush and, later, his son, George W. Bush, sought to restrict the expenditure and activity of federal institutions. A similar process occurred in Australia and many other countries. Governments are able to use the levers of state power, including law, to reshape their states. Where democratic politics operate, the power to do this is one of the powers over which contenders for government compete.

It is not necessary, however, for government to plan to restructure the state in order for its policies to have that effect. In seeking to join the EEC in the 1960s and 1970s, Harold Macmillan and Edward Heath were looking outward at the UK's place in the developing European order. They were not consciously seeking to reshape the UK's constitution; that was a consequence, but not an aim. Similarly, when Tony Blair's government in 1997–98 embarked on an ambitious programme of legislation which included devolution to Scotland, Northern Ireland (in pursuit of a treaty with Ireland) and Wales they produced a structure which A. V. Dicey, a century or so earlier, would not have recognised as a unitary UK. As Christopher McCrudden points out in his chapter, todays's United Kingdom owes more to James Bryce's idea of states as unstable balances between centripetal and centrifugal forces. It is unlikely, however, that Tony Blair or his government understood, much less planned, this outcome. As Vernon Bogdanor wrote in his study of the raft of constitutional changes which occurred in the decade or so after 1997, they provided the UK with a new constitution, but one in which reforms were enacted 'piecemeal . . . and seem without internal coherence'.[3] Margaret Thatcher, by contrast, knew how she wanted to change government and the state, and most of her policies were geared to achieving those changes.

Can law play a part in constituting the state, or is that entirely a political matter? In the UK, at least, the law for centuries carefully avoided developing a legal conception of the state. The Crown as a corporation was treated as a proxy for a legal or constitutional conception of the state. This caused some inconvenience early in the sixteenth century when King James VI of Scotland became King James I of England and Wales. The monarch represented two states with potentially conflicting interests and policies. The inconvenience was somewhat mitigated in 1707 when the two states became one, but continues to cause difficulty in relation to the Crown's responsibilities towards its colonies and dependencies. Was the Crown acting in relation to a dependency or colony the same as the Crown acting in relation to the UK? Judges have tended to answer these questions

---

[3] V. Bogdanor, *The New British Constitution* (Oxford: Hart Publishing, 2009), 271.

so as to minimise interference with the Crown's prerogatives, sometimes working on the basis of a divided Crown[4] and sometimes adopting a theory of the unity of the Crown.[5] It gives rise to further inconvenience in a devolved rather than purely unitary state. On the advice of which government should the Crown act and on what matters? In addition, the notion of an undivided Crown against which coercive legal remedies are not available (but only the petition of right) was a serious obstacle in the way of establishing and enforcing constitutional rules to govern the exercise of functions by different governmental institutions, whether at the same level or at different levels in the state. In England, such difficulties were addressed – unsystematically – in three ways: first, by treating officers of state as private individuals, personally liable in damages for legal wrongs committed in the Crown's service; secondly, by developing declaratory relief as a way of indirectly enforcing law against the Crown knowing that governments' commitment to the rule of law would normally lead them to act in accordance with their obligations as declared by the court; thirdly, by responding to the demands of EU law, which treats Member States from an external viewpoint as subject to EU law (even if their municipal law focuses on individual institutions, such as the Crown as a corporation in place of the state) and requires them to provide effective protection for Community rights.[6]

Other states approach this matter differently. Australian constitutional law quickly separated the state from the Crown, thus making possible effective judicial protection in a federal structure. The USA and France always rejected the Crown as a personification of or proxy for the state. This simplified the task of providing effective remedies in public law. It does not mean, however, that law constitutes the state in those countries. It means only that law has a conception of the state and so is more easily used to resolve conflicts concerning state actions.

The state and public law in the world order

The second contested area, the place of the state and public law in the world, is related to the first (as noted, for example, in relation to the UK's

---

[4] *R. (Quark Fishing Ltd)* v. *Secretary of State for Foreign Affairs* [2005] UKHL 57, [2006] 1 AC 529.

[5] *R. (Bancoult)* v. *Secretary of State for Foreign and Commonwealth Affairs* [2008] UKHL 61, [2009] 1 AC 453.

[6] *R.* v. *Secretary of State for Transport, ex parte Factortame Ltd* [1991] AC 603.

accession to the EEC in 1973). In recent decades certain public law and international law scholars have tended routinely to downplay the notions of state sovereignty and national self-determination. Modern states, it is said, are so interdependent for economic success and general security, and so subject to the vicissitudes of a global economy and power of international corporations and institutions, that we should focus attention on international governance, not national government. It is fair to acknowledge that national institutions' room for manoeuvre when choosing policies is affected by factors outside their control and often unforeseeable; the position of Eurozone states such as Greece, Cyprus, Italy, Spain and Portugal following the financial and banking meltdown in 2008 provides graphic evidence of this. External preferences and pressures may even have a major influence on the design of states and their constitutions. As Cheryl Saunders shows in her chapter on the architecture of states, these influences have a variety of sources, and are made effective through mechanisms which include direct intervention by international agencies following the collapse of states, conditions for funding from the World Bank or International Monetary Fund for state-(re)building, and the 'soft power' of culturally powerful societies in, for instance, the USA and Germany.[7]

It is equally true that states impose fetters on their own freedom of choice through treaties and other arrangements into which they enter with other states and international institutions. These arrangements may be economic and cultural as well as diplomatic or political. As the position of Member States in the EU shows, the deeper the bonds of international co-operation become, the more constrained national freedom of decision-making becomes. In terms of municipal public law, however, this does not necessarily dictate how the functions and powers of state institutions should be conceptualised. As Mark Elliott argues in his chapter, a notion such as the legislative supremacy of the UK's Parliament can be seen as operating within a context consisting of norms, which may or may not be legal, domestic or written, and which constrain political and legal choices, though the strength of a constraint appears different depending on one's institutional and geographical viewing point.

---

[7] See also D. Feldman, 'Modalities of Internationalisation in Constitutional Law' (2006) 18 *European Review of Public Law* 131.

Relationships between state institutions and officials

In some cases, law has nothing to say about relationships between institutions and officials of the state, and they have no impact on law. For example, the journalist and political commentator Walter Bagehot, writing in the 1860s, painted a picture of the British Cabinet as an institution composed of Ministers of equal status, the Prime Minister being merely *primus inter pares*, through which the 'efficient secret' of the constitution, 'the close union, the nearly complete fusion, of the executive and legislative powers', was able to work. Nearly a century later, Richard Crossman, a journalist, political commentator and politician who was soon to be a Cabinet Minister in Harold Wilson's government, argued that things had changed. The Prime Minister's power had grown at the expense of collective decision-making by the Cabinet. Prime Ministerial – almost presidential – government had, Crossman thought, replaced genuine Cabinet government, so the 'efficient secret' of the constitution had become a vehicle for what Lord Hailsham, a Conservative Lord Chancellor under Edward Heath and Margaret Thatcher, was (when out of office) to call 'elective dictatorship'.[8] This change (if indeed it had occurred) was fundamental, but had nothing to do with law. On the other hand, aspects of the relationship between Parliament and government can play out in ways which have legal, and justiciable, consequences. For example, judges have had to decide whether the government was legally entitled to use the power of the royal prerogative to legislate inconsistently with a provision in a statute which had not been brought into force because the government disagreed with it. (A majority in the House of Lords held that the statute, despite not having been brought into force, effectively restricted the government's use of prerogative powers.)[9] Judges can, and have, also been drawn into disputes between different tiers or within the same tier of government, where litigation can become a substitute for or complement to political action when institutions are unequally

---

[8] Walter Bagehot, *The English Constitution* (1867), ed. R. H. S. Crossman (London: Fontana, 1963), 65; R. H. S. Crossman, 'Introduction', in Bagehot, *The English Constitution*, 20–24, 33–39, 48–57; Lord Hailsham, 'Elective dictatorship', the BBC Richard Dimbleby Lecture for 1976, printed in *The Listener*, 21 October 1976, 496–500. See also N. St J. Stevas, *Walter Bagehot: A Study of his Life and Thought together with a Selection from his Political Writings* (London: Eyre & Spottiswoode, 1959).

[9] *R.* v. *Secretary of State for the Home Department, ex parte Fire Brigades Union* [1995] 2 AC 513.

powerful.[10] In the UK, this phenomenon is now more pronounced as a result of litigation concerning the extent of devolved legislatures' powers and the relationship between the powers of such bodies and those of the Westminster Parliament.[11]

In federal states, the relationship between federal and provincial (sometimes called state) institutions is usually governed by the constitution, and may be justiciable to the extent to which the constitutional norms are justiciable. This justiciability may not necessarily depend on a strict distinction between legal and non-legal standards. In Canada, as David Feldman notes in his chapter on the distinctiveness of public law, there is a procedure by which a court may be empowered to give an opinion on a constitutional reference concerned with the content and application of a convention, not a law, giving rise to interesting questions as to the status of the court's opinion. The role of lawyers and courts in relation to such claims is a result, as David Howarth suggests in his chapter, of strategic decisions about the relationship between law and politics; and, as Christopher McCrudden argues, it shows how constitutional lawyers work to increase centripetal forces and reduce centrifugal forces. It also supports Mark Elliott's suggestion that one cannot say how 'hard' or 'soft' constitutional constraints are unless one views them separately from the perspectives of each of the institutions concerned.

Legitimacy of institutions

At the level of the legitimacy of the acts of individual institutions of the state, there are different criteria of legitimacy depending on the nature of each institution. In principle, political institutions depend for their legitimacy on political values, such as democratic responsiveness and accountability, an ethos of public service, and commitment to an idea of the public

---

[10] See e.g. *Secretary of State for Education and Science* v. *Tameside Metropolitan Borough Council* [1977] AC 1014; *Bromley London Borough Council* v. *Greater London Council* [1983] 1 AC 789; *R.* v. *London Transport Executive, ex parte Greater London Council* [1983] QB 484; *R.* v. *Secretary of State for the Environment ex parte Nottinghamshire County Council* [1986] AC 240; *R.* v. *Secretary of State for the Environment ex parte Hammersmith and Fulham London Borough Council* [1991] 1 AC 521.

[11] See e.g. *AXA General Insurance Ltd and others* v. *HM Advocate* [2011] UKSC 46, [2012] 1 AC 868; *Attorney General* v. *National Assembly for Wales Commission* [2012] UKSC 53, [2013] 1 AC 792; *Attorney General for England and Wales* v. *Counsel General for Wales* [2014] UKSC 43, [2014] 1 WLR 2622

good. Administrative institutions found their legitimacy on an ethos of public service and methods of bureaucratic rationality. Judicial institutions rely for legitimacy on an ethos of public service, procedural equality, impartiality, principled consistency and public justification for decisions. In addition, any institution may bolster a claim to legitimacy by reference to the goodness of the outcomes which it produces (although their standards for assessing goodness may be very different).

In real life, an institution's legitimacy may become more complicated than that sketch suggests. As David Howarth shows in respect of the relationship between politicians and judges, people in different kinds of institutions tend to regard criteria of legitimacy which uncontroversially apply to them as being appropriate when assessing other institutions' legitimacy as well. For example, because democratic accountability is a criterion of the legitimacy of governments, politicians may assume that it is equally appropriate to the legitimacy of judicial action. But, as Tony Wright points out in his chapter on accountability, it is a mistake to think of accountabilities of all institutions in similar terms, or to assume that one kind of accountability is appropriate for all institutions. A similar reflection emerges from Aileen McHarg's review of the use of the standard of proportionality in adjudication on Convention rights under the Human Rights Act 1998. In reality, there are many forms of accountability – electoral, bureaucratic, and economic, to mention but three – and each has its own special merits and processes. When one type of institution fails to recognise this in relation to another, it causes mutual lack of understanding and inhibits useful discussion.

The problems are intensified when there is a direct dispute between two institutions with entirely different and inconsistent world views, as when the judicial ethos of government under law clashes with the governmental ethos of democratically responsible action in the public interest. There is an area in which their aspirations overlap, since governments like to use law to further political aims. But (as David Howarth points out) governments are not always as keen to recognise that their realm is subject to, much less constituted by, legal norms. The lack of common understanding and values makes it particularly important for public lawyers to mediate in the clash between what Sir John Laws has described as the morality of government and the morality of law.[12]

---

[12] Sir John Laws, 'The Good Constitution' [2012] *Cambridge Law Journal* 567.

The identity and worth of public law

The identity and worth of public law seem at first sight to be more legal than political. Yet the political may intrude at the most basic level. Martin Loughlin has argued, on the basis of a deep exploration of the history of the idea of public law, that public law is constituted by politics and the political.[13] That, as David Howarth notes in his chapter, is a view adopted by many politicians. On the other hand, many public lawyers see the law as autonomous and, sometimes, actually as constitutive of politics. The way in which this difference of view is resolved may change over time, and varies widely from place to place. But whichever view one takes, two major issues remain. First, what is public law (as distinct from other phenomena)? Secondly, how can one decide whether it is working well (which implies a prior question as to what it is for)?

The first question is explored in different ways by David Feldman, Richard Rawlings and Paul Craig. Feldman adopts a perspective internal to the legal system itself. Can public law be distinguished from the non-legal norms and processes which help to shape the state and government? He thinks that it can, on the basis of a positivist understanding of law. Richard Rawlings, on the other hand, adopts a more anthropological approach, looking functionally at the rich variety of norms (including but going far beyond legal norms) which together shape state and government. They pursue the aim of maintaining good, effective government in the face of multiple challenges, emerge from administrative and political discussions, and are implemented outside legal forms and procedures (although they may influence legal decisions, for example by giving rise to legitimate expectations which courts may protect). Rawlings shows how the political, administrative and legal processes for shaping government are complementary if not integrated at the level of the raw materials of governmental norms.

Feldman goes on to ask whether, within positive law, public law can be distinguished from private law. He suggests that public law is distinctive, if not distinct, because of its focus on public interests and governmental standards. Paul Craig deepens the understanding of public law by analys-ing it to see, among other things, whether (quite apart from the different types of relatively 'soft' and 'hard' law which Rawlings examines) the

---

[13] M. Loughlin, *The Idea of Public Law* (Oxford: Oxford University Press, 2003).

category of positivist public law is theoretically coherent. Is there a *system* of public law, at the level of either doctrine or principle, or are there different *systems* of public law for different administrative and governmental contexts and functions? To address this, he offers an analysis of the 'functional' which will help to clarify the issues raised by many of the other debates with which our contributors engage, and represents in itself a valuable contribution to the theory of public law. For example, one factor when evaluating rules concerning the scope and exclusivity of the procedure for judicial review of administrative action must be whether the rules help to ensure that judicial review discharges its function or functions.

This leads to the second issue. How can one assess whether a particular system or institution of public law is discharging its responsibility well? Until its function is understood, its effectiveness cannot be fully evaluated. But there is a more basic, empirical issue. Can we show that a particular institution or rule has any effect whatever? What evidence is there that the forms and processes of public law affect governmental and administrative activity, or do so for the better? This is at the heart of Maurice Sunkin's chapter. He assesses critiques of judicial review of administrative action which assert that judicial action has no, or no beneficial, effect either on the litigants or on the governmental process in which they are enmeshed. His conclusion, on the basis of a growing body of empirical evidence (for much of which he is himself responsible), is a cautious, but from the point of view of public lawyers reassuring, indication that judicial review has effects and that they tend to benefit public administration. These are not always direct effects of particular pieces of litigation, but can be more general, systemic effects flowing from recognition, and to a degree internalisation, of the standards which judicial review seeks to apply.

Conclusion

It will be clear from reading the work of our contributors that public law is dynamic not static, and richly varied in its norms, types of authority and procedures. Its variety flows from the protean character of states, politics and institutions in which public law moves and which it helps to shape. Inside and outside the state, public law and public laws are invoked by advocates of change and opponents of change. Is there an irreducible core, or some absolute value, intrinsic to public law? The contributions to this volume may not provide answers to those questions, but by helping us to understand the questions they may encourage readers to work towards their own answers.

The distinctiveness of public law 1

David Feldman

The nature of the problem

Attaching the adjective 'public' to 'law' suggests that one is making two distinctions: first, between 'public law' and 'non-public law'; secondly, between 'public *law*' and other tools for organizing the 'public' domain. This chapter attempts to identify what, if anything, distinguishes 'public law' in each of these ways. It suggests that the distinctions are loose, because they are drawn for different reasons and in different historical and institutional settings. When trying to make the various dividing lines coalesce, one inevitably produces a line which is blurry and wobbly, rather than one that is sharp and clearly focused. When such a line is converted into norms and those norms are applied to problems in the world, we should not be surprised or disappointed that they often leave room for doubt as to how to classify a particular issue, institution, process or claim. Recognizing that reality, however, does not entail discarding the idea that there are fundamentally important differences between law and non-law and between the public and non-public domains. There are core areas in which the classification is not in doubt, and, when it is contested, the dispute alerts us to the need to think hard about which norms and processes ought properly to be used in the circumstances. When people feel unease when trying to select mechanisms and rules with which to resolve controversies, we know that we are in the blurry area, and need to refer to meta-legal norms in order to clarify the issue.

When and why do the distinctions matter? From a practical lawyer's point of view, the distinctiveness of 'public law' matters when a state has a special procedure for implementing 'public law', or special rules of 'public law', or both. One needs to be able then to decide, and advise clients (who may be governmental bodies or ordinary people) as to whether it is more appropriate, or better for the client, to have an issue treated as one of 'public' rather than 'non-public' law, or as properly allocated to 'non-law' techniques of resolution, whether public or private. Lawyers advising clients want to help the clients to get the best possible outcome from their point of view. For individuals confronting governmental bodies, this usually means getting the best result in the particular case. For governmental bodies, and to some extent for third-sector players such as charities and campaigning non-governmental organizations (NGOs), the result in the particular case may be less important than the longer-term impact on their policies and goals; a government department, for example, can win cases in ways which damage the more general implementation of policies, and lose in ways which help for the future by clarifying the law.[1] But it is difficult for lawyers advising clients, and even for judges in *inter partes* litigation, to look holistically and disinterestedly at the distinctions between 'public law', 'non-public law', and 'public non-law' when those distinctions are being deployed partly as tactical weapons. For example, if X has brought proceedings against the Ministry of Y in the form of a straightforward claim in tort or delict, counsel for the Ministry might argue that the claim is properly regarded as a 'public law', one which should (therefore) be litigated in a 'public law' tribunal. X having brought the claim in the wrong form and the wrong tribunal, the tribunal should dismiss the claim. Counsel for the Ministry will focus on those aspects of the claim which make it appear 'public'; counsel for X on those which make it appear 'private'; and both will be concerned with the appropriateness of the forum for the claim, however that claim might be classified. If the tribunal is worried about its procedures and its caseload, it will introduce another set of pragmatic rather than philosophical considerations.[2] In any litigation, the tribunal's need to find a sensible, workable solution to a practical problem (rather than a philosophically coherent one) will make it unlikely that legal processes will yield a rounded picture of the distinction.

If we approach the matter as theorists rather than lawyers, it is easier to develop an approach from first principles. For instance, we might propose that 'public law' is concerned with the division, allocation and exercise of *the state's responsibilities and its distinctive claim to legitimate exercise of*

[1] T. Prosser, *Test Cases for the Poor: Legal Techniques in the Politics of Social Welfare* (London: Child Poverty Action Group, 1983); C. Harlow and R. Rawlings, *Pressure through Law* (London: Routledge, 1992); D. Seymour, 'Whitehall, Transparency, and the Law', in D. Feldman (ed.), *Law in Politics, Politics in Law* (Oxford: Hart Publishing, 2013).
[2] In England and Wales, see e.g. *R* v. *Secretary of State for the Home Department, ex parte Swati* [1986] 1 WLR 477, *O'Reilly* v. *Mackman* [1983] 2 AC 237, and *Cocks* v. *Thanet DC* [1983] 2 AC 286.

coercive force. On this view, its subject is how public officials should behave. But is 'public law' limited to conferral and regulation of the state's powers and responsibilities, or is it concerned more generally with organizing and regulating the exercise of a particular type of *function*, the exercise of coercive force, to try to ensure that its exercise works for *the benefit of, or at least not to the detriment of, the public* at large? Is the distinctive feature of the state and its institutions that it has an absolute obligation to act in the general interest of its citizens, not in the interests of particular individuals or groups? If 'public law' is concerned with this sort of function, its activities may have to go beyond regulating state institutions. Where the state discharges its public-interest obligation through procuring goods and services for people from, or relying on, private enterprises, rather than providing them directly through state institutions, one of the state's functions could be to regulate some or all kinds of 'private' enterprise. In different countries, this has brought about a partial merging of 'public law' and 'private law' in two ways: first, through states privatizing state-owned enterprises; secondly, through states using their position as owners and large-scale contractors to impose social-justice requirements on private enterprises by way of conditions for users of government-owned assets or tenderers for government contracts.[3] In these circumstances, property law and contract law are, or can be seen to operate as a form of, 'public law'. What are the practical implications of this? Should it affect the content of the contract or property law, or the tribunals before which claims may be brought?

One might respond to the notion of contract as 'public law' by saying that where neither party is a 'public' body (such as a government department) it cannot be right to subject them to 'public law' principles or force them into 'public law' procedures. But regarding a party as private or public involves adopting a defining characteristic for the 'public' as distinct from the 'private'. Is a 'public' party to be identified formally, as part of the apparatus of the state, or functionally, as a party helping a state institution to discharge its obligations? If 'public law' is concerned with the organization and use of state power, one party to it will be a state body or someone acting for such a body. That party may be on the receiving end of it, as

---

[3] See A. C. L. Davies, 'Public Law and Privatisation' (Chapter 9 in this volume); C. McCrudden, 'State Architecture: Subsidiarity, Devolution, Federalism and Independence' (Chapter 10 in this volume); C. McCrudden, *Buying Social Justice: Equality, Government Procurement, and Legal Change* (Oxford: Oxford University Press, 2007).

where someone challenges an exercise of power by a planning authority. Alternatively it may be using law as a tool for channelling and legitimizing the use of coercive force against people; the whole of criminal law is, in this sense, public law. On the other hand, if one adopts a functional approach, the parties on the receiving end of public law may be private individuals or associations, corporations or enterprises which have a type of function regarded as being one to which public law principles should attached. This, of course, would depend in turn on what the principles are.

'Law' and 'non-law' in governmental matters

The initial stimulant to attempts to distinguish 'law' from 'non-law' in relation to government in Westminster-model, common-law systems was the development of legal positivism in the early nineteenth century, led by Jeremy Bentham and John Austin, which portrayed law as a normative system of a particular state, independent of morality and history, and capable of scientific analysis in its own right. 'Public law' could then be seen as making a distinct contribution to the formation and operation of the state. Alongside this philosophical development went a pedagogical one: it became possible to establish English (or other national) law as a subject worthy of study in its own right, to establish law faculties in universities separate from faculties of history or moral philosophy, and to develop syllabuses for studying the distinctively legal aspects of national 'public law'. In the UK, studies of the constitution had treated it either as a branch of political history to which law might contribute peripherally, or as political science, the study of what happened in government and politics, emphasizing crucial differences between legal forms and practical realities. The first of Dicey's *Lectures Introductory to the Study of the Law of the Constitution*,[4] 'The true nature of constitutional law', published in 1885, was ground-breaking because he insisted upon examining the constitution as a lawyer, bringing out the distinctive contribution of law to the working of the state separately from the contributions undoubtedly made by political and administrative means. As junior counsel to the Inland Revenue before his election to the Vinerian Professorship at Oxford,

---

[4] A. V. Dicey, *Lectures Introductory to the Study of the Law of the Constitution* (London: Macmillan, 1885).

Dicey had had ample opportunity to see the distinctive operation of law in the British state. He did not suggest that other, non-legal norms were unimportant, only that they were not directly the concern of lawyers as such. Lawyers had constantly refreshed the constitution by reinterpreting the law for modern times, just as the genius of British politics had been to adapt to new needs through traditional, legal forms.

During the nineteenth and twentieth centuries, constitutional developments in British colonies and dominions as they moved towards independence and statehood tended to increase the centrality of positive constitutional law to the state. 'The corporate idea of the state became the ground on which an autonomous concept of public law was built.'[5] In the British Empire, colonial charters and constitutions had long constituted judicially enforceable limits to the competence of colonial legislatures. The judgment of the US Supreme Court in *Marbury* v. *Madison*[6] in 1803 put the Constitution of the USA on the same plane. When other former colonies secured their independence, their constitutions were codified, and, despite usually being built on the structures of the UK's uncodified constitution,[7] tended to be 'public law' in the sense of being judicially enforceable. For example, the High Court of Australia quickly decided that the Constitution of the Commonwealth of Australia, contained in the UK's Commonwealth of Australia Constitution Act 1900, was justiciable; it contained constitutional 'law'.

Back in the UK, however, the positivist approach to constitutional law faced two challenges. First, many political scientists and some lawyers resisted the idea that legal forms or norms controlled the state. The constitution, said Professor John Griffith, was what happened; any underlying norms were political, not legal.[8] From the perspective of the history of ideas, Professor Martin Loughlin locates public law as one of three 'orders' of political conflict. The first identifies the role of the state and politics as distinguishing between insiders and outsiders, and protecting the former against the latter. The second distinguishes between different orders within the state, such as governors and governed, or government and opposition.

---

[5] M. Loughlin, *Foundations of Public Law* (Oxford: Oxford University Press, 2010), 50.
[6] (1803) 5 US 137.
[7] In 1972, John Finnis gave a series of lectures in the University of Oxford entitled 'Essentials of a British Constitution' which focused on the constitution of St Kitts, Nevis and Anguilla. These were amongst the first lectures I attended as an undergraduate.
[8] J. A. G. Griffith, 'The Political Constitution' (1979) 42 *Modern Law Review* 1.

The third order makes the outcome of politics appear, to some extent, fair; this is done by utilizing constitutional and legal forms, and (says Loughlin) is driven 'mainly by prudential considerations'. Law is there to legitimate the result of politics.[9] Secondly, lawyers and legal theorists like Professor Trevor Allan and Sir John Laws, seeking to find moral authority for the use of state force, argued that the state's authority was founded on accepting certain moral principles which were reflected in, and (to a greater or lesser extent) could be enforced by, the common law and its courts. This tends towards the collapse of the distinction between 'law' and 'non-law', as it denies that political norms are different in kind from legal norms; but, in contrast to Griffith, these lawyers often seek to protect the authority of courts in 'public law' from encroachment by statute.[10]

In some circumstances, we thus face a threshold disagreement as to whether 'law', either 'public' or 'private', is an appropriate method of dealing with a problem at all. For instance, in Westminster-model systems of government, where the executive is directly responsible to a parliament for its acts, decisions and policies, government ministers, when challenged in a court or tribunal to justify the legality of their acts, may argue that the tribunal ought not to decide the case according to law because a minister's responsibility to Parliament provides a more constitutionally appropriate way of holding the minister to account than a judicial process.[11] In any system, the government may simply deny the court's capability to decide the question. Such arguments appear in different guises; they may use the language of justiciability (essentially, the appropriateness of a matter for judicial determination), or of separation of powers, or of 'deference' or 'variable intensity of review'. In times of deep social and political divisions (such as the 1930s and 1980s in the UK) or when the state is thought to face a pressing threat to its existence (as in wartime, during the IRA's bombing campaign from the late 1960s to the late 1990s, and in the present century), these arguments have sometimes been successful.[12] But they must always

---

[9] M. Loughlin, *The Idea of Public Law* (Oxford: Oxford University Press, 2003), 33–52.

[10] T. R. S. Allan, *Law, Liberty and Justice* (Oxford: Clarendon Press, 1993; Sir John Laws, *The Common Law Constitution* (Cambridge: Cambridge University Press, 2014).

[11] On accountability, see T. Wright, 'The Politics of Accountability' (Chapter 5 in this volume).

[12] See e.g. A. W. B. Simpson, *In the Highest Degree Odious: Detention without Trial in Wartime Britain* (Oxford: Clarendon Press, 1992, 1994); K. D. Ewing and C. A. Gearty, *The Battle for Civil Liberties: Political Freedom and the Rule of Law in Britain, 1914–1945* (Oxford: Oxford University Press, 2000); D. Dyzenhaus, *The Constitution of Law: Legality*

be viewed with suspicion and tested stringently to see whether they are justified by exceptional circumstances.

Dyson v. *Attorney General*, litigated in 1910 at a politically fraught time in the UK, is an example of what many perceive as a clash of moral or political imperatives. The Inland Revenue Commissioners required taxpayers to provide information about their property, threatening a financial penalty for refusal, although there was no statutory authority for levying such a penalty. When Mr Dyson brought an action against the Attorney General for a declaration that the demand was unlawful, the government objected that there was no precedent for seeking such a declaration as a remedy against the Crown. The Court of Appeal unanimously rejected the argument. Farwell LJ noted that the Attorney General's objection to the proceedings 'admits for this purpose the illegality of the inquiries, but claims for a government department a superiority to the law which was denied by the Court to the King himself in Stuart times', and that officers of the Crown had previously not put technical barriers in the way of people bringing points of difficulty before a court. He continued, 'I venture to hope that the former salutary practice may be resumed. If ministerial responsibility were more than the mere shadow of a name, the matter would be less important, but as it is, the Courts are the only defence of the liberty of the subject against departmental aggression.'[13] In other words, constitutional principles went beyond the brute facts of politics. If constitutional law has any normative content, this must always be so. Judges cannot properly leave it to the political class to police itself in matters of law, unless there is compelling evidence both that there is a pressing need for extraordinary action and that the political branches of government are up to the task of securing accountability for the use of special powers. Recent experiences in the UK, Australia, the USA and elsewhere give rise to serious doubts on both counts.

We should note a different point about the practical significance of the distinction between 'public law' and 'public non-law': it varies according to the position one occupies in the state. For people who want to challenge the acts of state institutions but have little direct access to the 'non-law' levers of political power and responsibility, 'public law' offers an important way of exerting pressure and bringing their concerns forcefully to the

---

in a Time of Emergency (Cambridge: Cambridge University Press, 2006); F. de Londras, *Detention in the 'War on Terror': Can Human Rights Fight Back?* (Cambridge: Cambridge University Press, 2011), chs 2, 3, 4.

[13] *Dyson* v. *Attorney General (No. 1)* [1911] KB 410, 422, 424.

attention of bureaucrats or politicians. To a bureaucrat or politician, by contrast, the distinction between 'public law' and 'public non-law' is likely to be almost irrelevant most of the time. These officers of the state work in a universe shaped by rules, some of which are imposed from elsewhere but often are self-imposed, but the juridical quality or pedigree of the rule has only peripheral significance to the bureaucrat when deciding how to do business. From within state institutions, a rule is a rule, whether administrative, political, social or legal. The question which bureaucrats face minute by minute is, 'What should I do?' Asking, 'By reference to what normative order should I decide what to do?' would be time-consuming and unproductive. The same is usually true in relation to politicians.[14]

This is, of course, an over-simplification. When politicians or bureaucrats want to use rules as instruments of policy, they have to decide not only what the rules should require, permit or institute, but also what *form* of rule is most likely to achieve their ends. They need to consider whether to use circulars, codes of practice, notes of guidance, memoranda of understanding, concordats, administrative directions, high-level principles, or legal norms. Each form offers its own distinctive advantages and costs, in terms of speed, adaptability, enforceability, accountability and legitimacy. Using law, for instance, legitimizes the use of force should that be needed, but automatically subjects the rule to constitutional and legal limits on law-making which apply in the state in question.[15] From a bureaucrat's perspective, the ideal is a piece of framework legislation which merely authorizes the bureaucrat to make rules with legal force, without tying the bureaucrat to any specific limits beyond those imposed by general law. From the perspective of a politician (or, at any rate, a conscientious parliamentarian, particularly if in opposition), however, this transfer of law-making power has disadvantages.

From the perspective of a lawyer, there is a very practical reason for examining the distinction between 'public law' and 'public non-law'. It is exceptional for courts to grant remedies in respect of alleged breaches of 'non-law'. Courts sometimes have an advisory jurisdiction (itself an

---

[14] This is an example of a wider point: the constitution does not exist as a single, abstract entity. Each institution operating it has its own perspective which shapes a distinctive conception of key features of the constitution: D. Feldman, 'None, One or Several? Perspectives on the UK's Constitution(s)' [2005] *Cambridge Law Journal* 329.

[15] See J. Black, '"Which Arrow?" Regulatory Policy and Rule Type' [1995] *Public Law* 94, and R. Rawlings, 'Soft Law Never Dies' (Chapter 11 in this volume).

oxymoron in the eyes of positivists, especially those in systems to which the notion of separation of powers is central, such as the Commonwealth of Australia[16]), but these are imposed on the court by constitution or statute. For example, in Canada the government may refer a constitutional question to the Supreme Court for an advisory opinion, and this may take the Court into areas of 'public non-law' such as the conventions relating to federalism.[17] The normal role of the court is strictly limited to deciding matters of law, including 'public law' and excluding 'public non-law'. It is true that sometimes an enterprising lawyer may persuade a court to extend 'law' (and, indeed, 'private law', with appropriate modification) into an area previously occupied only by 'public non-law'; *Attorney General* v. *Jonathan Cape Ltd*,[18] discussed later in this chapter, is an example of this. But if the court rejects such a request, the lawyer can hope for no help from the court. This is a matter of the court's jurisdiction (or as it is sometimes termed, especially in courts of theoretically unlimited jurisdiction like the English High Court, the justiciability of the issue). 'Non-law' is, in principle, no business of a court of 'law'.

'Public law' and 'non-public law'

The drive to distinguish 'public' law from other types of law is a legacy of the special powers reserved to rulers over ruled, and competition for control of them, particularly in monarchies when monarchs found their personal wealth, or *patrimonium*, insufficient to discharge their responsibilities to their subjects and sought additional resources from them, giving rise to a separate fund, the *fiscus*, subject to a different legal regime from the *patrimonium*. The *fiscus* consisted of assets held for public purposes, and had increasingly to be acquired, appropriated and used for those purposes. In the special character of the *fiscus* one can see the basis for a special system of law which could structure and sometimes limit, as well as

---

[16] See discussion of 'declarations of inconsistent interpretation' in the High Court of Australia in *Momcilovic* v. *R* [2011] HCA 34, (2011) 245 CLR 1.

[17] See e.g. the *Reference re Resolution to Amend the Constitution* [1981] 1 SCR 753, decided by the Supreme Court of Canada (SCC) on appeal from decisions of provincial courts on statutory references to them by the Governors of those provinces, and the *Reference re Secession of Quebec* [1998] 2 SCR 217, on a reference by the Governor General in Council under the Supreme Court Act, RSC 1985, c S-26, s 53.

[18] [1976] 1 QB 752, the *Crossman Diaries* case.

facilitate, the accumulation and exercise of power by rulers. Where rulers create institutions to implement their policies and exercise power on their behalf, the rulers also typically provide methods for overseeing the operation of those institutions. Such methods may, sometimes, involve making and applying laws which, alongside other means of direction and control, come to govern the acts of institutions which use resources from the *fiscus*; but the first and most direct form of oversight is that of accounting. The institution which controls financial accounting in government is in a good position to be the dominant power in the state. That is why, in the UK and other Westminster-model constitutions, the chief auditor, the Comptroller and Auditor General, is an officer of the House of Commons, not of the government.[19]

Even when a form of control involved legal forms, rather than a merger of accountancy and politics, this 'public law' was designed by rulers to be a method of accountability to them, not to their subjects. The ordinary processes of law applicable to the affairs of ordinary people were not suitable. There was no room for ideas of fair hearing and equality of arms when the issues related to the principal's (or ruler's) control over the principal's agent (or institution). If subjects were allowed access to these systems of institutional accountability, it was as petitioners, not as right-bearers. Subjects were admitted to help the ruler ensure that the ruler's institutions acted according to the ruler's directions. Only later, very gradually, and under conditions in which the subjects themselves became the ultimate rulers (or political sovereign) in democracies, did the character of these institutional processes change, allowing subjects to have access as of right to legal remedies for wrongs done to them rather than petitioning the ruler to do what was right by them. Sometimes this change was secured by legislation, sometimes (as in England and France) by judicial development, and sometimes not at all.[20]

Where and when that change occurs, it puts considerable pressure on the coherence of the notion of 'public' law. Where, as is typically the case in modern democracies, a citizen is allowed to use legal processes for

---

[19] See T. Wright, 'The Politics of Accountability' (Chapter 5 in this volume); S. Flogaitis, *The Evolution of Law and the State in Europe: Seven Lessons* (Oxford: Hart Publishing, 2014), Lessons 1 and 2. In the 1972 lectures, to which reference was made in n. 7 above, John Finnis argued that the Comptroller and Auditor General is the lynch-pin of a British constitution (a proposition which I now understand far better than I did then).

[20] Flogaitis (n. 19), Lesson 3.

challenging governing institutions, and the institutions challenged are seen as defendants in their own right, the shape of the procedure looks like a 'private' law procedure, and the substantive rules which apply may be those operating in 'private' law, albeit (as in the Crossman Diaries affair) with sometimes very significant adaptations to fit them to the new context. Where the procedure operates in a democratic state, and the challenged institution is an agent of that state, people may become uneasy at the inevitable tension between decisions in which the interests of individuals seem to dominate and the political sovereignty of the nation as a whole.

At various times and places the tension is expressed in different ways. But a desire to engage with, or more often finesse, the tension always seems to lie behind efforts to identify some distinctive field, function or nature for 'public law'.

In practice, the distinction between 'public law' and 'non-public law' operates in two areas. There are distinctively 'public' *rules* of law, and distinct *procedures and tribunals* for 'public law' matters. These are linked, in that one reason for providing specific procedures and tribunals is to make it easier to deal with the special features of 'public law' matters or rules. The rules establishing and regulating the activities of institutions of the state, for example, are different from those establishing and regulating, say, companies; whilst they share the characteristic of being corporate rather than human, state institutions have responsibilities for the common good which companies do not share (unless laws made by state institutions require them to act in the public interest in particular circumstances). A public institution's responsibility for, and often to, the public in general rather than particular individuals means that its legal obligations and legal proceedings in which it is a party must be shaped so as to ensure that the special responsibilities are taken into account.

In France, this led to the creation of entirely separate legal structures for dealing with 'public law' as distinct from 'private law'. The Constitution was scarcely the business of ordinary courts and tribunals, whether public or private. Until 2008, the *Conseil constitutionnel*, operating during the legislative process, alone determined the constitutionality of legislative Bills referred to it. Article 61–1 of the Constitution now allows ordinary courts and tribunals, deciding cases where it is thought that a legislative provision interferes with rights and liberties guaranteed by the Constitution, to ask the *Conseil constitutionnel* to determine the constitutionality of the provision; the

Conseil may abrogate a provision which it holds to be unconstitutional.[21] Many (though by no means all) modern constitutions in newly established states establish constitutional courts, some of which have exclusive jurisdiction to determine constitutional questions, while others have concurrent jurisdiction with 'ordinary' courts.

In common law Westminster-model systems, the distinctions between constitutional and other norms and procedures, and between 'public law' and 'non-public law' norms and procedures, tend to be rather less hard-edged. In Canada, every court is a constitutional court, in that every court must give effect to the Constitution. The same is true in the USA (where the law is influenced by the Westminster tradition, even though it would be wrong to say that it has a Westminster-model constitution), India, Australia and South Africa. In what follows I concentrate on England and Wales, that being the system with which I am most familiar, to illustrate the interplay of public and non-public in law and procedure.

In the UK, whilst the common law increasingly recognizes a difference between constitutional legislation and 'ordinary' law,[22] it has not so far generated separate procedures. Indeed, as already noted, the ability to pursue constitutional grievances through ordinary law and courts can be seen as part of the English model of the rule of law.

In relation to control of the administration on sub-constitutional grounds, the Napoleonic settlement in post-revolutionary France distinguished sharply between public administration and the regulation of dealings between citizens. The French model of separation of powers insisted on entirely separate systems to regulate each. Distinct sets of tribunals lead up to the *Cour de cassation* in 'private', non-criminal cases, and to the *Conseil d'état* (a governmental institution) in matters of public administration. In some cases, of course, the domains intersect. When a child is injured by a vehicle operated by a governmental institution, which tribunal should decide liability? A *Tribunal des conflits* allocates the case to the

---

[21] Art. 55 of the Constitution has long made reciprocal treaties and international agreements directly applicable and cognizable in ordinary courts and tribunals as long as they are sufficiently precise.

[22] *Thoburn* v. *Sunderland City Council* [2002] EWHC 195 (Admin), [2003] QB 151, [62]–[63] *per* Laws LJ. See further *R. (Buckinghamshire County Council)* v. *Secretary of State for Transport* [2014] UKSC 3, [2014] 1 WLR 324, [207]–[208] *per* Lord Neuberger PSC and Lord Mance JSC; D. Feldman, 'The Nature and Significance of "Constitutional" Legislation' (2013) 129 *Law Quarterly Review* 343; Laws (n. 10), 66–71.

tribunal regarded as more appropriate. But on what basis?[23] This is where one aspect of the distinction between 'public law' and 'non-public law' bites.

In the UK, by contrast, such cases were tried in ordinary, civil courts; particular remedies might have to be sought from special courts or tribunals, but in general the subjection of public officials to ordinary (that is, 'private') law alongside those remedies was thought to be essential to the rule of law and equality before the law as lawyers understood it.[24] This does not mean that there were no distinctions between remedies or forms of action. Historically, the whole of English law, whether private or public, could be understood as a system of remedies. If one had a grievance, one had to identify a remedy which might produce the effect one desired, bring one's self and one's case before the tribunal empowered to grant that remedy, and satisfy the conditions laid down by law (which often meant by the tribunal concerned) for the grant of the remedy. One chose courts for remedies just as one would choose horses for courses. What we now think of as public law remedies were originally mechanisms for the control of law-applying bodies by the royal courts, and the rules regulating standing and the range of bodies which the Court of King's Bench could control using each remedy were the foundation for what we now see as the principles of judicial review. The special remedies central to the state's control of the use of coercive power had their own distinctive procedures, although habeas corpus, certiorari, prohibition and mandamus were available from a court which also dealt with criminal matters (also the Crown's coercive control of the behaviour of inferiors), contracts, and other areas of 'private' common law. But differences between remedies were not dictated by a conceptual distinction between 'public' and 'private'. 'Private law' forms co-existed with 'public law' claims and remedies.[25] Each remedy had its own procedural requirements and adjectival law dealing with such matters as standing, delay, availability (or not) of discovery of documents, examination of witnesses, need for leave to apply, delay, and so on, and to a great extent their differences allowed them to complement each other.

---

[23] See e.g. the case of *Blanco, Tribunal des Conflits*, 8 February 1873; Flogaitis (n. 19), Lessons 2 and 3.

[24] Dicey (n. 4), 179–82.

[25] See e.g. *Dyson* v. *Attorney General (No. 1)* [1911] KB 410; *Ridge* v. *Baldwin* [1964] AC 40; *Anisminic Ltd* v. *Foreign Compensation Commission* [1969] 2 AC 147; *Blackburn* v. *Attorney General* [1971] 1 WLR 1037; *McWhirter* v. *Attorney General* [1972] CMLR 882; *Manuel* v. *Attorney General* [1982] 3 All ER 786; *R* v. *Secretary of State for Foreign and Commonwealth Affairs ex parte Rees-Mogg* [1994] QB 552.

When the 'private law' remedy of declaration was made available for deciding 'public law' questions about governmental power, it permitted cases to be
litigated which would never otherwise have got off the ground either because
of doubts as to whether prerogative orders lay against the challenged
decision-maker or because, without discovery of documents which was not
available in the prerogative writs, applicants could not find out what had led
to the decision going against them.[26] As a declaration does not quash
decisions but only declares their legal status, courts had to expand the
range of flaws in decision-making which would make a decision invalid in
order to make the declaration an effective remedy in 'public law'.

When the scope of and grounds for judicial review of administrative acts
began to expand in the 1960s and 1970s, however, two sets of concerns
collided. First, people pursuing grievances were frustrated at having to
start different proceedings in different courts subject to different rules in
order to access a range of remedies. Could they not all be available under
one roof? Secondly, public administrators and judges became concerned
that judicial caseloads were growing and administrative acts were being
reviewed by judges who were not sufficiently aware of the special needs of
public administration and in proceedings which denied public bodies the
protection against trivial challenges which procedure for prerogative writs
allowed them. Could judicial review of administrative acts be contained
within a single procedure with reasonable protection for the interests of
administrators, overseen by a specialist cadre of 'public law' judges?

These concerns produced the 'application for judicial review' (AJR)
procedure, in which the three main prerogative orders (as they became
known), prohibition, mandamus and certiorari, along with declarations,
injunctions and, in appropriate cases, private-law damages, could be
obtained in one set of proceedings regarding 'public law matters'. These
cases were heard by a small number of expert High Court judges in the
'Crown Office List'. Once this was achieved, the House of Lords decided
judicially that the AJR procedure should be the only way of litigating
'public law matters'.[27] The difficulty was that there was no clarity over
what 'public law matters' were. The courts went through doctrinal convul-
sions in attempting to find criteria for classifying matters as 'public law' or
'private law'. Possible criteria included the governmental nature of the

---

[26] Examples include *Ridge* v. *Baldwin* and *Anisminic* (n. 25).

[27] *O'Reilly* v. *Mackman* [1983] 2 AC 237; M. Aronson, 'Public Law Values in the Common
Law', (Chapters 7 in this volume).

body whose act was challenged, the governmental character of the function that the body was exercising, the statutory underpinnings of the
function being exercised, the source of funding for the activity in question,
the absence of a 'private law' (e.g. contractual) nexus between the parties,
and the monopolistic control which the challenged decision-maker exercised over access to a market. None of these was determinative, and in
many cases they pulled in different directions, so there was a degree of
uncertainty as to whether, for example, decisions of the Jockey Club, which
controls horse-racing but is not governmental, could be challenged by
AJR.[28] From an administrator's point of view, the advantages of the new
system were: challenges had to be brought within months rather than
years; a public body could quickly build up costs at an early stage in
proceedings, discouraging the challenger; there was a good chance that
the challenger would not get leave (now called permission) to apply for
judicial review; disclosure and examination of witnesses would be rare;
and, even if the body lost on the merits, remedies were discretionary.

With mainly cosmetic changes, the position today is the same under the
Civil Procedure Rules. The prerogative orders have been renamed (prohibitory order, mandatory order, quashing order); time limits have been
tightened; the Crown Office List is now the Administrative Court; the
need to cope with a growing caseload means that most judges hearing
cases in the Administrative Court are no longer specialists;[29] the
Administrative Court now deals with a good number of tort claims, particularly in relation to cases concerning detention of prisoners, immigration
detainees and people affected by military action in Iraq and Afghanistan,
so the procedures are having to be adapted in order to do justice between
the parties; and a judicial review jurisdiction has been conferred on the
Upper Tribunal, outside the ambit of the High Court. But the emphasis on
protecting public bodies remains, on the assumption that, unlike ordinary
litigants, they are acting in the public interest, as does the lack of clarity in
the dividing line between 'public law' and other matters.

In some respects, however, the dividing line has acquired additional
significance while becoming more blurred. A growing number of legal
obligations apply only to bodies which are 'public' in the sense that they

---

[28] The prevailing view is that they cannot: see *R. v. Disciplinary Committee of the Jockey
Club ex parte Aga Khan* [1993] 1 WLR 909; *R. (Mullins) v. Appeal Board of the Jockey Club
(No. 1)* [2005] EWHC 2197 (Admin).

[29] I am grateful to Sir Rabinder Singh for this point and the next one.

are treated as exercising functions or assuming obligations on behalf of the state, while the UK is well known to lack any developed notion of 'the state'. In EU law, for example, the state may be liable to private parties who are injured as a result of the state's failure to implement directives properly or otherwise to comply with obligations in EU law, and state institutions are bound by the terms of directives which the state has failed to implement properly. The Court of Justice has made it clear that affected bodies include all 'emanations of the state'; criteria for deciding whether or not a body is such an emanation have emerged, but are not always easy to apply, and overlap, without being identical to, criteria of 'publicness' developed for AJR purposes. Under the Freedom of Information Act 2000, 'public authorities' have duties in respect of information which they hold; the Act gives fairly detailed lists of bodies which are 'public authorities' for this purpose. By contrast, the Human Rights Act 1998 makes it unlawful for 'public authorities' to act in a manner incompatible with Convention rights (as defined in the Act), but only partly defines 'public authority', and leaves a fairly open category of normally non-public bodies which, however, exercise a 'public function', and are subject to the duty except when the nature of the 'act' on which they are engaged is 'private'. Courts have struggled to make sense of these provisions, and have developed indicators of 'publicness' and 'privateness' which, once again, overlap but are not identical to those used for AJR or EU law purposes. Finally, equality law imposes a 'public sector equality duty' (the duty to promote equality) on 'public authorities', defined by a list system supplemented by the general test imported from the Human Rights Act 1998; this gives the worst of both worlds, combining the unprincipled nature of lists with the uncertainty of the public function/private act analysis.

An illustration of the two distinctions in action

A well-known example illustrates the important yet problematic character of both the relationship between 'public law' and 'public non-law' and that between 'public law' and 'non-public law'. *Attorney General* v. *Jonathan Cape Ltd*[30] was a case in which the government tried to press law into service to support bureaucratic and political norms, rather than more

---

[30] [1976] 1 QB 752.

commonly discussed cases in which people try to use law against government; but this does not affect the usefulness of the example.

When Richard Crossman, formerly a Cabinet Minister in the Labour government of 1964–70, wanted to publish the diaries which he had kept during that period, the civil service sought to prevent the publication of his descriptions of dealings with civil servants and discussions in Cabinet and the Privy Council. It was acknowledged that a Cabinet Minister had an obligation not to disclose Cabinet discussions, but this was an aspect of the convention of collective Cabinet responsibility, or 'non-law'. Could the law be invoked to support it? When the Attorney General agreed to bring proceedings for an injunction to restrain publication, he relied on the (then barely formed) equitable doctrine of breach of confidence, previously used only to protect commercial confidences and information about family life. Was it applicable to governmental information? If it was, would there be special limitations on or conditions for its use in that context, in view of the public interest, in a democracy, in people knowing how their government was conducted? Was it inappropriate to use an equitable principle developed to protect commercial and familial interests in the context of government? In short, was it appropriate to use a 'private' law principle in a 'public' governmental setting?

In the event, Lord Widgery CJ decided that the principle could be used, but only if there was a strong 'public' interest in restraining disclosure (over and above the requirement in 'private' contexts that the information or the relationship affected should be of a confidential nature), and even if there was such a strong public interest, it could be (and in that case was) outweighed by countervailing 'public' and 'private' interests favouring publication.[31] Governmental activities were sufficiently like commercial and family activities in the need for a degree of confidentiality and secrecy to justify making use of the general equitable notion of breach of confidence in relation to advice to ministers from civil servants and discussions in Cabinet; but they were sufficiently different, on account of the distinctively public nature of governmental responsibilities and functions, to require the equitable doctrine to be tempered, in a governmental context, by a requirement for strong public interests to get a claim off the

---

[31] The same approach was later taken in Australia – see *Commonwealth of Australia* v. *John Fairfax & Sons Ltd* (1980) 147 CLR 39 – and other UK cases, including *Attorney General* v. *Guardian Newspapers (No 2)* [1990] 1 AC 109, and *Lord Advocate* v. *The Scotsman Publications Ltd* [1990] 2 AC 580.

ground at all and then to outweigh competing interests in disclosure. This extended and adapted the substantive principles of 'law' from 'private' to 'public' spheres, but did not affect the convention. Despite some claims to the contrary, 'law' (both 'public' and 'private') remained distinct from 'public non-law'.[32]

Conclusion

Can anything useful be said, then, about the distinctiveness of 'public law', given the protean idea of the 'public'? The discussion in this chapter prompts a number of reflections.

First, governmental bodies have, and see themselves as having, concerns which are usually different from those of ordinary people. They use money raised from or on behalf of the people as a whole for purposes which reflect a sense of what is 'in the public interest', meaning that the activity in question is calculated to improve the lot of a section of the people or the social conditions in which the people live. Acts of Parliament – or at any rate 'public general Acts', as distinct from private or local Acts – are not concerned with individuals, even though some individuals may benefit directly from them and some Acts confer rights directly on individuals. Likewise, public administration acts in the cause of a political conception of a good, or better, society. This justifies applying to public bodies a set of legal requirements different from, or at least additional to, those imposed on ordinary people, but also adapting the procedures and remedies of law as they apply to public bodies to limit the risk that an individual will be able to use 'private' or 'public' law to subvert public bodies' efforts to advance public interests.

One implication of this is that it is a mistake to try to put individual rights at the centre of 'public law' and its procedures. There is a place for rights in 'public law', but only as, first, a reflection of a view of what helps to make a good society, and, secondly, a sharp limitation on the means which public bodies may employ in pursuit of public interests so that they do not

---

[32] See the discussion in D. Feldman, 'Constitutional conventions', in M. Qvortrup (ed.), *The British Constitution: Continuity, Change and the Influence of Europe: A Festschrift for Vernon Bogdanor* (Oxford: Hart Publishing, 2013), 94–119. Compare the different view of T. R. S. Allan, *Law, Liberty, and Justice: The Legal Foundations of British Constitutionalism* (Oxford: Clarendon Press, 1993), ch. 10.

undermine the freedoms which are necessary for that conception of a good society.

A second reflection on the distinctiveness of 'public law' is that, turning on public interests, it is not undermined by the indisputable fact that one can identify some values underlying both 'private law' and 'public law'. That the commonality of values, persuasively explained by Professor Dawn Oliver,[33] is pervasive helps to give legality in all its forms, and, one may add, 'public non-law' too, their moral value. But they operate in different ways in different areas of law. In 'public law', the centrality of the public interest means that law draws on common values to different effect from 'private law'. Values may be the same, but rules and principles are different, because in 'public law' the rule of law operates in the shadow of the public-interest aims of public administrators and governments. As Sir John Laws has expressed it, the usually individualistic, right-based morality of courts has to reach an accommodation with the utilitarian morality of government.[34]

Thirdly, we should not assume that, because the need to reach this accommodation is at the heart of 'public law', it is limited to 'public law' proceedings. It can appear in many kinds of law and litigation. For example, the extent of tortious or delictual liability of public authorities raises the same issue. Does a local authority owe a duty of care in negligence to children, or to the parents of children, whom the authority's social workers remove from their homes? Does a constabulary owe a duty of care to someone who is injured when the constabulary fails to protect him or her against a foreseen or foreseeable threat? Is a Home Secretary liable to pay damages for false imprisonment to a person detained under a legal power where the decision is flawed on administrative law grounds? Faced with questions such as these, it does not matter whether the proceedings are classified as 'public' or 'private'. One cannot set the bounds of 'private law' liability without taking into account the 'public law' concern for the public interest, whatever that may be.

The importance of the public interest means that 'public law' is distinctive. Compared with 'public non-law', it is distinctively legal in terms of its rules and principles and its procedures, to the point where it is distinct. Despite occasional doubts as to where the boundary lies, to dispense with it would threaten both political sovereignty and the rule of law within the

---

[33] D. Oliver, *Common Values and the Public-Private Divide* (London: Butterworths, 1999).

[34] Sir John Laws, 'The Good Constitution' [2013] *Cambridge Law Journal* 567, and see also Laws (n. 10), 48–53, and Aronson (n. 27).

state. Accepting that Sir John Laws's legal and political moralities must be accommodated to each other does not entail allowing one to park its tanks on the other's front lawn. Drawing the boundary is the job of the legal rules regarding justiciability and legal accountability. By comparison, the boundary between 'public law' and 'non-public law' is softer. We should not expect that the primacy of the public interest in 'public law' will allow us to fashion rules and principles or procedures of 'public law' which can avoid the need to take the public interest of government into account in the 'private law' of tort, contract or trusts. 'Public law' is therefore not as distinct from 'non-public law' as it is from 'public non-law'; but that does not mean that it is not distinctive.

Further reading

J. W. F. Allison, *A Continental Distinction in the Common Law: A Historical and Comparative Perspective on English Public Law* (Oxford: Oxford University Press, 1996)

A. V. Dicey, *Introduction to the Study of the Law of the Constitution* 10th edn, ed. E. C. S. Wade (London: Macmillan, 1959), ch. 1

S. Flogaitis, *The Evolution of Law and the State in Europe: Seven Lessons* (Oxford: Hart Publishing, 2014)

Sir John Laws, *The Common Law Constitution* (Cambridge: Cambridge University Press, 2014)

M. Loughlin, *Foundations of Public Law* (Oxford: Oxford University Press, 2010)

D. Oliver, *Common Values and the Public-Private Divide* (London: Butterworths, 1999)

R. C. van Caenegem, *An Historical Introduction to Western Constitutional Law* (Cambridge: Cambridge University Press, 1995)

The politics of public law 2

David Howarth

Conflict between politicians and lawyers about the proper role of the law in political decision-making is not new, but events over the past twenty years in the United Kingdom suggest that some kind of breakdown is taking place. Political attacks on the judiciary, often connected with human rights and European Union law, are now commonplace. On the other side we see judicial musings about altering the accepted relationship between the rule of law and the supremacy of Parliament to the detriment of Parliament.[1] The situation is made worse by an apparent separation of law and politics, or at least a separation of politicians and lawyers, so that each group finds the perspective of the other increasingly difficult to understand.[2] In such circumstances, we should not be surprised to find that politicians interpret public law as essentially a political intervention by lawyers into politics and lawyers interpret it as a principled challenge to the lawlessness of politicians. The question this chapter poses is whether we can get beyond these two stereotypical characterisations and offer more nuanced descriptions of the relationship between public law and politics. In particular, can we treat the relationship between politics and public law not as a constant but as a variable, a relationship that can change over time and from place to place? If we can, we will at least have a more comprehensive way of describing the relationship that we might later be able to use to think about what the relationship should be.

An example

The difficulty of characterising the relationship between politics and public law can be illustrated by looking at one of the many confrontations

---

[1] E.g. *R. (Jackson)* v. *Attorney General* [2005] UKHL 56, [2006] 1 AC 262; *AXA General Insurance Ltd.* v. *Lord Advocate* [2011] UKSC 46, [2012] 1 AC 868.

[2] D. Howarth, 'Lawyers in the House of Commons', in D. Feldman (ed.), *Law in Politics, Politics in Law* (Oxford: Hart Publishing, 2013).

between a British Home Secretary and the judges. In February 2013 the Home Secretary, Theresa May, writing in the *Mail on Sunday*, declared:

[S]ome judges seem to believe that they can ignore Parliament's wishes if they think that the procedures for parliamentary scrutiny have been 'weak'. That appears actually to mean that they can ignore Parliament when they think it came to the wrong conclusion . . .

[T]he law in this country is made by the elected representatives of the people in Parliament. And our democracy is subverted when judges decide to take on that role for themselves.

Mrs May was annoyed about a decision of the Upper Tribunal, *Secretary of State for the Home Department* v. *Izuazu*.[3] The case concerned an issue that arose repeatedly in the early years of the twenty-first century. Unauthorised migrants who had formed relationships in the United Kingdom would argue that deporting them would break up those relationships, resulting in violations of Article 8 of the European Convention of Human Rights, which guarantees the right to 'family life'.[4] The issue was of great political importance. It brought together three topics of utmost interest to politicians on the nationalist right of British politics: immigration, the alleged iniquities of the European Convention on Human Rights, and, through the application of the same rules to deporting foreign offenders, crime. Those issues also fed into deeper political controversies about national identity and cultural diversity.

The Home Secretary, a member of the Conservative Party, had previously attempted to narrow the application of Article 8 by including a restrictive interpretation of it in the Home Office's Immigration Rules and had moved a resolution in the House of Commons endorsing that restrictive interpretation.[5] The motion passed without a division, although only after serious confusion broke out about what the House was debating and why.[6]

When the effect of the new rules came before the judges in *Izuazu*, Blake J, the President of the Upper Tribunal, was unimpressed. The Secretary of State had submitted that:

---

[3] [2013] UKUT 45 (IAC), [2013] INLR 733.

[4] See e.g. *Huang* v. *Secretary of State for the Home Department* [2007] UKHL 11, [2007] 2 AC 167. (Note that the right to family life might belong not only to the person threatened with deportation but also to the other members of that person's family.)

[5] Hansard, HC, 19 Jun 2012, columns 760ff.

[6] See especially the remarks of Pete Wishart MP at column 789.

[W]hile the Rules do not bind the Courts, in the same way as primary legislation, they are a clear, democratically endorsed, statement of public policy which must now be taken into account by the courts when assessing proportionality.

Blake J, however, took the entirely conventional view that resolutions of the House of Commons do not change the law. He noted that the Immigration Rules usually receive only 'weak scrutiny' in the form of the negative resolution procedure, but added:

There may have been more active debate of the new rules in the House of Commons than is often the case under the negative procedure resolution, but the House of Commons is not Parliament and it has long been the law that a resolution of the House of Commons is not given supremacy akin to primary legislation by the court: see *Stockdale* v. *Hansard* (1839) 9 A & E 1.

For Mrs May, such views constituted defiance of the will of the people. Her *Mail on Sunday* article continued:

Just think for a moment what this judge is claiming. He is asserting that he can ignore the unanimous adoption by the Commons of new immigration rules on the grounds that he thinks this is a 'weak form of parliamentary scrutiny'.

I find it difficult to see how that can be squared with the central idea of our constitution, which is that Parliament makes the law, and judges interpret what that law is and make sure the executive complies with it.

By the standards of UK Home Secretaries, Mrs May's choice of words was mild. Her Labour predecessor David Blunkett not only said that judges who refuse to accept ministers' public policy decisions constitute a 'threat to democracy', but also, allegedly, called the Lord Chief Justice 'a muddled and confused old codger'.[7] In terms of substance, however, Mrs May's actions were about as serious as one could imagine. She had attempted to change the most basic of constitutional rules, the rules about who is authorised to change the law. If the courts had conceded, the effect would have been as radical a reform of the legislative process as that of January 1649, when the Commons resolved that their ordinances had the full force of law even if the Lords and the King had not agreed them.[8]

---

[7] See R. Stevens, *The English Judges: Their Role in the Changing Constitution* (Oxford: Hart Publishing, 2005), 173.

[8] *House of Commons Journal*, 4 January 1648 (o.s.). The resolution in full reads:

Resolved, &c. That the Commons of England, in Parliament assembled, do Declare, That the People are, under God, the Original of all just Power:

Although the precise reasoning of *Izuazu* did not survive further analysis in subsequent cases, the courts refused to concede on the central point,[9] insisting that the law could not be changed by a resolution. The Home Secretary fumed, with the support of the media, but ultimately gave up, informing the Court of Appeal in a later case that:

The new Rules do not seek to change the law. What they seek to do is properly to reflect the Strasbourg jurisprudence when applied to the deportation of foreign criminals.[10]

The government subsequently introduced primary legislation repeating its interpretation of Article 8. The Home Secretary took the opportunity to make a final attack on the judges:

The Government first sought to address this issue in July 2012 by changing the immigration rules with the intention of shifting the weight the courts give to the public interest. This House debated and approved the new rules, which set out the factors in favour of deportation and the factors against it. The courts accept that the new rules provide a complete code for considering article 8 where we are deporting foreign criminals. However, some judges have still chosen to ignore the will of Parliament and go on putting the law on the side of foreign criminals instead of the public. I am sending a very clear message to those judges: Parliament wants a law on the people's side, the public want a law on the people's side, and this Government will put the law on the people's side once and for all. This Bill will require the courts to put the public interest at the heart of their decisions.[11]

Despite this grand rhetoric, however, the statute did not require judges to decide cases differently. It required them only to 'have regard' to the government's view of the public interest.[12]

A conventional legal account of these events would contend that the legal system defeated a political attempt to change basic constitutional

---

And do also Declare, that the Commons of England, in Parliament assembled, being chosen by, and representing the People, have the Supreme Power in this Nation:

And do also Declare, That whatsoever is enacted, or declared for Law, by the Commons, in Parliament assembled, hath the Force of Law; and all the People of this Nation are concluded thereby, although the Consent and Concurrence of King, or House of Peers, be not had thereunto.

[9] See e.g. *MF* [2012] UKUT 00393 (IAC) and *Ogundimu* [2013] UKUT 60 (IAC). For a fuller account see M. Gower, *Article 8 of the ECHR and immigration cases*, House of Commons Library SN/HA/6355 October 2013.

[10] *MF* v. *Secretary of State for the Home Department* [2013] EWCA Civ 1192, [34].

[11] Hansard, HC, 22 Oct 2013, column 162.   [12] Immigration Act 2014, s. 19.

rules. The Home Secretary enthusiastically espoused the view that democracy, as expressed through the House of Commons, should not be constrained by judges, but found herself constrained anyway by her inability to control the judges' insistence that instructions from the political system to the legal system should take specific forms.

A political account would be quite different. It would mainly concern the Home Secretary's political goals. The most straightforward goal would have been to change the law with the aim of causing a reduction in the proportion of cases in which the right to family life under Article 8 was used to resist deportation. There are reasons, however, for thinking her goal was not quite so straightforward. For one thing, the Home Office appears not to have known how many foreign criminals cited Article 8 in their appeals against deportation.[13] It is not unheard of for government to embark on a policy without knowing how its success or failure could be measured, but when it does so, it raises doubts about whether that was its only goal. Another complication is that even if the goal were to affect decisions in the tribunals, achieving it might not have depended on changing the law. Home Secretaries suspect, not without evidence, that judges react to political pressure, so that change can be effected outside the formal legal process. A former very senior civil servant, asked about the Home Secretary's *Mail on Sunday* article, recalled:

Someone in the Home Office did a chart which plotted the statements of Home Secretaries with the decisions of judges. It was quite extraordinary. In the 1980s and 1990s the correlation between big policy statements and sentences was quite breath-taking. Judges are very sensitive politically.[14]

Other civil servants were even more sceptical. 'She must know it's far-fetched, to put it charitably', said one. It would have been 'political cover rather than judicial influencing', said another. The explanation for the whole episode, according to a third, was that 'there is something politically interesting for a minister if they want to show particular virility in an area'. Her motives might have included, for example, showing the nationalist right of her party she was tough on the Human Rights Act 1998, immigrants and

---

[13] Hansard, HC, 7 Jan 2014, column 186W.
[14] Interviewed by the author and Shona Wilson Stark as part of the 'Reality of the Constitution' (a research project supported by the LeRoux Trust – for further details see e.g. D. Howarth and S. Wilson Stark, 'The Reality of the British Constitution: HLA Hart and what "officials" really think', available at http://ssrn.com/abstract=2466001).

criminals. It might also have been keeping those issues in the public mind, both for reasons of party advantage and for ideological reasons.

The problem with two accounts is not that either is necessarily wrong but that both are incomplete. From the point of view of the political account, the legal account is naive. It omits any explanation of what the political actors were trying to do and suppresses the possibility that judges can submit to political pressure. From the point of view of the legal account, the political account fails to take seriously the importance of the constitutional change being proposed.

The question is whether there is any way of reconciling these accounts, or are we doomed to a perpetual state of partial translation and misunderstanding?

Integrating law and politics

One way of approaching the question is to ask what the relationship between law and politics looks like at a more abstract level. Miro Cerar, for example, classified the relationships between law and politics into law conceived of as a goal of politics, as a means of politics and as an obstacle for politics.[15] Cerar's analysis, however, asks only what law looks like from the point of view of politics. It leaves undone a parallel analysis of what politics looks like from the point of view of law. One might propose, for example, that the law might see politics as a threat to legality, as a means of achieving legality and as a sphere outside legality. The first can be observed, for example, in the view that taking into account political considerations can taint public decisions.[16] The second is where the law demands that political processes, such as elections, take place. The third includes doctrines such as non-justiciability or deference, in which the law treats the political system as beyond the law's reach. Such further analysis would be interesting, but it would still leave the legal and political accounts unintegrated – still staring at each other in mutual incomprehension. One might, for example, construct a three-by-three table combining the three political views of law and the three legal views of politics, but it is not clear

---

[15] M. Cerar, 'The Relationship Between Law and Politics' (2009) 15 *Annual Survey of International & Comparative Law* 3, 37.

[16] E.g. *Roberts* v. *Hopwood* [1925] AC 578; *Bromley London Borough Council* v. *Greater London Council* [1983] 1 AC 768.

it would reveal anything but various kinds of incompatibility. The approach needs to be more integrated from the start.

We can achieve more integration if we see a public law system as the outcome of a series of strategic decisions about the relationship between law and politics. The idea would be to break down the overall relationship into a series of separate high-level decisions, allowing the overall picture to be made up from combinations of those decisions.[17] Instead of starting from separate legal or political perspectives, we can start from a unified perspective – namely asking what positions the law can take on the most important aspects of politics.

Politics – autonomous or constituted by law?

A central strategic question for a system of public law is whether it conceives of the political system as autonomous or as constituted by law. That question has engaged theorists as diverse as Carl Schmitt and H. L. A. Hart and continues in the UK in the form of the debate about whether we have a 'political' as opposed to a 'legal' constitution.[18] It is also connected to the debate about 'juridification', the extent to which the law should penetrate and seek to control social life.[19] But the point should not be to announce the intellectual victory of one side or another, but rather to see these debates as generating options among which a system can choose (and re-choose). There can be systems of public law that treat the political realm as socially constituted and not legally constituted and there can be

---

[17] This method is inspired by factorisation and systematic variation in engineering design. See G. Pahl, W. Beitz, J. Feldhusen, K.-H. Grote (K. Wallace and L. Blessing trans.), *Engineering Design: A Systematic Approach* (London: Springer, 2007), 3rd edn., 61. It is also close to the method of R. Clark in 'The Morphogenesis of Subchapter C: An Essay in Statutory Evolution and Reform' (1977) 87 *Yale Law Journal* 90.

[18] See e.g. J. A. G. Griffith, 'The Political Constitution' (1979) 42 *Modern Law Review* 1; R. Bellamy, *Political Constitutionalism: A Republican Defence of the Constitutionality of Democracy* (Cambridge: Cambridge University Press, 2007); T. R. S. Allan, 'Questions of Legality and Legitimacy: Form and Substance in British Constitutionalism' (2011) 9 *International Journal of Constitutional Law* 155; P. Craig, 'Political Constitutionalism and the Judicial Role: A Response' (2011) 9 *International Journal of Constitutional Law* 112 and T. Gyorfi, 'Between Common Law Constitutionalism and Procedural Democracy' (2013) 33 *Oxford Journal of Legal Studies* 317.

[19] See e.g. G. Teubner, 'Juridification: Concepts, Aspects, Limits, Solutions' in R. Baldwin, C. Scott, and C. Hood, *A Reader on Regulation* (Oxford: Oxford University Press, 1998).

systems that treat all political institutions, and thus all legitimate political activity, as having no existence outside the law.[20] In the former 'autonomist' conception, the law regulates political decision-making from the outside. In the latter 'constitutive' conception, political decisions cannot take place outside the law since the law makes politics possible. Most non-lawyers in politics seem to gravitate to the autonomist position, treating politics as an activity that would occur even in entirely lawless situations, as just something people do. But for lawyers, the constitutive position is far from unnatural. They would point to the example of the German Basic Law, which purports not only to bring the institutions of the state into existence but also to define the role of 'the people'.[21]

One way of determining which way a system has opted is to listen to how participants within it describe its political institutions. If even non-lawyers start their descriptions with the juridical foundations of political institutions, the system is likely to have opted for the constitutive view. One frequently hears EU officials, for example, begin descriptions of the EU with a discussion of the juridical nature of the Union, starting in international law. Descriptions of British political institutions, in contrast, rarely begin with juridical categories. Admittedly Bracton said the King was below no man but God and the Law, 'for the Law makes the King',[22] but that distinctly constitutive view is now uncommon. Largely because there has been no fundamental reset of the whole constitutional system for many centuries, 'Parliament', 'King', and even 'The Treasury' and 'The Home Office' are usually taken to be social realities whose existence owes nothing to the law. For example, in the Cabinet Manual, the UK Civil Service's guide to the constitution and the functioning of government, the chapter on 'The Sovereign' simply assumes the reader knows what kind of being a Sovereign is and launches straight into the monarch's 'ceremonial and

---

[20] I am using a broad conception of politics as the acquisition of power by human beings and its use over other human beings and a broadly positivist conception of law as a binding (i.e. non-voluntary) body of rules and principles for human action emanating from authoritative source.

[21] German Basic Law, Article 20(2). The US Constitution is constitutive with regard to political institutions but is arguably autonomist with regard to 'the People'. The ninth and tenth amendments treat 'the People' as an undefined pre-constitutional source of ultimate authority. There is, however, a counter-argument to the effect that 'We, the People' does not refer to a pre-existing social reality but is itself a self-authorising legal creation of the Constitution itself.

[22] H. de Bracton, *De Legibus Et Consuetudinibus Angliæ*, Thorne edition, vol. II, 33.

constitutional duties', the ceremonial duties seemingly on the same level as the constitutional.[23]

It is nevertheless possible for conflicts to break out about which direction the system should take. One way of interpreting the long struggle between the Commons and the courts about the nature of parliamentary privilege is that the Commons views its own existence and powers as owing nothing to the courts, whereas the courts, in cases such as *Stockdale* v. *Hansard*[24] and *R* v. *Chaytor*,[25] periodically assert that Parliament's privileges are constituted by the law. Parliament's view, as the Joint Committee on Parliamentary Privilege explained in 2013, is that privilege 'is, in effect, an exception to the general principle of the rule of law',[26] a view Parliament reinforces by referring to *Bradlaugh* v. *Gossett*,[27] in which the courts accepted that even the interpretation of statute law could fall within the exclusive cognisance of the Commons.[28] That is not the view of the courts, however. Backed by the European Court of Human Rights, which usually promotes the constitutive view,[29] the courts claim *Kompetenz-Kompetenz* over the extent of privilege, allowing to Parliament competence only over its application. Parliament seems now reluctantly to accept the courts' jurisdiction over extent,[30] although it darkly points to its undoubted power to enforce its own view by legislation.[31]

A similar conflict exists between the courts and the government. Judicial control over executive action is very well established in Britain. Judges treat judicial review of executive action as a fundamental part of the constitutional system, which, if threatened, might justify revision of the doctrine of parliamentary supremacy.[32] Within government, however, rather different views prevail. Civil servants when questioned about their view of the relationship between the courts and ministers express views that would surprise the courts – for example the view that court orders should only be obeyed if the Attorney General (a minister) says they should, or the view, not by any means universal but certainly held by some, that civil servants should obey ministerial instructions even if they

[23] *The Cabinet Manual* (London: Cabinet Office, 2011), 7. The treatment of the Government is similar (see p. 21).

[24] (1839) 9 Ad & E 1.   [25] [2010] UKSC 52, [2011] AC 684.

[26] Joint Committee on Parliamentary Privilege, *Parliamentary Privilege* (London: House of Commons and House of Lords, 2013), 7.

[27] (1884) 12 QBD 271.   [28] Above n. 26, 8.   [29] *A* v. *UK* [2002] ECHR 35373/97.

[30] Above n. 26, 10–11.   [31] Above n. 26, 11.   [32] Above n. 1.

believed those instructions to be in defiance of the law.[33] These views and the assumptions behind them go well beyond the debates, all too familiar to British public lawyers, about whether the courts should show 'deference' to the government on specific issues, for example on foreign and security policy. They reveal a rather more radical view that the power of the Crown and of those who act for the Crown – ministers and officials – exists autonomously without any reference to the law.[34] That view is the ultimate explanation of why the UK Civil Service keeps returning to proposals to restrict judicial review, proposals always viewed as scandalous by judges, but which seem nothing out of the ordinary to officials. Government, in the official view, does not proceed from law, and so there is nothing contradictory in it proposing changes to the law about itself.

Political dimensions

We can now turn to a number of other strategic decisions about the relationship between public law and politics, each of which relates to a different aspect of politics. Politics includes, for example, conflict over resources, competition between parties, ideological struggle (including conflict over the agenda of politics), and conflict over identity and allegiance.[35] We can construct strategic decisions for public law around each of these.[36]

Conflict over resources

The first strategic decision is whether the law will interfere in political decisions about the allocation of public resources. Will the courts abstain

---

[33] See Howarth and Wilson Stark (n. 14).

[34] Cf A. H. Birch, *The British System of Government* (London: Routledge, 2013), 20, who identifies a 'Whitehall' account of the constitution, namely the view of officials that Parliament has essentially no role in the government of the country. Much of Whitehall sees the courts in a similar way.

[35] For these dimensions of politics, see D. Howarth, 'Is Law a Humanity or is it more like Engineering?' (2004) 3 *Arts and Humanities in Higher Education* 9, 9. See further, on ideology and agenda control, S. Lukes, *Power: A Radical View* (Basingstoke: Macmillan, 1986).

[36] The provisional nature of the list should be emphasised. Other dimensions of politics might be added or used instead. The main purpose here is to illustrate the method of using strategic decisions.

from such interference or will they allow themselves to second-guess political institutions?

As Jeff King has pointed out, legal interference in resource allocation need not be confined to direct challenges to how public authorities allocate their budgets.[37] Many types of case can have serious financial consequences for government without direct challenge to resource allocation decisions, from damages awards in negligence cases to the cost of re-running a procedure following a successful judicial review. For that reason requiring the courts to have no effect at all on public expenditure would mean public law would become near impossible. That position nevertheless constitutes a theoretical possibility at one end of a scale, at the other end of which is allowing courts directly to review the discretionary budgetary decisions of democratically elected bodies.

The minimalist position attracts those who believe in a very strong version of the separation of powers, under which different branches should have no effect on one another. It was a view of that sort that led in France to the development of a system of public law entirely separate from the ordinary courts.[38] The maximalist position is advocated by those who favour strong social and economic rights or those who believe that inequality is a major threat to social peace.[39] In between, a system might rule out direct interference in discretionary budgetary decisions but allow any amount of indirect impact. Some human rights approaches might suggest a different rule, allowing court interference as long as it is necessary to avoid falling below minimum standards, for example the level of social security provision needed to preserve life.[40]

Again the object of the exercise is not to decide which approach is best but to plot where different systems of public law are positioned and where they might be moving. In England, for example, the position appears to be that direct challenges to budgetary decisions of public bodies are not

---

[37] J. King, *Judging Social Rights* (Cambridge: Cambridge University Press, 2012), 257; J. King, 'The Justiciability of Resource Allocation' (2007) 70 *Modern Law Review* 197.

[38] N. Brown and J. Bell, *French Administrative Law* (Oxford: Oxford University Press, 1998), 5th edn., 46–48.

[39] E.g. L. Arbour, 'Economic and Social Justice for Societies in Transition' (2007) 40 *NYU Journal of International Law and Politics* 1.

[40] E.g. V. Gauri and D. Brinks, 'Introduction: The Element of Legalization and the Triangular Shape of Social and Economic Rights', in V. Gauri and D. Brinks, *Courting Social Justice: Judicial Enforcement of Social and Economic Rights in the Developing World* (Cambridge: Cambridge University Press, 2010), 1.

permitted, even to the budgets of bodies not democratically elected,[41] but there is no limit to the degree to which budgets can be indirectly affected.[42] Human rights law, especially the concept of positive rights, looks capable of shifting the balance further in favour of intervention,[43] although the theoretical possibility of intervention does not necessarily change the outcome of cases.[44] Other systems seem to have gone further, though perhaps not as far as some have hoped. In South Africa, with its celebrated inclusion of economic and social rights in the constitution[45] (at least as a matter of 'progressive realisation' and 'within existing resources'), the case law seems to be moving towards positions more sceptical of judicial power.[46]

Party competition

The second aspect of politics is the struggle between parties for power. The strategic decision is whether public law recognises political party interests as legitimate. Is it, for example, a legitimate goal for a policy decision that it will generate a political advantage for the governing party? One extreme option is to treat all political considerations as a form of corruption and thus always unacceptable. The other extreme is to say that the central mechanism of representative democracy is politicians competing for votes, so that to condemn a decision for being 'political' is ipso facto anti-democratic. Intermediate positions might look to divide political considerations into the acceptable and the unacceptable, for example distinguishing between decisions taken to gain electoral support (acceptable) and decisions taken to interfere with informed political debate or to distort the electoral process (unacceptable).

---

[41] See e.g. *R. v. Cambridge DHA, ex parte B (No. 1)* [1995] 1 WLR 898 129; *R. (McDonald)* v. *Royal Borough of Kensington and Chelsea* [2011] UKSC 33, [2011] PTSR 1266.

[42] See e.g. *Breyer* v. *Department of Energy and Climate Change* [2014] EWHC 2257 (QB), in which the value of the claim, £132 million according to the claimants' solicitors (http://prospectlaw.co.uk/decc-held-liable-to-compensate-the-solar-pv-supply-chain-indus tries-for-its-unlawful-acts-in-prospect-laws-claim-for-132-million-brought-under-human-rights-legislation/), caused no comment from the court and a 'floodgates' argument was swiftly dismissed (at 41–43).

[43] *R. (Limbuela)* v. *Secretary of State for the Home Department* [2005] UKHL 66, [2006] 1 AC 396.

[44] See e.g. *R. (McDonald)* v. *Royal Borough of Kensington and Chelsea* [2011] UKSC 33.

[45] E.g. ss. 26, on housing, 27, on health, food, water and social security, and 29, on education.

[46] See e.g. A. Pillay, 'Economic and Social Rights Adjudication: Developing Principles of Judicial Restraint in South Africa and the United Kingdom' [2013] *Public Law* 606.

English public law has long contained a strong anti-political strain, for example condemning local authorities for setting wages on the basis of political beliefs,[47] or the Greater London Council for taking manifesto commitments into account when deciding its policy on public transport fares.[48] In addition, parliament itself increasingly treats not just current but past involvement in national electoral politics as a taint, for example barring appointment to certain types of public office.[49] But hostility to politics does not extend to all circumstances and the courts sometimes seem to apply a double standard – appearing on the surface to be severely anti-political but in reality being more accepting of politics. The *locus classicus* is the 'party whip' issue: whether a decision can be impugned on the ground that those voting for it did so on the basis of party political solidarity. Article 9 of the Bill of Rights prevents any judicial investigation of Parliament, but that protection does not extend to local government. The law is that a council decision can be attacked on the ground that councillors voted for it solely because of threats of disciplinary action against them if they voted against the party's line. That would amount to illegally fettering their discretion. But the key word is 'solely'. If they have other reasons for supporting the policy, or even if they vote with the party because they believe party solidarity is important while keeping open the possibility they might rebel, they are not acting illegally.[50]

Ideological struggle

We can now turn to politics as an ideological struggle, as a struggle over how people think about politics and what is properly on the agenda of

---

[47] See *Roberts* v. *Hopwood* [1925] AC 578, which treated the payment of what might now be called 'living wages' and 'equal pay' as illegal philanthropic gifts. The powers and duties of local authorities are now different, and the language of the court (referring disparagingly to 'socialistic philanthropy' and 'feminist ambition') is perhaps now out of date, but the principle of the case has been accepted as recently as 2012 – see *Charles Terence Estates Ltd* v. *Cornwall Council* [2012] EWCA Civ 1439, [2013] 1 WLR 466.

[48] *Bromley London Borough Council* v. *Greater London Council* [1983] 1 AC 768

[49] See Howarth (n 2).

[50] *R* v. *Waltham Forest London Borough Council, ex parte Baxter* [1988] QB 419. The leading judgment is by Sir John Donaldson MR, who had himself served as a local councillor (albeit as an Independent). Such political experience is now rare on the English Bench. For the most part, however, *Baxter* remains unchallenged – see e.g. *R (Island Farm Development Ltd)* v. *Bridgend CBC* [2006] EWHC 2189 (Admin); *R (De Whalley)* v. *Norfolk County Council* [2011] EWHC 3739 (Admin).

politics. Here it is more difficult to speak in terms of public law systems making strategic decisions since ideological struggles often proceed tacitly, by those engaged in them acting as if their preferred ideology was unchallengeable and simply assuming it to be right. But systems do adopt ideological positions in the sense of treating certain positions as unthinkable. It would be impossible, for example, to suggest in the US Supreme Court that capitalism itself violates the equal protection clause, or in the French *Conseil d'Etat* that 'liberté' requires the privatisation of all French state assets. Human rights approaches are themselves ideological in this sense – attempts to control the options available, not just the options taken. Often, the progress of an ideology across a public law system can only be judged historically, by tracing the decline, usually without comment, of other ways of thinking. And since the process is often silent and even unconscious, such histories will be contentious and disputed.[51]

Still arguably ideological, though more tractable, is what counts as 'public' for the purposes of deciding the purview of public law.[52] At one end of the spectrum lies the possibility that public law applies only to a very narrow range of entities, to those undoubtedly part of the state. At the other lies the possibility that public law applies to anyone exercising power over another person, regardless of official status or the form the power takes – whether political, social or economic. In between, a variety of positions can be taken as to what constitutes 'state action' or a 'public service'. US public law, for example, tends towards a very narrow view.[53] French public law takes a broader view, counting as 'public' the activities of any organisation delivering public services, regardless of legal form.[54] English law, although moving towards the French view under pressure from EU law,[55] takes an intermediate view, treating private suppliers of public services as generally outside the

---

[51] See e.g. J. Fishman and D. Law, 'What is Judicial Ideology and how should we Measure it?' (2009) 29 *Journal of Law & Policy* 133.

[52] For further discussion of this point, see D. Feldman, 'The Distinctiveness of Public Law' (Chapter 1 in this volume).

[53] See e.g. *Brentwood Academy* v. *Tennessee Secondary Schools Athletic Association* 531 U.S. 288; 121 S. Ct. 924 (2001). See further J. Miller, 'The Influence of Human Rights and Basic Rights in Private Law in the United States' (2014) 62 *American Journal of Comparative Law* 133.

[54] The precise criteria are controversial. See Brown and Bell (n. 38), ch. 6, especially pp. 129–135.

[55] *Foster* v. *British Gas plc* [1990] ECR I-3313.

scope of public law[56] but some formally private bodies as public if they carry out regulatory functions.[57]

Identity

Finally, there is politics as conflict over identity and allegiance. Loyalties to nations, ethnicities, localities, religions, social groups and classifications, and to individual leaders can lead to conflicts not only over material resources but also around symbolic confirmation of dominance and subservience (for example the conflicts in Northern Ireland about flying flags over public buildings and who can parade where). These loyalties are of very great importance but lawyers tend to treat them as irrational and so either legally irrelevant or antithetical to legal values. For example, public service is usually thought of as requiring a high degree of selflessness, one that excludes public servants from acting on loyalties to family or friends.[58] Equally, if one searches the corpus of English, European and European Court of Human Rights case law for mentions of 'nationalism', one frequently finds the word appearing in very negative contexts, often conjoined with 'extreme', 'hatred', 'triumphalist', 'accusations', 'descent' and 'outburst'.[59] But other stances are possible. A system of public law might treat as legitimate or even as required state activity aimed at promoting specified identities and loyalties. The 1780 constitution of Massachusetts, for example, specifically empowered the state legislature to require citizens to attend churches maintained at public expense.[60] The trend might be away from such provisions in the religious sphere, but systems do still recognise the legitimacy of measures designed to promote national solidarity or identity or even treating the constitution itself as an object of reverence or worship.[61]

---

[56] *YL* v. *Birmingham City Council* [2007] UKHL 27, [2008] 1 AC 95.

[57] *R.* v. *Panel on Takeovers and Mergers ex parte Datafin plc* [1987] QB 815.

[58] See e.g. the 'Nolan Principles' (*First Report of the Committee on Standards in Public Life* (Committee on Standards in Public Life, 1995), cited in e.g. *AB* v. *A Chief Constable* [2014] EWHC 1965 (QB); *R. (Leathley)* v. *Visitors to the Inns of Court* [2013] EWHC 3097 (Admin); *R. (Raabe)* v. *Secretary of State for the Home Department* [2013] EWHC 1736 (Admin).

[59] See e.g. *Cichopek* v. *Poland* (2014) 58 EHRR SE1; *Zdinjak* v. *Croatia* [2012] EWHC 1554 (Admin); *Mesopotamia Broadcast A/S METV* v. *Germany* [2012] 1 CMLR 32; *TK (Sri Lanka)* v. *Secretary of State for the Home Department* [2009] UKAIT 49; *Dean* v. *Burne* [2009] EWHC 1250 (Ch); *Spanovic* v. *Croatia* [2009] EWHC 723 (Admin).

[60] Massachusetts Constitution of 1780, Part I, Art. 3.

[61] See e.g. R. Bellah, 'Civil Religion in America' (1967) 96 *Dædalus, Journal of the American Academy of Arts and Sciences* 1. Oaths of office in the USA invariably include an

A specific example of the recognition of identity in public law concerns law about languages. Many systems accept as legitimate state action designed to promote the use of minority languages. Some still accept state action designed to promote the use of dominant languages.[62] A remarkable example of the latter is a 1999 decision of the French *Conseil constitutionnel* striking down French accession to the European Charter for Regional or Minority Languages. The *Conseil* said that recognising such languages would 'porte atteinte aux principes constitutionnels d'indivisibilité de la République, d'égalité devant la loi et d'unicité du peuple français'.[63]

A descriptive politics of public law

It should be possible on the basis of strategic questions such as these to provide a description of the politics of public law in any particular system, to describe the conflicts within the system and to trace directions of change. If we take as an example English public law, we would note that most actors within it assume that state institutions exist as social institutions without regard to law and that the idea they are constituted by law is largely rejected, although tendencies in the opposite direction are appearing. We would further note that English public law tends to an intermediate position on the legitimacy of court intervention in resource allocation decisions, to a mostly hostile stance to party politics, to moderately liberal ideological positions that increasingly import the assumptions of the human rights approach, to a patchwork position on what counts as 'public' and to a position on identity somewhat unreceptive to nationalism and religious solidarity, but with the former tempered by acceptance of protecting minority languages and the latter by the existence of an established

undertaking to uphold the constitution, in contrast to UK oaths of office, which are declarations of personal loyalty to the monarch (see e.g. Parliamentary Oaths Act 1866, Promissory Oaths Act 1868).

[62] See e.g. J.-G. Turi, Law, 'Language and the Multilingual State' in C. Brohy et al. (eds.), *Law, Language and the Multilingual State: Proceedings of the 12th International Conference of the International Academy of Linguistic Law* (Bloemfontein: University of the Free State, 2012) 71, especially pp. 75–79.

[63] Cons. const. décision n° 99–412 DC du 15 juin 1999. Also of interest are the Quebec language laws, which have given rise to significant litigation, e.g. *Ford* v. *Quebec (Attorney General)* [1988] 2 SCR 712 and *R.* c. *Entreprises W.F.H.* [2001] RJQ 2557 (CA). See generally M. Paz, 'The Tower of Babel: human rights and the paradox of language' (2014) 25 *European Journal of International Law* 473.

church. If one were to consider the USA or France, the set of answers would be very different. Both, for example, would take a constitutive view of the relationship between law and state institutions, though they would diverge on state action and on identity.[64]

How would this help with describing the Theresa May incident with which we began? It would help because it would remove much of the incomprehension with which both lawyers and politicians greet such incidents. The apparent insouciance of the Home Secretary towards established constitutional rules looks rather less surprising in the context of the belief that both the government and parliament do not owe their existence to the law. Theresa May's position, that the House of Commons is the democratically elected voice of a sovereign people and so should be obeyed by judges regardless of how it communicates its wishes, predictably found no favour with judges, but proposing it is not, from her point of view, necessarily illegitimate. The government and parliament, as living social entities, are entitled to try to change their terms of trade with the courts. But the courts' response is also not surprising. Even though the results of the relevant cases might have been costly for the government, the courts would not have seen themselves as directly challenging the government's resource allocation decisions. At the same time their generally anti-political stance would have led them to give no credit at all to the party political motives the political account of the episode emphasises. In terms of ideology, the basic conflict arises from the courts' absorption of human rights thinking, whereas politics is, if anything, moving in the opposite direction. Finally, the courts are not predisposed to see promoting national identity as a legitimate goal of policy, unlike the Home Secretary.

Next steps – a normative politics of public law

There remains the matter of a normative politics of public law. What *should* the relationship between public law and politics look like? A vast literature exists on that issue, from what should count as a 'political question' in the USA to 'republican' interpretations of the UK constitution via debates

---

[64] For example, US courts are mostly hostile to 'English-only' laws, at least where they restrict the use of other languages. See e.g. R. Levy, 'Introduction: Watch your Language! The Kansas Law Review survey of official-English and English-only laws and policies' (2009) 57 *University of Kansas Law Review* 669.

about the 'margin of appreciation' afforded governments in European human rights law. What can the strategic decision approach possibly add? The answer is that it provides a clearer starting point. By combining different routes through the decisions, we can generate new options and generate new insights into what we really want. Do we prefer, for example, a combination of the autonomist view of the relationship between law and political institutions, judicial abstention from resource decisions, a favourable view of party politics, an egalitarian ideology, a broad view of state action and a sympathetic view of national identity over a combination of the constitutive view, interventionism in resource allocation, hostility to politics, a property-rights libertarian ideology, a narrow view of state action and hostility to all forms of solidarity-based politics? Some of the combinations might already have names. For example the former combination seems close to the 'republican' view of how public law should work.[65] But there is no reason to restrict debate to named combinations. Unnamed combinations might turn out to be more attractive.

Another contribution is that combinations of decisions are more important than each individual decision. The answer to the question of which is the best combination might not be answered by merely listing the best option for each decision individually. Possible trade-offs between different decisions make that unlikely. For example, the breadth of application of public law might interact with the desirability of intervention in budget decisions. The normative question if it is to be answered at all should be answered holistically.

Further reading

T. R. S. Allan, 'Questions of Legality and Legitimacy: Form and Substance in British Constitutionalism' (2011) 9 *International Journal of Constitutional Law* 155

M. Cerar, 'The Relationship Between Law and Politics' (2009) 15 *Annual Survey of International & Comparative Law* 3

D. Feldman (ed), *Law in Politics, Politics in Law* (Oxford: Hart Publishing, 2013)

---

[65] Admittedly Adam Tomkins, a leading proponent of 'republican' interpretation of the British constitution, is uncomfortable with the party basis of British politics and advocates abolishing the party whip (see A. Tomkins, *Our Republican Constitution* (Oxford: Hart Publishing, 2005), 137–38). Parties, however, are crucial to the system of accountability he puts at the centre of his republicanism.

V. Gauri and D. Brinks, *Courting Social Justice: Judicial Enforcement of Social and Economic Rights in the Developing World* (Cambridge: Cambridge University Press, 2010)

J. King, *Judging Social Rights* (Cambridge: Cambridge University Press, 2012)

R. Stevens, *The English Judges: Their Role in the Changing Constitution* (Oxford: Hart Publishing, 2005)

A. Tomkins, *Our Republican Constitution* (Oxford: Hart Publishing, 2005)

3 The rule of law in public law

Jeremy Waldron

Is the political ideal we call 'the rule of law' biased towards private law? There are definite tendencies in that direction and these tendencies make it difficult to develop an understanding of how the rule of law applies in the realm of public administration. The tendency towards private law also introduces an unwelcome ideological element, inasmuch as the rule of law can all too easily become associated with special respect for the rights of property owners, employers, and investors in cases of conflict between these rights and the business of public administration.

Of course the business of public administration is not self-justifying. And the rule of law is not doing its proper normative work unless it disciplines and constrains the way that business is carried out. Still, we should consider the prospects for a normatively robust conception of the rule of law that does not minimize or deprecate the mission of public administration. That is what I shall undertake in this chapter.

A unified ideal?

The task of developing a conception of the rule of law that applies to public law in particular faces an immediate challenge from those who deny the importance of the traditional distinction between public and private law.[1] Maybe there is no distinction. Maybe we should say that in the last analysis all law involves the operation of the state on society; all law is public law in some ultimate sense.[2] If so, then perhaps the rule of law should be conceived as an entirely general idea, prescribing the uniform application of a

---

[1] For further discussion of this matter, see D. Feldman, 'The Distinctiveness of Public Law' (Chapter 1 in this volume).

[2] Cf. H. Kelsen, *Pure Theory of Law*, trans. Max Knight (Berkeley: University of California Press, 1967), 282: 'The Pure Theory of Law ... sees in the private legal transaction just as much as in an administrative order an act of the state.'

discipline of legality to state action across the board. After all, whether the state is operating in the field of public administration or whether it is resolving private disputes, we have to face the possibility that it might be acting extra-legally, without reference to legal rules, principles, and procedures. We might say, normatively, that the point of the rule of law is to foreclose that possibility – again across the whole field. We might say that; but should we? When we subject the state's operation in the field of public administration to the discipline of the rule of law, should we use exactly the principles we use when we apply the discipline of legality to the resolution of private disputes?

Philosophers of law have usually assumed that the rule of law is a unified ideal, albeit one that consists of a list of items (Lon Fuller's eight principles of 'the inner morality of law', for example).[3] On the unified approach, one would begin an essay of this kind with a very general definition of the rule of law and then try to derive various aspects of its application to the specific case of the activity of the state and its agencies. So we might say something like the following. The rule of law comprises a requirement that people in positions of authority should exercise their power within a constraining framework of public norms. It also includes a requirement that there be general rules laid down to govern the conduct of ordinary people, rules whose public presence enables people to figure out what is required of them and what the legal consequences of their actions will be. And the rule of law insists on the role of courts, operating according to recognized standards of due process, and offering an impartial forum in which disputes can be resolved in an even-handed way.

So far as private law is concerned, these principles generate a demand for clearly defined rights of property and contract that can form a basis for stable expectations upheld and enforced by the courts. And so far as public administration is concerned, these same principles are supposed to generate limits on official discretion, a requirement of fair and consistent administration of existing rules by officials dealing with individual cases,

---

[3] See L. Fuller, *The Morality of Law* (New Haven: Yale University Press, 1969), revised edn., 33–94 (listing generality, prospectivity, publicity, consistency, practicability, clarity, stability, and congruence with official action, as the eight principles of the inner morality of law). See also the eight principles identified by Joseph Raz in 'The Rule of Law and its Virtue' in his collection *The Authority of Law* (Oxford: Oxford University Press, 2009), 2nd edn., 210–31.

and the establishment of procedures that allow people to challenge the legality of official action when it impacts adversely upon their interests.

All this seems fine as a preliminary understanding. But how far can we take these abstractions? A more elaborate understanding of the rule of law will inevitably reflect the jurist's path to that abstraction. For example, the array of principles cited by Fuller seems to betray a preoccupation with the direct application of rules to the conduct of individuals, a preoccupation that is perhaps most at home in criminal law. It may be less obviously applicable to the constitutional or legislative regulation of administrative agencies.[4] By contrast, an emphasis on legal certainty is likely to betray its private law origins: predictability matters most in areas of contract and property, where businessmen crave security of expectations and financiers need to be able to calculate what they can count on in the enterprises into which they have invested their funds.

In addition, we must bear in mind that the rule of law is a contested concept.[5] It is likely that the direction from which one tries to reach a neutral conception of legality will be reflected in the way one deals with some of the contested issues. These include: debates about the distinction between the rule of law and the rule of men; the distinction between the rule of law and rule *by* law; instrumental versus non-instrumental understandings of legality; and debates about the inclusion of substantive as well as formal and procedural elements in the rule of law. This is not just academic contestation: the way one approaches these debates affects one's view of judicial law-making, official discretion, and the respect due to regulatory legislation. It is likely to make some considerable difference to how one approaches these issues whether one begins from a public law or a private law standpoint.

Is the rule of law essentially a private law idea?

The quest for abstraction is one thing. It is another thing to associate the rule of law with private law and to say frankly that in public law the rule of

---

[4] See E. Rubin, 'Law and Legislation in the Administrative State' (1989) 89 *Columbia Law Review* 369.

[5] See the discussion in J. Waldron, 'Is the Rule of Law an Essentially Contested Concept (in Florida)?' (2002) 21 *Law and Philosophy* 137.

law represents the normative dominance of private law considerations when public and private come into conflict.

I have heard civil law formalists say that private law is the epitome of law and that what the rest of us call public law is a relatively marginal phenomenon.[6] On this view, *law as such* takes the security of private rights very seriously: it consists of a formal structure in which disputes are resolved and in which private interests of various sorts are adjusted to one another while still preserving their fundamental character as rights. And the rule of law, on this account, represents a determination to uphold these private rights in *every* area of governance. Now, there is no reason to suppose that public administration in and of itself will be sensitive to private law concerns; indeed there is a standing danger that private law concerns will be sidelined. So – according to this view – the point of the rule of law as a normative ideal is to bring these concerns to the attention of officials and to insist that everything they do should be constrained by law in this sense.

Should we accept this? Public lawyers do have to come to terms with the interpenetration of private and public concerns. Much of the regulatory activity of the administrative state affects the content and exercise of private rights, in the public regulation of property, for example, or in the governance of employment relations. And the rule of law must have something to say about this. Still, although public administration needs to take proper account of private law rights, it is not necessarily the job of the rule of law in public law to make our administrators back down whenever a pre-existing right rears up in their path. The role of the rule of law is not just to be representative of private rights or to stand sentinel for the protection of private property rights in the face of public law regulation. Certainly, it is the job of the rule of law to be *alert* to the way in which individual rights, including property and contractual rights, may be affected by public regulation. Its job is to stand against any arbitrariness. But this not a way of protecting private law rights from the impact of public law as such; it is a way of protecting them from the *arbitrariness* of public law. So we need to develop a sense of the distinction between arbitrary and non-arbitrary state action that can be applied in this domain.

---

[6] For example B. Sirks, 'Civil Law and Common Law' in his valedictory lecture on 14 July 2014 as Regius Professor of Civil Law at Oxford.

Ideological manipulation of the rule-of-law ideal

What I am criticizing here is quite a common view. Societies in which the rule of law is thought to flourish are supposed to be societies where rights of ownership are protected, contracts enforced, and a predictable environment established for enterprise and investment. And the idea that the rule of law must make sure that private rights are not sidelined helps explain the curious imbalance of some of the conceptions of the rule of law that we find in political economy. Consider, for example, the following account. According to James Wolfensohn, former President of the World Bank, the rule of law means that a

> government must ensure ... it has an effective system of property, contracts, labor, bankruptcy, commercial codes, personal rights law and other elements of a comprehensive legal system that are effectively, impartially, and cleanly administered by a well-functioning, impartial and honest judicial and legal system.[7]

What is missing from Wolfensohn's definition is any reference to public law – where law's effectiveness includes compliance with legal regulations by business, industry and commerce, and the application and enforcement of such regulations by the agencies of the state. These regulations include health and safety requirements, limits on contracts (for example in labour markets), and environmental legislation affecting use of property. Respect for legislation and the enforcement of regulations – these aspects are deafening by their silence in Wolfensohn's definition. Yet they are surely exactly the issues we need to address if we are to understand the relevance of the rule of law for public law.

Sometimes it is not just silence. Some ways of conceiving and measuring the rule of law are actively hostile to any sort of respect for regulation. An organization called the Center for Financial Stability offers a reading of the rule of law which measures as one key factor the 'Burden of Government Regulation', a measure obtained by asking businesses: 'How burdensome is it for businesses in your country to comply with governmental

---

[7] J. D. Wolfensohn, in his proposal for a 'Comprehensive Development Framework' (21 January 1999), 10–11, available at http://web.worldbank.org/archive/website01013/WEB/0__CO-87.HTM. I have discussed views of this kind extensively in J. Waldron, 'Legislation and the Rule of Law' (2007) 1 *Legisprudence* 91, and in J. Waldron, *The Rule of Law and the Measure of Property* (Cambridge University Press, 2012), 76–111.

administrative requirements (e.g., permits, regulations, reporting)?'[8] If we take this seriously, it seems to follow that a society's score on a rule-of-law index should be diminished by the effective enforcement or self-application of these requirements. On this approach, regulation of this kind is inherently subject to suspicion and the rule of law seems to require that such requirements be kept to a minimum.

The case that is made for this conception is sometimes quite cynical. The real aim, we are told, is to persuade governments to uphold substantive values such as property rights, investment values, and the principle of free markets. And since everyone happens to be in favour of 'the rule of law' at the moment, we might as well use the good vibrations associated with that phrase to drive home these points about markets and property.[9] Indeed on this account, it might be better to forget the traditional rule-of-law principles (which, in the hands of someone like Fuller, seem to presuppose a pro-legislation mentality) and just link the phrase 'the rule of law' with market values. That seems to be the strategy. Economists are ingenuous about the advantages of this approach. Defending the use of rule-of-law indices like those of the Centre for Financial Stability, Harvard economics professor Robert Barro observes that '[t]he general idea of these indexes is to gauge the attractiveness of a country's investment climate by considering the effectiveness of law enforcement, the sanctity of contracts, and the state of other influences on the security of property rights'.[10] By 'the attractiveness of a country's investment climate', Barro means its attractiveness to foreign investors. And he believes 'the willingness of [such] customers to pay substantial amounts for this information is perhaps some testament to their validity'.[11]

---

[8] Center for Financial Stability 2012–13 Rule of Law Index, available at www.centerforfi nancialstability.org/rli.php.

[9] See, for example, World Bank, 'The Rule of Law as a Goal of Development Policy', available at http://web.worldbank.org/WBSITE/EXTERNAL/TOPICS/EXTLAWJUSTINST/0,, contentMDK:20763583~menuPK:1989584~pagePK:210058~piPK:210062~theSitePK: 1974062~isCURL:Y,00.html:

'The main advantage of the substantive version of the rule of law is the explicit equation of the rule of law with something normatively good and desirable. The rule of law is good in this case because it is defined as such. This is appealing, first because the subjective judgment is made explicit rather than hidden in formal criteria, and, second, because the phrase "rule of law" has acquired such a strong positive connotation.'

[10] R. Barro, 'Determinants of Democracy' (1999) 107 *Journal of Political Economy* 158, 173.

[11] Ibid.

Is this an inappropriate perspective from which to develop an account of the rule of law to apply to public administration? The Barro perspective is that of an extractive and predatory investor, looking to the society and the interests of its members for what it can get out of them.[12] As such it is quite different from the perspective of someone who lives in the society and who cares about the quality of life among his or her fellow inhabitants. We should be wary of adopting any conception of the rule of law that is designed to push this latter perspective to one side.

A fresh start

What is needed is an understanding of the rule of law that is not opposed in principle to the mission of public administration and is not just the shadow of private or external concerns.

Some elements in a public law conception of the rule of law will be familiar. It will involve, in the first instance, an emphasis on rules in the governance of conduct. The familiar principles of Lon Fuller's 'inner morality of law' specify that laws must be general, prospective, public, clear, consistent, practicable, and stable.[13] These principles have obvious application in any domain where conduct is being legally regulated. A public law conception of the rule of law will also involve an emphasis on judicial procedures. The importance of such procedures has always been a key concern about public administration in the rule-of-law tradition. At the end of the nineteenth century, jurists like A. V. Dicey watched with dismay the replacement of what were previously judicial or quasi-judicial tribunals with more managerial boards and inspectorates.[14] It is a fault of Fuller's analysis in *The Morality of Law* that the chapter in which he presents his 'inner morality' says so little about procedures. Analytic legal philosophers have tended to follow him in this (whether they are

---

[12] For example, see I. Shihata, 'Relevant Issues in the Establishment of a Sound Legal Framework for a Market Economy' in I. Shihata, F. Tschofen and A. R. Parra (eds.), *The World Bank in a Changing World: Selected Essays*, vol. II (Dordrecht: Martinus Nijhoff, 2000), 205: 'An over-regulated economy undermines new investment, increases the costs of existing ones and leads to the spread of corruption.'

[13] Fuller (n. 3), 33–94.

[14] See A. V. Dicey, *Introduction to the Study of the Law of the Constitution* (Indianapolis: Liberty Fund, 1982), 8th edn. [1915], lv–lxi.

supporting or criticizing his account).[15] Elsewhere in his work, however, Fuller has placed more emphasis on the procedural aspect. And it is plain that both the formal and procedural sides will need to be emphasized in a conception of the rule of law that is fit for public law.

Notice, however, that Fuller's account so far presupposes that one is already in the business of making law and ruling through law and legal tribunals. But as Fuller himself concedes, it may not be appropriate to use law or legal methods for every task of public administration:

As lawyers we have a natural inclination to 'judicialize' every function of government. Adjudication is a process with which we are familiar and which enables us to show to advantage our special talents. Yet we must face the plain truth that adjudication is an ineffective instrument for economic management and for governmental participation in the allocation of economic resources.[16]

Something could be said along the same lines about the issuance and enforcement of rules. Officials may find they can be more effective using well-informed discretion rather than the mechanical application of rules. Rules may be too simple to take into account all the circumstances that ought to make a difference to the way particular situations are resolved. Laying down rules in advance, without knowing what kinds or combinations of circumstances will have to be faced, and applying those rules through rigid judicial procedures may not be what fair and effective administration requires.

Now, it is possible to interpret these possibilities as simple opposition to the rule of law. The rule of law, after all, is a controversial ideal, and there is controversy not only as to what it involves, but also as to whether we ought to be following any version of it at all. Some are happy to dismiss it altogether as archaic legalism in favour of a more frankly managerial approach.

However, instead of abandoning the idea of law altogether, we might reconceive the rule of law so that it is more sensitive to the needs of administration. So, for example, we might insist on the use of promulgated rules and legalized due process in some areas but not others – in areas where something like a penalty is in the offing, but not in areas where interventions of a non-punitive kind are involved. Or one might imagine an array of cases, ranging from purely administrative decisions at one end,

---

[15] For a general discussion, see J. Waldron, 'The Rule of Law and the Importance of Procedure' in J. Fleming (ed.), *Nomos 50: Getting to the Rule of Law* (New York: New York University Press, 2011).

[16] Fuller (n. 3), 176.

through cases that require a modicum of due process, all the way up to cases that represent in effect the full application of criminal law standards.

Something similar may be said about tribunals. In the view of A. V. Dicey, the rule of law required that 'no man is punishable or can be lawfully made to suffer in body or goods except for a distinct breach of law established in the ordinary legal manner *before the ordinary Courts of the land*'.[17] The phrase I have emphasized seems to preclude specialist administrative tribunals. But other apostles of the rule of law have been more accommodating in this regard. F. A. Hayek regarded Dicey's condemnation of dedicated administrative tribunals as unfortunate. That dispute may seem obsolete today, but only because Anglo-American jurists have now been able to reconcile the two positions that Dicey thought incompatible: tribunals embodying dedicated specialist familiarity with some field of public administration along with the judicialized operation of such tribunals and a reasonably clear set of standards for them to apply.[18]

In this connection, we may also want to say that the norms deployed in public administration can range from highly operationalized rules to general norms that have more the character of standards and require argument and judgment in their application. The kind of individual thoughtfulness sponsored by norms of this latter kind need not be regarded as incompatible in principle with the rule of law, provided one is alert to the kinds of cases in which their application might prove arbitrary.[19] (Cases in which there is reasonable congruence between the judgments of citizens and the judgments of officials are cases in which the use of standards is consistent with non-arbitrary administration; but if, on account of animus or asymmetries of expertise, there is no expectation of congruence, then rules are preferable.)[20]

So too with administrative discretion. It is natural to contrast official discretion with the application of rules, but there is a range of possibilities in between and some of the intermediate possibilities seem compatible with

---

[17] Dicey (n. 14), 110.
[18] F. A. Hayek, *The Constitution of Liberty* (Chicago: University of Chicago Press, 1978), 200–04.
[19] See the discussion in C. Sunstein, 'Rules and Rulelessness' *Coase-Sandor Working Paper Series in Law and Economics* (Chicago: University of Chicago, 1994), available at http://chicago unbound.uchicago.edu/cgi/viewcontent.cgi?article=1434&context=law_and_economics and J. Waldron, 'Thoughtfulness and the Rule of Law' (2011) 18 *British Academy Review* 1, available at www.britac.ac.uk/events/2011/BritishAcademyLawLecture.cfm.
[20] There is a useful discussion in R. Post, 'Reconceptualizing Vagueness: Legal Rules and Social Orders' (1994) 82 *California Law Review* 491.

a moderate conception of the rule of law. Discretion need not be free-standing. It can be guided by standards or left unguided. It can be framed, authorized, and constrained by legislation. Earlier exercises of it can inform subsequent exercises. It can be subject or not subject to review. In each of these dimensions, the element of sheer human wilfulness can loom larger or smaller compared to the considerations of legality.[21]

The role of legislation

Inevitably, if law is to play any significant role at all, the landscape of public administration will be dominated by legislation and by rules made by agencies under the auspices of legislation, both of which will frame, authorize, guide, and constrain the official discretion that is needed for intelligent and effective governance.

We noted earlier that some conceptions count the burden of state regulation as something that tends to diminish the rule of law. But it is not the function of the rule of law to assess the substantive justifiability of particular measures, to say whether their benefits are worth the burdens they impose or whether the burdens and benefits are distributed equitably. The rule of law deals with the way we are governed, not with the justification of governmental measures.

Nevertheless, it is worth saying something general about this form of governance if only because certain rule-of-law theorists have condemned most forms of legislation as incompatible in principle with the rule of law.[22] They condemn it for its complicity with state power and its voluntarism: something becomes law on the basis of nothing but a political determination that the law should be thus-and-so. But these characterizations are tendentious. We might say – more favourably – that legislation involves the representatives of the community taking responsibility for the conditions under which members of the community live their lives and

---

[21] I am grateful to Peter Strauss for discussion of these matters.

[22] In his later work, Friedrich Hayek contrasted law with legislation. He said that the legislative mentality is inherently managerial; it is oriented in the first instance to the organization of the state's own administrative apparatus; and its extension into the realm of public policy means an outward projection of that sort of managerial mentality into society at large. See F. A. Hayek, *Law, Legislation and Liberty, Vol. 1: Rules and Order* (Chicago: University of Chicago Press, 1973), 72–73 and 124–44.

conduct their business. In most countries, legislation is organized democratically, and it is not accident that theorists of the rule of law who
deprecate legislation also regard democracy and democratization as low
priorities in nation-building. Economists like Robert Barro have suggested
that we should strive to establish legal protections for property rights and
markets first, before establishing democracy institutions. On this account,
the function of the rule of law is to protect property, contracts, and markets
from the depredations of democracy.[23]

Now it is true that the rule of law does not necessarily entail democracy.
The two are distinguishable stars in the constellation of our political ideals.
But this does not mean the rule of law should be understood as inherently
hostile to democratic governance. The view that I am criticizing seems to
regard it as undesirable for the people of a country to act collectively
through the medium of (what we would ordinarily call) law to pursue social
justice, diminish inequality, or take control of the conditions of their social
and economic life. That, I think, is not a healthy proposition to associate
with the rule of law.

Stability in public law

If the role of law in public administration means a legal environment
dominated by legislation, and if rule-of-law complaints about the volun-
taristic and political character of these legal arrangements are rejected,
then what becomes of the rule of law's investment in stability and the
security of expectations?

The rule of law has always been associated with the value of predictability in human affairs. The most important thing, we are told, that people
need from the law that governs them is predictability in the conduct of their
lives and businesses. Tom Bingham observed that '[n]o one would choose
to do business, perhaps involving large sums of money, in a country where
parties' rights and obligations were undecided'. That sounds like a private
law concern, but a similar point is made insistently in the area of public law
as well. It is, according to F. A. Hayek, a matter of freedom:

---

[23] R. Barro, 'Democracy and the Rule of Law' in B. Bueno de Mesquita and H. Root (eds.),
Governing for Prosperity (New Haven: Yale University Press, 2000).

[G]overnment in all its actions [must be] bound by rules fixed and announced beforehand, rules which make it possible to foresee with fair certainty how the authority will use its coercive powers in given circumstances and to plan one's individual affairs on the basis of this knowledge.[24]

One is free so far as the impact of government action is concerned not because one's choices are completely untrammelled by regulation, but because one can predict when and how the state will intervene and work around, just as one works around the laws of nature.[25]

The demand for stability is important but it cannot be absolute.

The rule of law seeks as stable a set of legal arrangements as it is reasonable to expect in the circumstances. Law must not change so often that people lose the opportunity to come to terms with it and organize their lives around it. But 'reasonableness' here cannot be divorced from an awareness of the tasks of legislation and rule-making in a changing world. What counts as arbitrary or unreasonable must be predicated on an understanding of the inevitable rhythms of changing circumstances and political possibilities.

At any given time, a society faces its problems with a given heritage of customs, statutes, case law, and regulative arrangements. Now, however serviceable this array may have been in previous times, there is no guarantee it will continue to work in the future. New problems may emerge or be identified. As the society develops socially and economically, new frameworks and institutions may be necessary. Old ways of dealing with existing problems may prove limited or counterproductive in new circumstances. New ways may emerge for evaluating both problems and solutions and old ways may be contested. The balance of concern for different sections of the community may shift, posing difficult questions of equity. None of this is straightforward; much of it is contested; and all of it is important.

No society capable of self-government can remain passive or inert in the face of these changes. And legislation – the deliberate alteration of a society's rules and structures – is the proper way of responding to these developments. To its detractors, legislation may seem too much a matter of will, or of processes (like election and majority-decision) which combine wills to produce a politically contingent result, to deserve celebration under the auspices of a political ideal – the rule of law – whose purpose many understand to be the taming of will in politics.

---

[24] F. A. Hayek, *The Road to Serfdom* (London: Routledge Classics, 2001), 75.
[25] Hayek (n. 18), 153.

But law *is* changeable. That is one of the ways we contrast law with morality, even positive morality.[26] Morality changes over time, but it cannot be the subject of deliberate or intentional change. Setting up a legal system, however, establishes the possibility that changes may be made intentionally in the way that a society is ordered. It involves the union of primary rules of conduct, which may once have been immemorial, with secondary rules that empower a society to take responsibility for the primary order, adapting it flexibly to changing social conditions and keeping track of the changes that stand in the name of us all. That is what law essentially is and the principle we call the rule of law cannot in its essence be antagonistic to that.

This helps us understand why private law rights cannot be insulated from the impact of these changes. It is not reasonable to demand an extent of legal stability that precludes such impact. Some of the changes that a society has to face up to legislatively will involve reconsideration of the overall effect on the environment of the private use of resources. From time to time this will involve some alteration in the content of property rights. Also societies may have inherited distributions of land and other resources that are massively inequitable and represent the residue of injustice that in other regards has been repudiated. The rule of law cannot impose obstacles to the responsible remediation of this.[27] Similarly, contractual rights will accumulate in a way that defines the structure of markets and these too may need to be limited or regulated when a society confronts market failure, market crisis, or market inequity.

How one evaluates all this in regard to the rule of law will depend on one's perspective. Considered purely as an investor, unconcerned with the side of conditions of human life in a given society, a person might be impervious to concerns of this kind and expect that his private rights will be secure and available for exploitation by him at any time on the same basis as they were when he acquired them. And from this point of view, it might seem that the function of the rule of law is to underpin such expectations with legal certainty. The point of view of a member of the society in question may be quite different. The responsible citizen knows that there is such a thing as a public agenda confronting a changing world

---

[26] See H. L. A. Hart, *The Concept of Law* (Oxford: Clarendon Press, 2012), 3rd edn., 92–96 and 175–78.

[27] See the helpful discussion in R. Cass, 'Property Rights Systems and the Rule of Law' in E. Colombatto (ed.), *The Elgar Companion to Property Right Economics* (London: Edward Elgar Publications, 2003).

with evolving ideas about what is needed for the fair pursuit of the public good. He knows that these changes and the legislation they elicit are bound to affect the environment in which property rights are held and exercised, contracts enforced, and investments secured.

That matters like those I have mentioned may need collective attention from time to time is not an anomalous or socially destructive position; it is the ordinary wisdom of human affairs. No conception of governance, no conception of law or the rule of law that fails to leave room for changes and adjustments of this sort can possibly be tolerable. And it seems to me that any conception of the rule of law which denigrates the very idea of such changes and which treats their enactment and application as an inherent derogation from the rule of law has to be wrong.

True – any particular proposal for change will have its opponents, and sometimes the opponents will be right. They may be right because a proposed environmental regulation proves unnecessary or hysterical, or because a given piece of social legislation represents nothing more than cynical rent-seeking by one faction exploiting another. But the opponents are not necessarily right, and certainly not right simply on the ground that once property rights have been established, any change or regulation is out of the question.

No more than rule by law?

Does all this amount to anything more than rule by law? I mentioned earlier that some commentators draw a distinction between the rule of law and rule *by* law.[28] The one is supposed to lift law above politics. The other – rule by law – involves the instrumental use of legal forms and procedures as tools of political power. On this account, rule by law is a version of rule by men since it is comfortable with the highest authority being wholly unconstrained in the measures it lays down.

My own view is that this distinction between rule of law and rule by law is overblown, involving as it does a mythic quest for forms of law which come into existence and operate without any human agency.

But perhaps the more demanding idea of the rule of law is not altogether inapplicable. Perhaps, in certain pockets of public law, it can be used to

[28] See, e.g., B. Tamanaha, *On the Rule of Law: History, Politics, Theory* (Cambridge: Cambridge University Press, 2004), 3.

consecrate a form of constitutionalism – the idea that the legislature as well as the state is subject to substantive constraints (constraints based on individual rights, for example) in its law-making.[29] That is a possibility and the further the framers of the constitution are from us in time, the more this might seem like law itself ruling us. In fact, constitutional constraints are usually few and negative and mostly they leave legislative and regulatory discretion untouched.[30] And, anyway, even if we forget about the human framers, there is no getting away from the role of human judges in interpreting and applying these constraints. Does the empowerment of the judiciary represent the rule of law or the rule of men? Some think that a ruling counts as the rule of law provided it is done through the hierarchy and procedures of courts: short of the fantasy that the laws themselves might rear up and render their own objective decision, this is the most the rule of law could possibly entail. Others say that there is always a danger that activist judges will take advantage of the authority given to them to make themselves into the very despots whose rule the rule of law is supposed to supersede. The issue remains bitterly disputed.[31]

Beyond the rather meagre and contested constraints of the constitution, the rule of law in the public realm certainly opposes prerogative power and it supports the practice of judicial review of executive action. This certainly represents the subordination of the powerful to the rule of law: 'Be you never so high, the law is above you.'[32] Still, this is almost always review on the basis of legislation, and it cannot be denied that the statutes appealed to in these reviews are themselves laid down in the first instance under the model of rule by law.

In any case, we should not accept the disparagement of rule by law that the contrast with the rule of law is supposed to suggest. Sometimes the phrase 'rule by law' is used to describe Singapore-style regimes, as though it were just a fig leaf for authoritarian rulers.[33] And the impression is given

---

[29] See, e.g., F. Fukuyama, *The Origins of Political Order: From Prehuman Times to the French Revolution* (New York: Profile Books, 2011), 246: 'The rule of law can be said to exist only where the preexisting body of law is sovereign over legislation.'

[30] For an account of the significance of negative as opposed to positive constraints, see Hayek (n. 18), 152.

[31] See Waldron (n. 5), 137–38, 142–44, and 147–48.

[32] Thomas Fuller in 1733 as quoted by Lord Denning in *Gouriet* v. *Union of Post Office Workers* [1977] QB 729, 762.

[33] T. Ginsburg and T. Moustafa (eds.), *Rule By Law: The Politics of Courts in Authoritarian Regimes* (Cambridge: Cambridge University Press, 2008). See also J. Rajah, *Authoritarian Rule of Law: Legislation, Discourse and Legitimacy in Singapore* (Cambridge: Cambridge University Press, 2012).

that rule by law serves only the instrumental purposes of the regime and that it cannot be understood as a political ideal that inures to the benefit of those being governed. In fact an insistence on being ruled by rules and by legal procedures serves the interests of citizens at least as much as their rulers. By imposing a reasonable amount of stability, it lets people know where they stand, and as a mode of rule it treats with the dignity of responsible agents capable of self-applying the rules that are made for the community. There is always the possibility that these values might be neglected in public administration and it is the function of the rule of law in public law to see that they are taken seriously.

Constructing a conception

A final word about the methodology that has been used here. One has to feel a little self-conscious about constructing an understanding of the rule of law that is dedicated to governance in the public realm and that is intended to see off some dominant ideological conceptions that apparently have a problem with the very idea of public administration. Defenders of those conceptions will denounce what I have set out in this chapter as incompatible with what the rule of law really requires.

But there is no 'really' here: there is no commanding exemplar, no canonical authority for conceiving of the rule of law one way rather than another. There is a heritage dating back to Aristotle of concern for legality and enthusiasm for the possibility that legal modes of rule may take the edge off human power. And there are various ways of interpreting that heritage in regard to the challenges of governance faced by every generation.[34] I have argued that it is possible to construct a moderate understanding of the rule of law that takes seriously the mission of the modern administrative state. That understanding is built up out of the heritage of the rule-of-law tradition, but it reserves the right to think anew about what the rule of law requires in this particular environment. The grounds for criticizing other understandings as inadequate or ideological is not that they fail to embody what the rule of law objectively entails, but that they are predicated on perspectives and concerns that are quite inappropriate for good faith elaboration of this ideal – an ideal

---

[34] There is a useful discussion of interpretive methodology in relation to the rule-of-law heritage in R. Dworkin, 'Hart's Postscript and the Character of Political Philosophy' (2004) 24 *Oxford Journal of Legal Studies* 1, 23–26.

that is, after all, supposed to serve the needs and promote the freedom and dignity of those who live in a given society and are engaged in the responsible endeavour of self-government.

Further reading

T. R. S. Allan, *Constitutional Justice: A Liberal Theory of the Rule of Law* (Oxford: Oxford University Press, 2003)

T. Bingham, *The Rule of Law* (London: Penguin, 2011)

P. Craig, 'Formal and Substance Conceptions of the Rule of Law: An Analytical Framework' [1997] *Public Law* 467

J. Raz, 'The Rule of Law and its Virtue' in J. Raz, *The Authority of Law: Essays on Law and Morality* (Oxford: Oxford University Press, 2009), 2nd edn.

J. Waldron, 'Is the Rule of Law an Essentially Contested Concept (in Florida)?' (2002) 21 *Law and Philosophy* 137

J. Waldron, 'Legislation and the Rule of Law' (2007) 1 *Legisprudence* 91

Legislative supremacy in a multidimensional constitution 4

Mark Elliott*

Few questions in public law are as fundamental as those which relate to the source and extent of the authority wielded by the state. Defining the parameters of such authority is a core function – if not *the* core function – of constitutional law, and is a task that is usually discharged via the terms of a 'written constitution'. But this is not invariably so, not least because not all states possess such a governing text.[1] Indeed, the distinction between legal systems that respectively do and do not possess texts that allocate and restrain state authority represents a significant fissure in constitutional design. In the common-law world, this is reflected by the apparently stark contrast between countries like Australia, Canada, South Africa and the United States, in which state authority is allocated and restrained by a constitutional text, and those, like New Zealand and the United Kingdom, in which other arrangements obtain.

Prominent among those other arrangements is the doctrine of parliamentary sovereignty. At the core of that doctrine lies the ostensibly outlandish claim that legislators' legal authority is boundless. Everything that is enacted is legally valid; nothing that is enacted can be questioned in legal (as distinct from political or moral) terms. At least on the face of

* I am grateful to David Feldman, Aileen McHarg, Dawn Oliver and Scott Stephenson for comments on an earlier draft of this chapter. The usual disclaimer applies.

[1] It must be acknowledged at the outset that even states with 'written constitutions' do not necessarily possess a single governing text that authorizes judicial invalidation of legislation that conflicts with the terms of the constitution. Constitutions may be poly-textual; they may not be wholly self-executing; and they may not authorize judicial invalidation or disapplication of incompatible legislation. When I refer in this chapter to 'written constitutions' or to the 'governing-text model', I am therefore primarily concerned with self-executing, text-based constitutions that assert priority over other law and contemplate judicial intervention in the event of legislative infraction of the constitution. However, the fact that other models exist simply serves to underscore the point, which will be made in the chapter, that exceptionalist characterizations of the UK constitution may be misplaced, not least because the UK system cannot straightforwardly be characterized as the binary obverse of a single competing model.

it, the parliamentary-sovereignty and governing-text models of constitutionalism are mutually exclusive, an all-powerful legislature and a
power-allocating (and power-limiting) constitution being uncomfortable
bedfellows. However, this chapter will argue – with particular reference
to the contemporary constitution of the UK – that the contrast between
these two paradigms may not be as stark as is sometimes supposed. In
doing so, it will suggest that the exceptionalism that is sometimes
invoked, at least implicitly, when characterizing constitutions like the
UK's may, at least to some extent, be misplaced.

Contemporary 'challenges' to legislative supremacy

Such exceptionalism can be manifested through the notion that the dominant tradition in the UK is one of *political* constitutionalism, an approach
that falls to be contrasted with the *legal* constitutionalism associated with
systems based upon a governing constitutional text. There is, of course,
something in this point, the apex legislature in a system based upon political
constitutionalism – the Westminster Parliament in the UK – enjoying authority that is neither allocated nor delimited by a governing constitutional
instrument. However, while this may seem to produce a situation radically
different from that which is bequeathed by the governing-text model, the
distinction should not be overstated. Even Dicey – revered, perhaps unfairly,
as the high priest of parliamentary sovereignty – acknowledged that political
constraints upon legislative power might be as real as, if different from, legal
constraints.[2] As a result, legislation ordaining the killing of all blue-eyed
babies[3] remains as unthinkable in a country like the UK as it does in a state
that enshrines the right to life in the text of a power-limiting constitution. Yet
this insight, though important, leaves untouched the basic distinction according to which the two types of constitutional system respectively rely upon law
and politics as restraints of final resort, cautioning only against exaggerating
the *implications* of that distinction.

However, the position that obtains in the UK today is in fact more
complex than can be accommodated by bald distinctions between the

---

[2] A. V. Dicey, *An Introduction to the Study of the Law of the Constitution* (London: Macmillan, 1959), ch. I.
[3] An example famously given by Leslie Stephen in *The Science of Ethics* (London: Smith, Elder & Co, 1882), 137.

governing-text and parliamentary-sovereignty institutional models and the legal and political forms of constitutionalism to which (on the face of it, at least) they respectively give rise. This is so because, looked at in one way, the UK's constitution is in the process of being legalized, such that law increasingly encroaches upon, and perhaps diminishes, legislative authority. One way of putting this is to characterize certain contemporary features of the constitutional landscape – four of which are sketched in the following paragraphs – as 'challenges' to parliamentary sovereignty.

First, there are the legal implications of the UK's membership of the European Union. Looked at in one way, the EU supremacy principle, according to which Union law enjoys primacy in the event of a conflict with the law of a Member State,[4] is in tension with the UK Parliament's claim to legislative supremacy. The spectacle of a British court 'disapplying' an Act of Parliament on the ground of its incompatibility with EU law, as the Appellate Committee of the House of Lords did in *Factortame*, might be thought more reminiscent of legal/governing-text constitutionalism than of the political/parliamentary-sovereignty model.[5] However, British courts have tended to treat EU law's hierarchical superiority to domestic law as a product of the will of the UK Parliament[6] – an approach that has been endorsed by Parliament itself through the enactment of subsequent legislation that seeks to clarify Parliament's own understanding of the status of EU law in the UK.[7] In this way, the paradoxical possibility arises of explicating EU law's effective domestic primacy in a manner that is consistent with the sovereignty of the UK Parliament. This is so (the argument goes) because EU law has domestic effect only on the terms set by Parliament, meaning (among other things) that it is open to the still-sovereign Parliament to derogate, selectively or wholesale, from EU law

---

[4] See, e.g., Case 6/64 *Costa* v. *ENEL* [1964] CMLR 425.

[5] *R* v. *Secretary of State for Transport ex parte Factortame Ltd. (No. 2)* [1991] 1 AC 603.

[6] *Thoburn* v. *Sunderland City Council* [2002] EWHC 195 (Admin), [2003] QB 151; *R. (HS2 Action Alliance Ltd.)* v. *Secretary of State for Transport* [2014] UKSC 3, [2014] 1 WLR 324. See further M. Elliott, 'Constitutional Legislation, European Union Law and the Nature of the United Kingdom's Contemporary Constitution' (2014) 10 *European Constitutional Law Review* 379.

[7] Section 18 of the European Union Act 2011 provides that: 'Directly applicable or directly effective EU law (that is, the rights, powers, liabilities, obligations, restrictions, remedies and procedures referred to in section 2(1) of the European Communities Act 1972) falls to be recognised and available in law in the United Kingdom *only by virtue of that Act* or where it is required to be recognised and available in law *by virtue of any other Act*.' (Emphasis added.)

provided that it makes its intention to do so sufficiently plain. This possibility, which inhabits the world of domestic-constitutional theory, is of course without prejudice to the fact that such explicit national-legislative renunciation of an EU provision would cut no ice as a matter of EU law, which would continue to bite (as a matter of international law) upon the UK for as long as it remained a Member State.

Second, a similar analysis can be applied to the status within the UK legal order of the rights set out in the European Convention on Human Rights (ECHR). Just as the European Communities Act 1972 provides for the applicability in domestic law of directly effective EU measures, so the Human Rights Act 1998 (HRA) gives effect in national law to certain of the Convention rights. That the two pieces of legislation make *different* provision – the priority accorded (albeit ambiguously) to EU law by the European Communities Act has no analogue in the Human Rights Act, which makes it clear that Acts of Parliament incompatible with the ECHR may only be declared to be so[8] – is less important for present purposes than the fact that it is UK legislation that specifies the domestic legal effects of each of these international-law regimes. On one view, this establishes that parliamentary sovereignty continues undiminished, since it is Parliament, in the first place, that has licensed – and limited – the domestic legal force of the Convention. Yet this analysis, which evidences a domestic-legal focus, does not (because it does not attempt to) account for the legally binding effect of the Convention rights upon the UK as a matter of international law, or the potential of legally non-binding domestic declarations of incompatibility to operate as substantial political constraints upon legislative freedom.[9] Viewed from these perspectives, rather than from a purely domestic-legal standpoint, the human-rights regime established by the ECHR and the HRA may be considered a greater challenge to – or at least a less comfortable fit with – legislative supremacy.

Although EU law and the ECHR/HRA regime are legally distinct, they are, at one level of abstraction, merely two examples of one phenomenon: namely, the capacity of the UK's international obligations to limit

---

[8] Section 4(6).

[9] The high level of legislative response to declarations of incompatibility issued under the HRA, so as to remove incompatible provisions from primary legislation, is indicative of the domestic constraining effect of Convention rights. See further Ministry of Justice, *Responding to Human Rights Judgments* (Cm 8727, 2013).

Parliament's room for manoeuvre (if it wishes to avoid placing the UK in breach of those obligations). EU law and the ECHR/HRA regime thus illustrate a form of constraint that is much more general in nature, and which long precedes the UK's ratification of the Convention and the EU Treaties. What sets those instruments apart, however, is the fact that domestic legislation provides for national courts to apply EU law and Convention rights as benchmarks against which to measure domestic law. In this way, the constraining effect of international law is (to some extent, at least) domesticated, placing it in tension with legislative supremacy more transparently and directly than in contexts in which international law exists in exotic distinction from the national legal order.

A third matter that might be characterized as a challenge to the legislative supremacy of the UK Parliament arises from the devolved systems of government in Northern Ireland, Scotland and Wales. Suggestions to the contrary notwithstanding,[10] this does not amount to the federalization of the UK's constitution: authority is allocated to devolved institutions by nothing more than UK legislation,[11] while the UK Parliament, at least technically, has merely shared its power with devolved bodies,[12] relinquishing none.[13] On this analysis, no challenge to the supremacy of the UK Parliament is evident, the powers – indeed, the very existence – of devolved institutions being a function of, and so vulnerable to curtailment or abolition by, that Parliament. However, while no legal inhibition upon parliamentary sovereignty is implicit in the devolution settlements,[14] it is strongly arguable that the institutional landscape wrought by the devolution legislation effectively forecloses upon the possibility of unilateral interference by the UK in (let alone abolition of) those settlements. Looked at in this way, the constitutional significance of the devolution

---

[10] Baroness Hale, 'The Supreme Court in the UK Constitution' (Legal Wales Lecture, 12 October 2012).

[11] As a result, the UK Parliament remains, in law, in unilateral control of the devolution settlement – a state of affairs that is inconsistent with any conventional understanding of the federal model.

[12] In contrast, federalism would entail a division (rather than a sharing) of authority.

[13] See, e.g., Scotland Act 1998, s. 28(7), which provides that conferral of legislative competence on the Scottish Parliament 'does not affect the power of the Parliament of the United Kingdom to make laws for Scotland'.

[14] It has recently been proposed that UK legislation should provide that the Scottish Government and Parliament are 'permanent' institutions, which may imply that the UK Parliament would not be legally competent to abolish them. On this point, see further nn. 28–29 below and the accompanying text.

legislation – and, in particular, its implications for the UK Parliament – substantially outstrips its status viewed through a conventional domestic-law lens.

Fourth, there is the question whether the legislative authority of the UK Parliament might be qualified by constraints that are latent within the unwritten constitutional order.[15] It is well established that that constitutional order embodies fundamental norms, including what have come to be known as common-law constitutional rights.[16] The orthodox view, however, is that the existence of such rights is consistent with legislative supremacy because they amount to nothing more than interpretative constructs. Parliament's capacity to qualify or even abrogate common-law rights therefore remains intact, albeit that such legislative endeavour may, if it is to succeed, require the use of particularly clear language so as to preclude an interpretation that would leave the right undisturbed. There are, however, two reasons why this analysis – which seeks to reconcile common-law constitutional rights with unqualified legislative authority – might be questioned.

Even if the essential proposition – that common-law rights are vulnerable to parliamentary manipulation provided that the statute is sufficiently clear – is accepted, it does not necessarily follow that no qualification of legislative authority is entailed. That such manipulation is, on this view, technically possible in legal terms is clear: but the need for the legislature, in effect, to confront the rights issue through the use of express (or at least very specific) language necessarily implies a political cost.[17] As such, the legal violability of common-law constitutional rights may, at least in some circumstances, obscure their political inviolability – or at least overstate the extent to which they are in practice vulnerable to legislative disturbance. In this way, the doctrine of common-law constitutional rights may serve to erode the distinction between political and legal forms of constitutional constraint by erecting a legal barrier to interference with

---

[15] See, e.g., D. Oliver, 'Parliament and the Courts: A Pragmatic (or Principled) Defence of the Sovereignty of Parliament' in A. Horne, G. Drewry and D. Oliver (eds.), *Parliament and the Law* (Oxford: Hart Publishing, 2013).

[16] See, e.g., *R.* v. *Lord Chancellor, ex parte Witham* [1998] QB 575; *R. (Osborn)* v. *Parole Board* [2013] UKSC 61, [2013] 3 WLR 1020.

[17] Of course, circumstances could well arise in which it was judged that such a cost would be worth paying, e.g. if the political branches were reflecting public concern relating to the conduct of a minority.

rights – in the form of an explicitness requirement – that is politically, albeit not legally, insuperable.

It may, however, be possible to go further than this. The notion that common-law rights are legally vulnerable in the face of sufficiently clearly worded legislation has long been questioned by some constitutional theorists.[18] On this view, certain values, including certain rights, possess a degree of fundamentality that makes them immune to legislative displacement, notwithstanding that they are not enshrined in any governing constitutional text. Such an analysis reduces substantially, if not to vanishing point, the distinction between the governing-text and parliamentary-sovereignty models of constitutionalism sketched above. It suggests that the UK's constitution discharges the power-allocation and power-limitation functions usually associated only with the governing-text model by postulating the existence of implicit constitutional restraints upon legislative authority in the absence of a text in which such constraints may explicitly feature. Theorists' suggestions along these lines are now accompanied by judicial *dicta* to similar effect,[19] although this view is certainly not the subject of curial unanimity (or even plurality).[20] In any event, whether such implicit constraints are actually to be found within the UK's unwritten constitutional order is a question shrouded in empirical uncertainty, not least because, on the whole, Parliament is careful to avoid the sort of gross breaches of basic constitutional standards that might make that question other than moot, and because, when such an infraction is arguably discernible, courts prefer to frame their response in terms of statutory interpretation rather than constitutional confrontation.[21] That this is the courts' preference is hardly surprising, not least because no constitutional roadmap determines what would happen in the event of such a showdown. The obvious risk

---

[18] E.g. T. R. S. Allan, *The Sovereignty of Law* (Oxford: Oxford University Press, 2013), ch. 5. Although Allan argues that 'notions of conflict . . . between parliamentary supremacy and the rule of law are false', his interpretive theory ascribes a role to fundamental values that extends beyond one capable of accommodation by orthodox notions of parliamentary sovereignty.

[19] See, e.g., *R. (Jackson)* v. *Attorney-General* [2005] UKHL 56, [2006] 1 AC 262, [102] (Lord Steyn), [107] (Lord Hope), [159] (Baroness Hale); *AXA General Insurance Ltd* v. *Lord Advocate* [2011] UKSC 46, [2012] 1 AC 868, [51] (Lord Hope).

[20] See, e.g., Lord Neuberger, 'Who are the masters now?' (Second Lord Alexander of Weedon Lecture, 6 April 2011), arguing that 'it is clear that parliamentary sovereignty is absolute'.

[21] As Lord Phillips frankly conceded in evidence to the House of Commons Political and Constitutional Reform Committee: *The Constitutional Role of the Judiciary if there were a Codified Constitution* (HC 802, 2013–14), [41].

arises, therefore, that the courts might end up the losers in an institutional standoff with Parliament.[22]

Given that there is so much uncertainty about the fundamentality of common-law rights, it would be rash to argue that they *are* legal constraints upon the UK Parliament's legislative competence, whatever stance is adopted in relation to the normative question whether they *ought* to operate in such a way. Yet the very *possibility* that a court might – as Lord Steyn put it in the *Jackson* case – be willing to recognize 'constitutional fundamental[s] which even a sovereign Parliament . . . cannot abolish' is significant.[23] It arguably creates an institutional tension between the legislative and judicial branches which, in turn, demands a form of institutional comity that requires legislative respect for fundamental constitutional values as well as judicial respect for Parliament's legislative authority.[24] In the absence of textually demarcated constitutional domains, each organ has a vested interest in securing its own territory by preserving the *status quo*, including by according to other organs respect whose withdrawal would likely precipitate a constitutional crisis with unpredictable results. Viewed from the perspective of the legislative branch, this, in itself, can plausibly be characterized as a restraint upon its authority, notwithstanding that the form of any such restraint is other than straightforwardly legal.

Hard and soft constitutionality

One way of looking at developments such as those sketched above is to place them in opposition to a pristine notion of parliamentary sovereignty, according to which Parliament's legislative freedom is unbounded. The narrative implicit in that classical doctrine seems far-fetched when the constraining influence of such developments is factored into the analysis. Can Parliament really legislate in opposition to its obligations under the ECHR? Could it reverse – or even abolish – devolution, or (more modestly) override the wishes of a devolved legislature in a particular field? Without leaving the EU, is it realistic to propose that a 'sovereign' Parliament is free to derogate from EU law, provided that it expresses its intention to do so in sufficiently clear terms? Does Parliament have the authority, in anything

---

[22] See further Oliver (n. 15).   [23] *Jackson* (n. 19), [102].

[24] See further M. Elliott, 'Interpretative Bills of Rights and the Mystery of the Unwritten Constitution' [2011] *New Zealand Law Review* 591.

other than a technical or theoretical sense, to eviscerate basic constitutional values or rights (by, for example, entirely abolishing judicial review of administrative action)?

The answers to those questions may be 'no', but the questions are arguably ones that do not implicate the notion of parliamentary sovereignty; to the extent that Parliament may be unable to do some or all of these things, the reasons for its incapacity may consist in factors that leave the doctrine of parliamentary sovereignty untouched. This is not to suggest that that doctrine is an adequate account of relevant aspects of the modern British constitution; it may, however, be that its inadequacy derives not from the fact that it is unsustainable viewed on its own terms, but from the fact that the terms on which it is viewed are *themselves* inappropriately confined. The matters sketched in the previous section of this chapter might therefore be better viewed not as 'challenges' to parliamentary sovereignty, but as factors that should prompt us to question whether the constitutional lens through which the doctrine of parliamentary sovereignty is revealed – and made a, if not *the*, focal point of the UK's constitutional architecture – is an adequate one.

An alternative way of understanding the notion of legislative supremacy – and, hence, constitutions like the UK's in which that doctrine prominently figures – is to acknowledge that it forms part of a wider constitutional landscape in which the idea of constitutionality is itself more nuanced than an orthodox understanding of legislative supremacy permits. Viewed thus, phenomena such as those sketched in the previous section, and which may be conceptualized as challenges to the sovereignty of the UK Parliament, might be better understood as matters that give rise to or presuppose a network of constitutional norms – legal and extra-legal, written and unwritten, domestic and international – that, while not technically inconsistent with parliamentary sovereignty, supply crucial features of the context within which Parliament's legislative authority is to be understood and the legitimacy of its exercise assessed.

An analogy may be drawn with the way in which constitutional conventions operate – and, in particular, with their mode of interaction with the legal powers upon which they bite. Take, for instance, the convention which holds that the monarch will grant royal assent to bills duly approved by Parliament. That convention – which has not been departed from in three centuries – has the effect of converting the monarch's apparent discretion to grant or withhold assent into an obligation to do so. And while a monarch who breached that obligation would act *lawfully*, they would almost certainly be considered to be acting *unconstitutionally*. Dicey himself recognized – indeed, championed – the distinction between convention and law, arguing that conventions were legally unenforceable and that conduct in breach of conventions was legally unimpeachable.[25] Understood thus, conventions – and the norms underpinning them – may be treated as non-legal standards by reference to which the constitutionality of actors', including Parliament's, behaviour may be measured. From a legal perspective, then, conventions can be regarded as a soft-constitutional constraint: one that may inhibit conduct that breaches the convention (or the underlying norm) but which does not impinge upon the lawfulness of such conduct.

An equivalent point can be made about parliamentary sovereignty and its relationship with constitutional features that might otherwise be characterized as challenges to it. From a domestic-legal perspective, the existence of hard-constitutional limits upon a sovereign legislature is a logical impossibility. But this does not exclude the possibility of what might be considered – from a domestic-legal perspective – to be soft constraints. Take, for instance, the capacity of the UK Parliament to legislate in breach of EU law. As a matter of domestic law, the capacity of the UK Parliament to legislate in such a way persists, the EU principle of the supremacy of Union law notwithstanding. This does not foreclose the possibility – realized in *Factortame* – of national courts preferring EU over national law in the event of a conflict between the two. However, it presupposes that any priority accorded to Union law is attributable to domestic legislation, such that any sufficiently clear attempt by the national legislature to escape the strictures of Union law would necessarily succeed. Yet it would be naïve to assert that the UK Parliament is therefore 'free' to legislate contrary to Union law (just as it would be misleading to assert monarchical freedom to decline royal assent). The absence of a hard domestic-law constraint notwithstanding, Parliament's freedom of action is curtailed by (what is, viewed from a domestic-legal perspective) a soft constraint deriving from the UK's obligations under the EU treaties.[26]

---

[25] Dicey (n. 2), ch. XV. See R. Rawlings, 'Soft Law Never Dies', Chapter 11 in this volume.

[26] A rich seam of such soft constraints – which impact upon the propriety and feasibility not only of legislative but also of executive action – arguably exists. For examples, see J. Simson Caird, R. Hazell and D. Oliver, *The Constitutional Standards of the House of Lords Constitution Committee* (London: The Constitution Unit, 2014); the *Ministerial Code*

From hard and soft constraints to multidimensional constitutionalism

There is, however, a potential – and perhaps compelling – objection to the distinction between hard and soft constraints elaborated above. Whether a given constraint is hard or not (or, more subtly, exactly *how* hard it is) depends, at least in part, upon the perspective from which one approaches the question. Inherent within the distinction between hard and soft constraints is a hierarchical ordering that reduces factors that may condition – but not legally impinge upon – the exercise of the UK Parliament's legislative authority to a lesser, softer, status. For instance, on such an approach, devolved legislatures are subject to hard-constitutional constraints that preclude them from legislating on matters reserved to the competence of the UK Parliament, whereas the latter is subject to what might be characterized as soft constraints that inhibit but do not, as a matter of law, preclude unilateral interference by the UK Parliament in matters engaging devolved competence.[27]

The question arises whether the ordering of constitutional norms and considerations implicit within the distinction between hard and soft constraints – and which, on an orthodox understanding, precludes the sovereign legislature from being subject to anything more than soft constraints – is one that fully reflects the reality of the contemporary constitution. Issues of this nature are thrown into sharp relief by the proposal to enact UK legislation making the Scottish Parliament and Government 'permanent' institutions.[28] Orthodox analysis suggests that even if enshrined in primary UK legislation, any guarantee as to the permanence of the Scottish governing institutions could not form a hard constraint upon the sovereign UK Parliament – as Laws LJ put it in *Thoburn* v. *Sunderland City Council*: 'Being sovereign, [the UK Parliament] cannot abandon its sovereignty.'[29] However, when matters

---

(London: Cabinet Office, 2010); the 'seven principles of public life' set out in *Standards in Public Life: First Report of the Committee on Standards in Public Life* (Cm 2850, 1995).

[27] Indeed, this 'soft' constraint was quickly acknowledged through the adoption of a constitutional convention (the so-called Sewel convention): Office of the Deputy Prime Minister, *Memorandum of Understanding and Supplementary Agreements* (Cm 5240, 2001), 8.

[28] *Report of the Smith Commission for Further Devolution of Powers to the Scottish Parliament* (2014), 13

[29] *Thoburn* (n. 6), [59].

are examined in this way, it is arguable that only part of the constitutional picture may emerge.

This difficulty is attributable to the fact that conventional analyses, by presupposing and making central the supremacy of the UK Parliament, necessarily adopt a domestic-legal lens, treating considerations of a domestic-legal nature paradigmatically. That accounts of the constitution which place sovereignty front and centre proceed in this way is, at one level, unremarkable. Indeed, the position could not be otherwise, since to say that the UK's Parliament – or that any legislature – is 'sovereign' is and can only be a claim rooted in and about domestic law. For all that the claim is extravagant, in that it contemplates the legal validity of legislation no matter how objectionable it might be in moral terms, it is simultaneously modest. It asserts no more (but no less) than that legislation duly enacted by the body in question represents valid domestic law, and (consequently) that the domestic judiciary lacks any legal authority to deny that such enactments enjoy that status. Viewed from *within* this domestic-legal paradigm, factors that might in some sense constrain or sit uncomfortably with the idea of legislative supremacy cannot be other than soft in nature if they relate to matters that are not domestic-legal in character. They may *discourage* the enactment of certain legislation, but they do not – cannot – impose constraints upon the legislature that amount to hard limits on its authority viewed according to the terms of the operative paradigm. This is so because, as factors operating on some *other* legal or constitutional plane, they are necessarily incapable of cutting across a construct such as parliamentary sovereignty which can meaningfully exist only on the domestic-legal plane.

For instance, the UK's post-devolution constitution clearly acknowledges devolved autonomy as a significant constitutional value – one that is institutionalized by means of a constitutional convention requiring local assent to UK legislative involvement in devolved affairs.[30] However, that principle (at least for now) exists other than as a hard-legal restraint upon the authority of the UK Parliament – the terms of the devolution legislation explicitly, and the doctrine of parliamentary sovereignty implicitly, ruling out the possibility of such hard restraint. The (likely) political-constitutional impossibility of unilateral UK interference in devolved matters thus conditions, but does not impinge in legal-constitutional terms

---

[30] See n. 27.

upon, the extent of the UK Parliament's authority. For purists, such an account would continue to hold even if the legislation outlined above – contemplating the 'permanence' of the Scottish governing institutions – were enacted. Such legislation, viewed from a perspective that takes the sovereignty of the UK Parliament as a given, could amount to nothing more than an aspirational statement: a signal of Westminster's intent, but not a brake upon its authority. Put in different terms, such legislation would reflect – but would not make legally binding – a *political* understanding concerning the relationship between UK and Scottish institutions.

A similar point may be made in relation to constraints that, whilst legal in nature, are extra-domestic. For instance, from a domestic-legal perspective, the claims implicit in the doctrine of parliamentary sovereignty are wholly reconcilable with the constraining effect upon the UK of international law.[31] It is therefore possible to argue that there is no tension between the doctrine of parliamentary sovereignty and the doctrine of the primacy of EU law. The former represents a claim about the status of the UK Parliament – or, more precisely, about the status of its enactments – within the domestic legal system. In contrast, the primacy doctrine is a construct of EU law. The latter may, and does, have the effect of constraining the UK as a state in international law, but this leaves untouched the sovereignty of the UK's Parliament viewed from within the domestic-legal paradigm to which that doctrine relates. Similarly, the fact that the UK is obliged by international law to amend domestic law found to breach the ECHR presents no challenge (on this view) to the doctrine of parliamentary sovereignty. The obligation in question exists on an international plane, such that no head-on collision between it and the domestic doctrine of parliamentary sovereignty ensues.

However, while it is possible in this way to shield the notion of legislative supremacy from non-domestic and non-legal factors that might otherwise be characterized as challenges to it, it is less clear whether this is a helpful way of looking at things. Reducing factors that are not domestic-legal in character to the status of merely soft constraints that do not directly impinge upon the doctrine of legislative supremacy makes sense only when the constitution is viewed from the specifically domestic-legal dimension of the constitution that parliamentary sovereignty inhabits.

---

[31] See further D. Feldman, 'Sovereignties in Strasbourg' in R. Rawlings, P. Leyland and A. Young, *Sovereignty and the Law* (Oxford: Oxford University Press, 2013).

Yet that aspect of the constitution is not exhaustive of it: the British constitution is, in reality, multidimensional in nature. That multidimensionality consists not only in the multilayered character of the modern constitution – which encompasses or intersects with several tiers of authority at the domestic and international levels – but also its sometimes Janus-like politico-legal nature, according to which norms and factors that may not exist in legal form – but which may, for instance, be institutionalized as constitutional conventions – nevertheless operate as constraints upon legislative capacity. It follows that once the traditional tendency to place domestic-legal considerations centre-stage is dispensed with, influences rooted in other dimensions of the constitutional order are less readily dismissible as merely soft constraints. The inferiority ascribed to them from within the domestic-legal paradigm may have little or no purchase when they are viewed from the perspective of some *other* (e.g. non-legal or non-domestic) paradigm. This is not to suggest that they cast doubt upon the legislative supremacy of Parliament: merely that that supremacy does and can only bite within the particular dimension of the constitution to which it relates.

Multidimensionality and the exceptionalism of the unwritten constitution

It was suggested towards the beginning of this chapter that the parliamentary-sovereignty model of constitutionalism adopted in countries like the UK might be considered to contrast starkly with the governing-text model found in many other countries in the common-law world (and beyond). However, the foregoing analysis suggests that the differences between those two models are not as great as is commonly supposed. One reason for this is that, as noted above, the governing-text model is itself a broad church: one that, while encompassing what might be considered to be classical manifestations such as the US system, also includes approaches that structure the relationship between constitutional and regular law – and between courts and lawmakers – more subtly.[32]

A second reason is that a multidimensional understanding of the UK system serves to contextualize – and so diminish – the apparently

---

[32] Above (n. 1).

excessive claim about legislative authority that is implicit in the doctrine of parliamentary sovereignty. It does so not by disputing the correctness of the claim – that the sovereign legislature's enactments are necessarily valid laws that the courts are bound to apply[33] – viewed in its own terms. Rather, it shows that the claim only bites within the domestic-legal dimension of the constitution to which it relates, and that its broader significance can only properly be assessed once the wider picture – which extends to non-legal and non-domestic matters – is factored in. Viewed thus, the apparently extravagant notion of legislative supremacy is rendered a more modest one, albeit that this is secured otherwise than by calling into question its accuracy as a statement of domestic constitutional law. In turn, this means that a constitution that acknowledges legislative supremacy may differ less radically than might be assumed from systems that adhere to the governing-text tradition. This follows because the authority of a sovereign legislature may nevertheless be limited once it is recognized that constraints may exist outwith the domestic-legal dimension that constitutes the home territory of the doctrine of parliamentary sovereignty.

Even if those constraints do not, viewed from within the domestic-legal dimension, amount to hard-legal constraints, that does not prevent them, on a more holistic view of the constitution, from operating as benchmarks of constitutionality and so as constraints that determine the boundaries within which the legislature may legitimately act. Of course, the practical effect of those constraints may be other than to result in domestic-judicial invalidation of legislation enacted in breach of them. However, for two reasons, that does not rob them of significance or undermine the suggestion that acknowledging multidimensionality erodes the apparent distinction between the parliamentary-sovereignty and governing-text systems.

First, although some (but not all) systems of the latter type provide for judicial invalidation when legislators exceed their authority, this does not inevitably ensure that such limits reduce to absolutes. At the most pragmatic level, this may be so because of difficulties in relation to enforcement and compliance. And in legal terms, governing-text systems

---

[33] This does not detract from the fact that courts may sometimes have to choose between such enactments. As noted above, the manner in which priority was given to EU law in the *Factortame* case can be rationalized by reference to the House of Lords' willingness in that case to give effect to the European Communities Act 1972, by virtue of which EU law enjoys legal force within the UK's domestic legal system, rather than to subsequent legislation that was inconsistent with EU norms.

that demarcate the limits of legislative authority may nevertheless do so in ways – for instance, by supplying law-makers with override powers – that stop short of wholly foreclosing upon the possibility of legally effective legislative infraction. It follows that even governing-text systems may delimit legislative authority by reference to benchmarks of constitutional legitimacy that do not amount to constraints whose transgression inevitably results in effective judicial invalidation.

Second, just as the efficacy of constraints deriving from governing constitutional texts may be limited, so the efficacy of constraints applicable within a parliamentary-sovereignty model may exceed expectations. Perhaps most obviously, constraints that derive from the political dimension of the constitution may operate so as to disincentivize – or even practically preclude – the enactment of legislation that would cut across broadly shared values. Meanwhile, constraints that exist within the legal-non-domestic realm, as well as similarly disincentivizing legislative infractions, may – if transgressed – result in judicial enforcement and legal liability, albeit on the international[34] rather than the domestic plane.[35]

However, these points notwithstanding, the parliamentary-sovereignty model of constitutionalism remains, in a significant respect, distinctive. It necessarily ascribes an inferior status to factors that might loosely be regarded as restraints upon legislative freedom. Constraining forces are thus to be found only in constitutional dimensions (e.g. political or international) other than that (i.e. the domestic-legal dimension) which, from an orthodox standpoint, is considered paradigmatic. It is this characteristic of the legislative-sovereignty model that enables exercises of sovereign legislative authority to be considered legally valid even if they cut across constraints (e.g. fundamental (political) values or international legal norms) that are anchored in other dimensions.

In contrast, the governing-text tradition necessarily reduces legislative authority and (at least some of) the factors that constrain it to phenomena that exist within a *single* constitutional dimension. By virtue of nothing other than its *constituting* effect, the governing text establishes the

---

[34] E.g. through proceedings in the European Court of Human Rights or the Court of Justice of the EU.

[35] A further possibility, concerning the constraining potential of legally acknowledged fundamental constitutional rights and values within the legislative-supremacy model is considered below.

constitutional realm and determines the ordering of norms and institutions within it. As a result, factors that may, within a legislative-supremacy system, be open to characterization as soft constraints might instead take the form of unambiguously hard constraints. An obvious example lies in the distinction between the devolution scheme found in the UK and the allocation of power by a written constitution according to federal principles. As already noted, within the former system, central interference in legislative matters is precluded by constraints lying outwith the constitution's domestic-legal dimension. In contrast, in a governing-text/federal system, the federal distribution of power operates as a hard constraint upon the powers of the central legislature. This is so because that federal distribution of power is ordained by law that occupies the same constitutional space as – and so impinges upon – the federal legislature's legal authority. A similar point can be made by contrasting governing-text models that recognize fundamental rights as hard constraints operating on the domestic-legal plane with the British model, in which the rights contained in the ECHR sit on another (international) plane, thus acting as hard-legal constraints upon the UK as a state, but not upon the UK Parliament as a matter of domestic law.[36] Understood thus, it is the capacity of the governing-text model to situate legislative authority within a unified constitutional realm that also accommodates constraining forces which sets it apart from the parliamentary-sovereignty model in which legislative authority and constraints upon it occupy different constitutional dimensions.

However, for two reasons, the distinction should not be overstated. First, for reasons explored above, whether constraining influences sit within the same constitutional dimension as that which accords authority to the legislature may be less important than first appears, given that constraints found in other dimensions may nevertheless impinge upon, even if they do not directly cut down, legislative authority. Second, the distinction between the legislative-supremacy and governing-text systems does not straightforwardly map onto a corresponding distinction between multidimensional and unidimensional models of constitutionalism. Although the governing-text tradition is likely to situate some constraining forces

---

[36] The rights contained in the ECHR are, of course, presently given limited legal effect in the UK by the Human Rights Act 1998, but in a way that does not formally detract from the UK Parliament's legislative competence. The extent to which fundamental rights exist as part of the common law, thus operating upon the domestic-legal plane, is considered below.

within the constitutional space in which legislative authority is acknowledged, this does not foreclose the possibility of other constraining forces existing within other constitutional dimensions. Such forces may take the form of non-legal constraints such as conventions (an obvious example being the two-term convention that prefigured the 22nd amendment to the US Constitution) or, at least in dualist systems, international law that constrains the state on the international plane without eroding the authority of the legislature viewed through a purely domestic lens. It follows, then, that even in governing-text systems, the domestic-legal dimension may not be exhaustive of the constitution. All constitutions, on this view, are multidimensional, the crucial difference being between those that locate *some* constraints upon legislative authority within that phenomenon's home dimension and those in which such constraints exist *only* in other dimensions.

The legislative-supremacy model and the possibility of domestic-legal constraints

This leaves a final question to be addressed. According to the analysis advanced so far, the defining feature of the parliamentary-sovereignty model is that such constraints upon legislative authority as exist are situated outwith such authority's home constitutional dimension. Might, however, the possibility arise of constraints situated *within* that dimension? The obvious answer is 'no', since the existence of such constraints would appear to be inconsistent with the very essence of legislative supremacy. However, for two reasons, the position is more complicated.

The more straightforward of those reasons is that legislative supremacy does not necessarily fall to be asserted against the background of a wholly blank domestic-law canvas. Even if, pursuant to the notion of parliamentary sovereignty, there are no *insurmountable* legal obstacles to legislative erosion or displacement of fundamental values or rights, it does not follow that there are no obstacles whatever. The domestic legal environment may prove to be a hostile one that is not especially receptive to legislative erosion or displacement of fundamental values or rights, even if, in the final analysis, there is no absolute impediment to such legislative intervention. The most obvious way in which this phenomenon may become manifest is through the application of principles of interpretation in a way that skews the playing field in favour of constitutional values which are potentially threatened by legislation. Canons of interpretation may thus equip courts to protect constitutional norms against infraction by a legislature lacking the political capital needed to effect the sort of full-frontal, explicit assault upon fundamental norms that would be necessary to achieve their displacement. In this way, the domestic-legal dimension of a system that recognizes legislative supremacy may turn out be a relatively complex constitutional space that accords a degree of legal security to fundamental values, even if they are not embedded so firmly as to be wholly beyond the possibility of legislative infraction.

This is certainly the position in the UK today. Common-law rights and values are openly recognized by the courts as matters that enjoy a high degree of constitutional security, rendering them immune from interference save by very specific provision in primary legislation.[37] Importantly, such thinking has survived the greater focus that is now placed upon Convention rights as a result of the enactment of the HRA.[38] Equally, it has been judicially suggested that legislation may be constitutional in character when (for example) it enshrines fundamental constitutional arrangements or values, such legislation being resistant to casual repeal.[39] It has even been suggested by the Supreme Court that there might be a hierarchy *within* the category of constitutional legislation and norms, some species of the genus being more fundamental – and so more resistant to erosion by regular or less-fundamental constitutional legislation – than other such species.[40] All of this is consistent with the notion that the domestic legal environment might be *hostile* to legislation that infringes constitutional rights and norms without going so far as to *preclude* such measures. In this way, the existence of genuinely fundamental constitutional values can be accommodated within a system premised upon a doctrine of legislative supremacy, albeit that the degree of fundamentality enjoyed by such values is ultimately limited.

However, the extent to which such values' fundamentality is constrained by legislative supremacy falls to be assessed by reference to a further

[37] See, e.g., *Witham* (n. 16); *R.* v. *Secretary of State for the Home Department ex parte Pierson* [1998] AC 539; *R.* v. *Secretary of State for the Home Department, ex parte Simms* [2000] AC 115.

[38] See, e.g., *Osborne* (n. 16); *Kennedy* v. *The Charity Commission* [2014] UKSC 20, [2014] 2 WLR 808; *A* v. *British Broadcasting Corporation* [2014] UKSC 25, [2014] 2 WLR 1243.

[39] *Thoburn* (n. 6).   [40] *HS2 Action Alliance* (n. 6).

consideration – the second of the two complications mentioned above. It is one thing to say that courts will strive to interpret legislation consistently with constitutional norms, thereby ensuring a (necessarily qualified) degree of fundamentality, but what if such construction is impossible? If legislative supremacy is genuinely a feature of the constitutional system in question, then the answer must be that courts would be obliged to – and would in fact – enforce such legislation. Yet, at least in the UK, the picture is less certain. That much is evident from the willingness of some senior members of the judiciary to voice doubts about what the courts would do if Parliament were to enact legislation inconsistent with a fundamental constitutional value or feature. In particular, in decisions issued by the UK Supreme Court and its predecessor, the Appellate Committee of the House of Lords, judges have countenanced the possibility of refusing to apply legislation were Parliament to seek to abolish or substantially curtail the courts' powers of judicial review of administrative action.[41]

There is a risk that this discourse reduces to a 'what if' debate that has an all-or-nothing character: one that seeks to furnish a definitive answer to the question: 'Is Parliament sovereign?' Lord Hope appeared to answer that question in the negative when, in the *Jackson* case, he said that although the UK constitution remains 'dominated by the sovereignty of Parliament', the doctrine of 'parliamentary sovereignty is no longer, if it ever was, absolute'.[42] This is a curious formulation given the ostensibly binary nature of legislative supremacy: the natural inference is that if parliamentary sovereignty is *not absolute*, then Parliament is not sovereign *at all*. However, the ambiguity inherent in Lord Hope's view perhaps hints at a more subtle way of looking at this matter. Perceiving such judicial interventions through a binary optic may oversimplify, and so distort, the discourse about legislative supremacy. Instead, it is possible to situate them within a paradigm that acknowledges a further, and arguably crucial, feature of uncodified systems: namely, uncertainty.

There is no novelty in the suggestion that such systems are inherently more uncertain than those based upon a governing text (albeit that the extent of the certainty purchased by such a text can easily be overstated). The form of uncertainty that is generally associated with uncodified constitutions relates to *content*. For instance, the content of the category of common-law constitutional rights in the UK is substantially less certain

---

[41] *Jackson* (n. 19) and *AXA* (n. 19).   [42] *Jackson* (n. 19), [104]

than the content of the catalogue of textual rights given effect by the HRA (or by constitutional bills of rights in systems that possess such texts). However, a second, deeper form of uncertainty can be identified: one that pertains not to the content of uncodified constitutional norms, but to their status, and, in particular, to the extent to which they are embedded so as to be shielded from legislative erosion or displacement. The other side of the coin of which this normative-hierarchical uncertainty forms one face is a corresponding form of institutional-hierarchical uncertainty: doubts about the extent of constitutional norms' fundamentality produce a resultant uncertainty about the institutional relationship between legislators and courts.

These matters are captured well by frank extrajudicial remarks made by Lord Phillips, who was the inaugural President of the UK Supreme Court. Asked what would happen 'if Parliament did the inconceivable' by legislating contrary to a fundamental constitutional principle, he said that 'we [the judges] might do the inconceivable as well'.[43] This might appear to be, but is not in fact, an unvarnished assertion of judicial supremacism. As Lord Phillips explained more recently, there would have to be a 'constitutional crisis before you could envisage the courts purporting to strike down primary legislation' – and before the possibility of strike-down could be contemplated, an elaborate interpretative dance would first have taken place. The court, said Lord Phillips, would ascribe to the legislation an interpretation that it could not bear, so as to say to Parliament: 'We have pulled you back from the brink. Are you really going to persist with this?'[44] The reality is that were a constitutional crisis of the type contemplated by Lord Phillips to eventuate, the outcome could not be predicted with any certainty. What is more important, however, is that such a crisis is rendered less likely in the first place by virtue of that uncertainty.

Viewed thus, the interlocking phenomena of normative-hierarchical and institutional-hierarchical uncertainty that can be – and, in the UK's case, are – found in uncodified constitutions may be considered a form of restraint in themselves. They strongly discourage both legislators and judges from stepping over the constitutional brink (albeit that its precise location may be somewhat vague), while drawing upon and sustaining means by which constitutional brinksmanship can play out in ways that

---

[43] BBC radio interview, 2 August 2010.
[44] *The Constitutional Role of the Judiciary if there were a Codified Constitution* (n. 21), [46].

stop short of the kind of confrontation for which there is no roadmap. Whether that is a strength or a weakness of such systems is a question of perspective. For present purposes, however, the important point is that the uncertain status of constitutional norms can be understood as a form of constraint upon legislative (as well as upon judicial) authority. How that constraint should be characterized is a difficult question to answer. To the extent that this form of uncertainty arises from the possibility of domestic-legal limits being articulated and enforced by the judicial branch, it might be thought to reduce to a constraint sitting within the very constitutional space that the sovereignty doctrine itself inhabits. But even if that is so, it is a constraint that is different in character from the sort of legal limits upon legislative authority which are found in governing-text systems: one that relies upon an unrealized prospect of judicial activism rather than the policing of extant legal boundaries. Indeed, it is arguable that the effect of judicial kite-flying of the type outlined above is ultimately political in nature, in that it may serve to shift the course of political debate.[45] This only serves to demonstrate the permeability of the distinctions that separate the constitution's different dimensions – and so the futility of attempting to understand it from the perspective of only one of them.

Final thoughts

There is, unsurprisingly, no straightforward answer to the question whether the UK Parliament is sovereign. While that may seem a rather unsatisfactory position, the question itself is arguably misconceived – both because it frames the issue in terms whose binary nature is perhaps inapt, and because it implicitly presupposes that there is a single paradigm by reference to which the issue can be definitively resolved. The reality is more subtle than the all-or-nothing assumption underlying the question thus conceived. The legislative authority of the UK Parliament is a phenomenon that can be appreciated only when examined in terms that embrace not only domestic-legal but also international and extra-legal considerations. Viewed through those distinct – albeit overlapping and interlocking – lenses, the picture turns out to be a complex one.

---

[45] An extra-judicial warning issued by Lord Woolf about proposals to oust judicial review of immigration and asylum decisions had precisely such an effect: Lord Woolf, 'The Rule of Law and a Change in the Constitution' [2004] *Cambridge Law Journal* 317.

This, in turn, places in sharp relief the extent of the distinction between a constitution like the UK's and the governing-text model. That a distinction exists is undeniable; but its starkness can easily be overstated. As far as the extent of legislative authority is concerned, the distinction appears to set up limited and unlimited notions of legislative competence in opposition to one another. Yet the reality, as this chapter has attempted to show, is more nuanced. The nature of the limits that may operate in the absence of a governing text are certainly different from those liable to derive from such a text – but it would be wrong to suppose that the absence of a governing constitutional instrument, and the associated embrace of legislative supremacy, necessarily implies a dearth of any such limits. That that is so in relation to the UK is apparent once its doctrine of legislative supremacy is understood within the wider context of multidimensional constitutionalism that characterizes the British system today.

Further reading

T. R. S. Allan, *The Sovereignty of Law: Freedom, Constitution, and Common Law* (Oxford University Press, 2013)

N. W. Barber, 'The Afterlife of Parliamentary Sovereignty' (2011) 9 *International Journal of Constitutional Law* 144

J. Goldsworthy, *Parliamentary Sovereignty: Contemporary Debates* (Cambridge: Cambridge University Press, 2010)

N. MacCormick, *Questioning Sovereignty: Law, State, and Practical Reason* (Oxford: Oxford University Press, 1999)

A. Young, *Parliamentary Sovereignty and the Human Rights Act* (Oxford: Hart Publishing, 2009)

5 The politics of accountability

Tony Wright

Accountability has recently been described as 'the *uber*-concept of modern times'.[1] In politics it has certainly become ubiquitous. There are daily demands for someone or something to be 'held to account'. The routine response to a whole range of political issues is a call for 'more accountability'. Yet this political usage of the word is relatively recent. What began life as the language of the counting house, as dry as financial dust, has been converted into the stock language of the political and constitutional arena. Even more interestingly, what was once a means by which medieval monarchs could count the assets of their subjects has been transformed into the means whereby modern citizens can hold to account those who rule them.

So pervasive has the language of accountability become – and so synonymous it now is with every desirable attribute of democracy and good government – that the concept is in danger of losing all critical meaning. For example, it would be a very brave politician (or commentator) who would dare to suggest that good governance might even benefit from somewhat less accountability in certain respects. This is not the place to explore all the conceptual complexities of accountability, but it is necessary to pin down a core meaning.[2] It involves a relationship between an account-holder and an account-giver, so that the latter has to provide explanations to the former, with the possibility of consequences. Obviously legal accountability is a 'hard' form of accountability, with enforced consequences, but the primary focus here is on the political accountability that is intrinsic to democratic politics and which takes a variety of forms.

---

[1] M. Flinders, *Defending Politics* (Oxford: Oxford University Press, 2012), 26.
[2] For discussion of the core meaning of accountability, see M. Bovens, 'Analysing and Assessing Accountability: A Conceptual Framework' (2007) 13 *European Law Journal* 447 and the extended discussion in M. Bovens, R. Goodin and T. Schillemans, *The Oxford Handbook of Public Accountability* (Oxford: Oxford University Press, 2014).

It is intrinsic because the idea of democracy carries with it the belief in the popular control of power. This in turn acts to prevent abuse of power and corruption, promotes learning and nourishes legitimacy. Accountability is therefore both the lubricating idea and the practical toolkit that gives effect to the idea. In the case of political accountability, the relationship is usually described as that between principal and agent. The principal is the electorate and the agent is their elected representatives. There then follows a chain of delegation, with ministers accountable to the elected representatives and civil servants accountable to ministers. At least that is the theory. In practice, of course, each link in the chain needs to be examined and its efficacy tested.[3] Moreover, it has been found necessary to supplement this formal accountability chain with a wide assortment of additional power-controlling mechanisms.

It is now necessary to bring this rather general discussion of accountability down to earth by looking at how it has been played out in recent British politics. It will be suggested that there was believed to be a particular problem about accountability in Britain, with a political executive that was too powerful and with inadequate power-controlling checks on it. In many ways the history of the last twenty years or so has been of a process in which a variety of steps have been taken to remedy this accountability problem. It is even possible to describe an accountability explosion during this period. Yet at the end of this period it can be argued that there remains an accountability problem, though of a rather different kind. The rest of this chapter fleshes out this story and identifies some of the central issues involved.

Accountability and the British political tradition

It has been conventional to describe the British political tradition in terms of an attachment to strong government. This could be explained historically by the unbroken transfer of the prerogative powers of monarchs to modern executives, constitutionally by the absence of formally separated powers or a codified constitution, and electorally by a system designed to produce majority party governments. All this gave a British government an

---

[3] This is explored in K. Strom, W. Muller and T. Bergman (eds.), *Delegation and Accountability in Parliamentary Democracies* (Oxford: Oxford University Press, 2003).

exceptional freedom of action. I once described this system of government as a 'dominocracy';[4] others have referred to it as an 'elected dictatorship'.[5]

It seemed to have produced a particular kind of political culture too, in which the business of governing took precedence over any concerns about holding to account. In the words of the journalist, Hugo Young: 'This preference, which is for strong government over accountable government, is to be found throughout the British parliamentary system.'[6] It was a system built upon the doctrinal rock of parliamentary sovereignty, which put judges (and others) firmly in their place.

By the final decades of the twentieth century this way of governing found itself under increasing attack from those who wanted to find a better balance between governing and holding to account. Yet it is a mistake to think that conventional understandings of British politics lacked any attachment to accountability (or 'responsibility' as it was usually described). It is rather that it was an essentially simple conception, in which ministers were responsible to Parliament and Parliament was responsible to the people. Anything which cut across and complicated this simple accountability chain was therefore to be resisted. There is much to be said for having such a clear and direct line of accountability. It is captured in a wonderful phrase coined by Bagehot in the 1860s in his *The English Constitution* when he proclaimed that in every constitution 'the sovereign power must be *come-at-able*'.[7] This ability to combine accountability with effective government became a central claim of the 'Westminster model'.

If we jump across a century, to the 1960s, we can see the continued force of this conception of accountability in the parliamentary debates on the Labour government's proposal to establish an Ombudsman to take up complaints from citizens about 'maladministration leading to injustice' in relation to services provided by the state. Leading for the Conservative opposition, Quentin Hogg (who, as Lord Hailsham, was later to denounce 'elective dictatorship') declared his belief that 'the new machinery will undermine the position of the individual Member of Parliament vis-à-vis the Executive, and ... it will undermine his position vis-à-vis his constituents'.[8] This was an authentic expression of the simple view of

---

[4] T. Wright, *Citizens and Subjects* (London: Routledge, 1994).
[5] Lord Hailsham, *The Dilemma of Democracy* (London: Collins, 1978).
[6] *The Guardian*, 15 September 1988.
[7] W. Bagehot, *The English Constitution* (London: C.A. Watts, 1964), 127.
[8] Hansard, HC, 18 October 1966, vol. 734, col. 74.

political accountability. It was a view which did not prevail, but it helps to explain why the Ombudsman was tied so closely to Parliament, having to account to a select committee and with citizens having to make their complaints through a Member of Parliament, and why there was no power to compel redress.

If the Ombudsman was one constitutional innovation designed to supplement a traditionally simple conception of political accountability, another came at the end of the 1970s with the proposal (arising out of a report from the House of Commons Procedure Committee) that the scrutiny and accountability function of the Commons needed to be strengthened by the establishment of select committees for each government department. Introducing the Commons debate on the report, and speaking for the committee, Sir David Renton MP set out the central argument: '[W]e say that the balance of advantage in the working of our constitution is now weighted in favour of the government ... to a degree which arouses widespread anxiety.'[9] Yet, rather like Hogg's view on the Ombudsman proposal earlier, Labour's Michael Foot believed what was being proposed would subvert a traditional model of political accountability:

> The proposal is for a range of select committees which are supposed to deal with the major question of the disbalance between the executive and the legislature. That is not a minor matter; it is a proposal for dealing with a major question. If those committees, applied to each department, are to rectify such a disbalance, they will have a predominance in our parliamentary affairs which will be different from anything that we have previously experienced.[10]

In particular Foot believed the committees would devalue the Commons chamber, which was the proper arena of political accountability. It was therefore left to the Conservative government elected in 1979 to introduce the new select committee system. The significance of the debates from this period – whether on the Ombudsman or select committees – is that behind the particular institutional and procedural proposals were competing understandings of the nature of political accountability. On one side were those who asserted the merits of clarity and simplicity of the traditional model and resisted changes which they thought would complicate and subvert it; while on the other side were those who pointed to the inadequacies of that traditional model and argued that it needed to be

---

[9] Hansard, HC, 19 February 1979, vol. 963, col. 45.
[10] Hansard, HC, 20 February 1979, vol. 963, col. 292.

strengthened and supplemented by institutional innovations. Nor are these merely ancestral arguments, for they remain central to contemporary debate on a range of fronts.

Politics and law

A major front in this debate has been the boundary line between politics and law, and between political and legal constitutionalism.[11] While political constitutionalism asserts the primacy of democratic politics as the arena of accountability and the necessary limitations of the role of unelected judges, legal constitutionalism points to the dangers of mere majoritarianism and the need for the protective accountabilities that only an independent judiciary can provide. In Britain, in simplest terms, the debate centres on the relationship between the axial constitutional doctrine of the sovereignty of Parliament and a conception of the rule of law. Except that until relatively recently there was no real debate, for the law knew its deferential constitutional place in relation to the supremacy of Parliament. This was the settled position for the first half of the twentieth century.

It rapidly became unsettled. On one side, there was the constitutional shock administered by EU membership to the sovereignty of Parliament, as the courts were called upon to uphold the supremacy of EU law over domestic law in all areas of competence.[12] The fact that Parliament had assented to this arrangement in joining the EU, coupled with the claim that sovereignty was preserved because there always remained the option of leaving, did little to diminish the continuing political impact of the shock. In terms of accountability, it fuelled the argument that a domestic political accountability over a range of policy areas had been transferred to an unelected and unaccountable supranational institution which could have its powers enforced in the courts. To those attached to a traditionally simple model of political accountability, this was a complication too far. To others, it represented a pooling of sovereignty in the interest of shared goals and a recognition that accountability took a variety of different forms. This argument rumbles on.

---

[11] On related matters, see D. Howarth, 'The Politics of Public Law' (Chapter 2 in this volume).
[12] See, e.g., the landmark decision of the House of Lords in *R* v. *Secretary of State for Transport Secretary ex parte Factortame (No. 2)* [1991] 1 AC 603.

Yet this was not the only side on which the accountability debate between politics and law was being tested. On the domestic front, a new judicial activism was underway, challenging the old deference. This was seen most strikingly in the expansion of judicial review of ministerial and administrative action. The changing terms of trade between government and the courts was reflected by the title of a guide issued within Whitehall: *The Judge Over Your Shoulder.*[13] In part at least, this development was a response to what was described earlier as the perception in the latter decades of the twentieth century that there had become a constitutional imbalance, in which the power of government had grown too strong and the political checks on it, notably Parliament, too weak. If there was an accountability vacuum that had developed, then it was constitutionally necessary that it should be filled; and this encouraged at least some in the judiciary to think that they might have a larger role to play.

This larger role was then guaranteed by the Human Rights Act 1998.[14] Originally presented as simply 'bringing rights home', so that domestic courts could take cases concerning the European Convention on Human Rights that previously had to go to the Strasbourg court, the effect has been to bring the courts into some of the most contentious political territory. Despite the constitutional ingenuity that went into the construction of the Human Rights Act, preserving parliamentary sovereignty by having 'declarations of incompatibility'[15] by the courts rather than powers to strike down legislation, this has not prevented politicians and the courts having a running battle, especially on terrorism issues, as they assert their rival legitimacies: on this side, parliamentary sovereignty; on that side, the rule of law. Who should decide? Should political or legal accountability prevail? Or are these the wrong questions? Perhaps the real task is to recognise that, in a mature constitutional democracy, these accountabilities are complementary rather than competing.[16]

The precise balance between political and legal versions of accountability swings back and forth in response to changing circumstances. The

---

[13] The first edition was issued in 1987; the most recent edition, the 4th, was issued in 2006. It is available at www.gov.uk/government/publications/the-judge-over-your-shoulder-joys-edition-4.

[14] See further A. McHarg, 'Rights and Democracy in UK Public Law' (Chapter 6 in this volume).

[15] Human Rights Act 1998, s. 4.

[16] On parliamentary sovereignty, see further M. Elliott, 'Legislative Supremacy in a Multidimensional Constitution' (Chapter 4 in this volume).

perception that executive power in Britain was insufficiently checked contributed to the extension of judicial review and the legal protection of human rights. Yet a more recent perception has warned of the democratic dangers of pushing this rebalancing too far. As Lord Bingham, the former Lord Chief Justice, put it: 'The British people have not repelled the extraneous power of the papacy in spiritual matters and the pretensions of royal power in temporal in order to subject themselves to the unchallengeable rulings of unelected judges.'[17] In particular there has been a reaction, not just from politicians but from some judges, against what is seen as the Strasbourg court over-reaching itself (as on the voting rights of prisoners) in a way that offends against democratic decision-making, especially in Britain where there exists, in the words of one senior judge, 'a deep sense that matters of state policy are in essence the responsibility of the elected arms of government'.[18]

It is through politics that interests and values are contested and mediated, in a way (if done openly and fairly) that enables elected politicians to be accountable for them and, even when outcomes are disliked, for the process to be regarded as legitimate. As Supreme Court Justice Lord Sumption recently expressed this: 'Politics is quite simply a better way of resolving questions of social policy than judge-made law.'[19] This is clearly so, although it tells us little about the proper relationship between politics and law in a well-functioning constitutional framework. For example, even those who dislike Strasbourg and want a home-grown British Bill of Rights are recognising the need for judicial protection of human rights and not just for their political protection. It may well be that the best protection comes from the creative tension between law and politics on this front, or what is sometimes described as constructive dialogue.

However, the claim for the centrality of politics depends upon politics working well. Where politics is corrupt, intolerant or oppressive, then people will naturally look for remedies elsewhere. Elections are a necessary but not sufficient condition for a functioning democracy. A democracy which oppresses minorities or is contemptuous of basic rights may be majoritarian but is not the kind of democracy which deserves the name. All this is a preamble to the argument that it is not enough to assert the

---

[17] T. Bingham, *The Rule of Law* (London: Allen Lane, 2010), 168.

[18] Sir John Laws, *The Common Law Constitution* (Cambridge: Cambridge University Press, 2014).

[19] Lord Sumption, 'The Limits of Law' 27th Sultan Azlan Shah Lecture, 20 November 2013, available at www.supremecourt.uk/docs/speech-131120.pdf.

centrality of political accountability without also examining whether the nature of this accountability is effective in practice. As has already been seen, this has been a major question in recent political debate in Britain, glimpsed in those discussions of the Ombudsman and select committees and with a direct bearing on the boundary disputes between politicians and judges. So how effective is political accountability in Britain?

The effectiveness of political accountability in Britain

It is certainly not as straightforward as simple versions of the principal and agent model of accountability might suggest, nor of the chain of democratic delegation that is supposed to flow from them. It turns out that there are complications at every stage. This is clearly true of elections, which are the bedrock of political accountability. The fact that governments are put there by the electorate, and have to account to the electorate for their performance, is fundamental to democratic politics. Elections are therefore decisive instruments of accountability. They provide a mandate to rule. Parties present their programmes to the electors, who choose between them, with the winner forming the government. This process is repeated at regular intervals. In Britain, with its organised party system and majoritarian electoral system, this seemed to represent a clear, direct and brutal form of political accountability.

In that phrase of Bagehot, it meant that power was 'come-at-able'.[20] Accountability could not be dodged or fudged. There might be complaints in some quarters that the simple plurality electoral system was insufficiently representative of the range of electoral opinion, but in terms of a direct line of accountability from governors to governed, it was precisely the simplicity of the system that delivered this. What it lacked in representativeness was more than made up for by what it gained in accountability. This was reinforced by a party system which gave clear governing choices, with parties themselves rooted in mass memberships which both connected them to the wider society and produced an additional dimension of accountability. For most of the twentieth century this was the way in which electoral accountability in Britain could be described.

---

[20] Bagehot (n. 7), 127.

In fact, matters were never quite so straightforward (not least because of the difficulty of knowing exactly what people were voting for or against), but this did not diminish the governing accountability of the system. Subsequent developments have radically altered this picture. Electoral participation has sharply declined. Political allegiances and attachments have fractured. Parties have shrunk, both in membership and support. The nature of politics has therefore changed. This trend is not unique to Britain (in fact, it has been described as 'the hollowing of Western democracy'),[21] but it has been especially marked here and has a direct impact on the way in which electoral accountability is described. Elections remain, but the supporting building blocks have been substantially eroded. The effect is to make electoral accountability much less effective than it once was.

This has been compounded by a further (and related) development. The failure of any party to win a majority in the 2010 general election, thereby producing the first coalition government in the period since the Second World War, meant that it could no longer be claimed that the electoral system had the singular merit of delivering clear outcomes which, in turn, ensured a clear line of accountability. A government had been formed which nobody had voted for, on a governing programme assembled after the election, and with the coalition parties able to tell different stories to the electorate at the next election about what they had done. All this may be inevitable; but it shattered a version of electoral accountability that had long been regarded as a hallmark of the British political tradition. If this pattern of politics becomes normal, it will have implications for political accountability which remain to be worked out.

If elections are necessary but not sufficient for accountability, a major reason is that they are episodic (although the prospect of facing the electorate acts as a permanent discipline). Holding power to account is a continuous process, not just the matter of an electoral moment. Elections enable rulers to be kicked out; but there should also be an ability to kick them while they are in. Political accountability is therefore not just vertical, but also horizontal; not just episodic, but continuous; and not just about elections, but about all the ways in which power is held to account. Some of these ways (for example, the media in all their various forms, along with campaign and pressure groups), though fundamental to the activity of scrutiny, are beyond the focus here. There are then an array of institutions

---

[21] P. Mair, *Ruling the Void: The Hollowing of Western Democracy* (London: Verso, 2013).

and mechanisms that are engaged in one way or another with the formal business of accountability. There are the courts of course, but there is also the whole world of watchdogs, auditors, inquiries, ombudsmen, commissioners, inspectorates, regulators and all the rest of the modern account-holding universe.

Parliament

These all contribute to the continuous activity of accountability; but they also raise accountability issues of their own. Who brings this accountability universe together into some kind of politically manageable shape? Who guards the guardians? The obvious candidate is Parliament, the institution charged with the central function of continuous political accountability. It has been said that Parliament should sit at 'the apex of accountability'.[22] But does it? Or has it been by-passed by these other accountability mechanisms? It is the constitutional task of Parliament to hold ministers and governments to account, but the question is how effectively this is done – and whether it could be done better.

It certainly gives the appearance of doing it. The daily interrogation of ministers, and weekly of the prime minister, is the most visible expression of Parliament's accountability role. It can be a challenging experience. Tony Blair has described it as 'the most nerve-racking, discombobulating, nail-biting, bowel-moving, terror-inspiring, courage-draining experience in my prime ministerial life, without question'; although then adding that 'it's also rather a myth that it's a great way of holding the prime minister to account'.[23] There is a general point here. In many ways Parliament is organised as a great accountability machine. Questions are asked and answered, statements made and examined, debates conducted, legislation scrutinised and votes taken. This is all accountability in action, and should not be undervalued. Yet much of it is also a ritualised kind of accountability, in which appearance is not the same as the reality, which makes it less effective than it might be.

It is not difficult to identify why this might be so. Although scrutiny is a key parliamentary function, this operates in a particular context. This

---

[22] Hansard Society, *The Challenge for Parliament: Making Government Accountable* (London: Hansard Society, 2001), ch. 8.
[23] T. Blair, *A Journey* (London: Hutchinson, 2010), 109.

context is one in which, with no formal separation of powers, the executive routinely controls the legislature. MPs are not primarily scrutineers but government-supporting or opposition-supporting party politicians. Much of the scrutiny and accountability of government that takes place is of the partisan kind undertaken routinely by the opposition. This permanent adversarialism performs a valuable accountability function, but its partisan character is also a limitation. Not surprisingly, when MPs are asked to rate the importance of scrutiny among their various roles, it receives a higher rating when their party is in opposition and a lower rating when it is in power. Of course there are independent-minded MPs, and more 'dissidence' in the division lobbies than when party government was at its tightest, but this remains the essential context within which scrutiny and accountability takes place.

This is seen most clearly in the legislative process, which consumes a vast amount of parliamentary time but which (despite some recent changes) is structured by adversarial politics rather than a commitment to making legislation as good as it can be. The partisan character of scrutiny is often cited as the reason why much legislation turns out to be defective.[24] It is also advanced as a main justification for the House of Lords (even in its semi-reformed state) as it takes the business of scrutiny seriously and enables amendments to legislation to be made. All this directs attention back to the wider political context. On one view, here is a political system in which scrutiny is embedded and in which accountability is relentless and often ferocious. On another view, it is a system in which neither scrutiny nor accountability is as effective as it might be.

This is usually discussed in terms of the 'balance' between executive and legislature; and proposals for parliamentary reform have invariably taken the form of an argument for balance-shifting of various kinds.[25] In particular this has been the argument for extending and strengthening the system of investigatory select committees. It was believed that these committees would be able to keep a much closer eye on what ministers and officials were doing than was possible in the political theatre of the Commons chamber, and to do so in a way that was more collaborative and less partisan. So it has proved, although the committees have also had

---

[24] See, e.g., A. King and I. Crewe, *The Blunders of our Governments* (London: Oneworld, 2013).

[25] See T. Wright, *Doing Politics* (London: Biteback, 2012), 165–90.

severe limitations which have made them less effective than they might have been. Political commitment to them was weak, resources were limited, and they were appointed by the party machines. They had clearly had some impact, but how much – and of what kind – was difficult to assess.[26]

However, recent changes, particularly those made in the wake of the parliamentary expenses scandal, have strengthened the select committee system (and the Commons as a whole). A Reform Committee set up in 2009 announced that it was time for the Commons to become 'more vigorous in its task of scrutiny and accountability'[27] and proposed that the select committees (and their chairs) should be elected and that backbenchers should control more of the House business. The implementation of these reforms does seem to have energised the Commons. The profile of the select committees has certainly been raised, as they have put themselves at the centre of the big issues of the day in televised hearings, armed with their new legitimacy, and with the election of some independent-minded chairs who would not have emerged under the previous whip-appointed system. At the same time, the ability of backbench MPs to control part of the agenda of the House has produced debates and votes on issues which the party machines might well have preferred to avoid.

These are real gains for accountability, but it does not mean that weaknesses have gone. There is a danger that the desire of select committees to be at the centre of every political issue will be at the expense of the more prosaic scrutiny work of departments that should be their bread and butter. They are also not well equipped to undertake the more detailed and forensic investigation of issues that other kinds of inquiry are called upon for, often lacking the necessary coherence or skills, although the recent Parliamentary Commission on Banking Standards (a joint committee of Commons and Lords, with extra powers and resources) is an interesting innovation that could be built on. The Public Accounts Committee is effective because it has all the resources of the National Audit Office behind it; other committees are poorly resourced by comparison, despite the establishment of a 'scrutiny unit' to support them. Perhaps most fundamental of all, MPs themselves still need to commit themselves to the scrutiny function as a central activity. A Parliament that was

---

[26] For a recent assessment, see M. Russell and M. Benton, *Selective Influence: The Policy Impact of House of Commons Select Committees* (London: The Constitution Unit, 2011).

[27] House of Commons Reform Committee, *Rebuilding the House* (HC 1117, 2009).

determined to sit at the apex of accountability would need to address such weaknesses.

The accountability explosion

However, not only are these recent accountability gains real, but they should be seen as part of a process through which the accountability of government has been extended and expanded over the past two decades in a whole variety of ways. It is not too much to say that this process has been the leitmotif of the period. There has been an accountability explosion. The following is an outline sketch of some of what this has involved in the period 1994 to 2014:[28]

- **Ethical watchdog.** Establishment of Committee on Standards in Public Life as standing watchdog on standards of conduct in public life; has promoted ethical regulation in a number of areas of public life.
- **Elections and party funding.** Rules on party funding, donations and election spending introduced, monitored and enforced by a statutory Electoral Commission.
- **Human rights.** Passage of Human Rights Act 1998 incorporates European Convention on Human Rights and enables human rights issues to be heard and decided by the courts.
- **Information and transparency.** Passage of Freedom of Information Act 2000 gives right of access to official information, supported by an Information Commissioner; a Public Sector Transparency Board established to promote open data in central and local government; legislation to protect whistleblowers.
- **Public appointments.** Public appointments by ministers governed by a Code of Practice and monitored by a Commissioner for Public Appointments.
- **House of Commons.** Parliamentary Resolution on Ministerial Accountability; vetting of major public appointments by select committees; new powers (previously prerogative) on war-making and treaty

---

[28] This list is not intended to be exhaustive, but to illustrate some of the main ways in which accountability has been strengthened and extended in the past twenty years. Some of these changes are statutory, others not.

approval; election of select committee chairs and members; and control of backbench business.

- **Parliamentary Standards.** A Parliamentary Commissioner for Standards established to monitor financial interests and Code of Conduct, and to investigate complaints about MPs; and an Independent Parliamentary Standards Authority established to regulate MPs' expenses and remuneration, and to enforce compliance with the rules.
- **House of Lords.** House of Lords Appointments Commission established to appoint independent cross-bench peers, and vet all peerage nominations for propriety, including nominations from the political parties. Removal of hereditary peers strengthens scrutiny and revision role.
- **Judges.** Establishment of independent Judicial Appointments Commission strengthens judicial independence by removing role of Lord Chancellor; and establishment of Supreme Court transfers judicial authority from House of Lords.
- **Civil Service.** Civil Service Commission put on statutory basis (previously royal prerogative) to protect key civil service values under the Civil Service Code.
- **Prime Minister.** Publication and revisions of Ministerial Code, with a Prime Minister's independent adviser on ministers' interests to investigate alleged breaches. Convention established that a Prime Minister appears before a committee of select committee chairs on regular basis.
- **Statistics.** Establishment of UK Statistics Authority to safeguard integrity of official statistics by independent scrutiny and monitoring, including investigation of alleged abuses.
- **Referendums.** Convention established (and by law in relation to EU) that major constitutional changes will require referendums, with their operation – and the questions – regulated by the Electoral Commission.
- **Security Services.** Parliamentary oversight of security services introduced by establishment of Intelligence and Security Committee.
- **Economy.** Interest rate policy transferred to independent Monetary Policy Committee of Bank of England; and Office for Budget Responsibility established as independent fiscal watchdog.
- **Fixed-term parliaments.** Legislation on fixed-term parliaments introduced, replacing previous prerogative discretion on dissolution.
- **Complaint and redress.** Proliferation of ombudsman-type complaint and redress schemes across public sector, including independent complaints body for the police; along with new inspectorates and regulators.

This makes sorry reading for those attached to the traditionally simple model of political accountability; but it makes more cheerful reading for those who thought this model was inadequate and needed to be supplemented by additional accountability mechanisms. If, at the beginning of this period, the nature of power in Britain could be described as an elective dictatorship, at the end of the period it could be authoritatively declared that 'the power of the executive ... has been cut into pieces'.[29]

A convenient starting point for this period is the establishment by John Major in 1994 of the Committee on Standards in Public Life as a response to the 'sleaze' allegations surrounding his party at that time. This began a process of ethical regulation of public life that brought important consequences. In its first report in 1995 the Committee announced its Seven Principles of Public Life, one of which was accountability: 'Holders of public office are accountable for their decisions and actions to the public and must submit themselves to whatever scrutiny is appropriate to their office.'[30] Even more significant was the constitutional reform programme implemented by the Blair government after 1997, which included such major accountability measures as the Human Rights Act 1998 and the Freedom of Information Act 2000. Other measures, big and small, have followed; and the cumulative effect has been to make governments, parties and politicians subject to many more external accountability checks on their actions than was the case previously.

What has this meant for ministerial accountability? This doctrine is the ark of the covenant as far as political accountability in Britain is concerned, the key element in the chain of delegation linking the people to those who govern them. Ministers have to account to the people's representatives for their actions, and officials have to account to ministers. However, as has often been pointed out, the constitutional simplicity of the doctrine disguises many practical difficulties and ambiguities. Accountability for what exactly? And with what precise consequences? This territory is well explored,[31] not least in relation to the shift from 'government' to 'governance' in the management of the modern state

---

[29] V. Bogdanor, *The New British Constitution* (Oxford: Hart Publishing, 2009), 289.

[30] Committee on Standards in Public Life, *Standards in Public Life: First Report of the Committee on Standards in Public Life* (Cm 2850, 1995), 14.

[31] A recent exploration is G. Drewry, 'The Executive: Towards Accountable Government and Effective Governance?' in J. Oliver and D. Oliver (eds.), *The Changing Constitution* (Oxford: Oxford University Press, 2015), 8th edn.

and what this complexity means for an essentially simple doctrine of political accountability. Nor is this an abstract question, as it goes live whenever there is political dispute about who is responsible for what. (A recent example is the spat between a government minister and the chair of the Environment Agency in early 2014 about responsibility for flood protection.)

What is much less explored is the way in which the accountability explosion of the last two decades has impacted upon ministerial account-ability. In some respects it has been strengthened, not least because of the greater energy of the select committees in holding ministers to continuous account and the greater information available to account-holders. However, in other and more significant ways, the doctrine has been chal-lenged. This is a reminder of the Janus-faced nature of ministerial account-ability itself. On one side, it is the indispensable instrument with which Parliament holds government to account. In that sense it belongs to the conventional armoury of Parliament. On the other side, it is the instrument with which government has kept Parliament (and others) at bay and blocked incursions into its territory. In this sense it belongs to the consti-tutional armoury of government.

This last point needs explanation. The compression of formal political accountability into the simple and narrow channel of ministerial account-ability made it politically visible but also enabled it to be employed to choke off other kinds of accountability. For example, it provided the justification for keeping the actions of officials away from the scrutiny of Parliament, for protecting the patronage power of ministers in making appointments and preventing Parliament having any kind of vetting role, and for shielding the prime minister from the kind of scrutiny by select committees that other ministers were exposed to. In all such cases the demand from Parliament could be met with the assertion that what was being proposed was incompatible with the axial constitutional principle of ministerial accountability. In this way a doctrine that was supposed to embody the accountability role of Parliament was used, for a long period, to contain and restrict that role.

It is against this background that the more recent developments in accountability should be seen. Ministerial accountability remains funda-mental, but it now sits within a much larger framework of political accountability. What this meant was nicely illustrated when freedom of information provisions (first in an access code, then in legislation) produced complaints by MPs that citizens now enjoyed better information rights than their own questions to ministers. Partly in response to such external developments, Parliament has grown more assertive in its own claims and has not allowed ministerial accountability to prevent it finding a role in key public appointments or encroaching on prerogative powers (as seen most vividly in the parliamentary vote that prevented military action in Syria in 2013). There is also pressure, including from the Public Accounts Committee, to open up the Civil Service to more parliamentary scrutiny.

Two paradoxes

This suggests that the accountability explosion is not yet exhausted. Indeed in a range of areas (from the scrutiny of the security services to the recall of MPs) the demand is for more and better accountability. Yet there is a paradox here. It might have been expected that the accountability growth of recent times, reflected in the range of power-checking bodies and measures that now exist, would have produced greater public confidence and trust in how government works. This was, after all, the reason usually given for their introduction. Yet not only has this not happened, but the reverse seems to have taken place. The period during which accountability has expanded has also been the period during which political trust has contracted. 'Is it possible', asks Flinders, 'that the growth in the "account-ability industry" (constitutional watchdogs, audit processes, ethical guardians, investigatory agencies, regulatory boards, freedom of information legislation, quasijudicial commissions, etc) has actually contributed to the erosion of public support for politicians, political processes and political institutions?'[32]

This is certainly possible. Perhaps what was previously hidden has been brought into public view, and people do not like what they see. Perhaps accountability has been reduced to finding someone to blame. Or perhaps an excess of the wrong kind of accountability crowds out the capacity for good government. Certainly there are frequent lamentations from public service professionals that this is so, that a preoccupation with process is at

---

[32] M. Flinders, 'Daring to be a Daniel: The Pathology of Politicized Accountability in a Monitory Democracy' (2011) 43 *Administration and Society* 595.

the expense of purpose. Hence the identification of the baleful effects of what has been described as an 'audit explosion';[33] and the plea for an 'intelligent accountability'.[34] This takes us wider than the discussion of political accountability here, but it does provide a reminder that the political demand for ever more accountability should not automatically be equated with the advance of good government. Accountability is a fundamental constituent of good government; but rather than simply demanding 'more' of it, it may be more useful to explore what kind of accountability is most appropriate.[35]

However, there is also a second paradox, more telling even than the first, which is associated with the recent expansion of accountability devices; and which is central to the whole issue of political accountability. This is that the multiplication of accountability has been accompanied by a sense that direct, visible and effective accountability has somehow been dissolved by diffusion. 'Never before in British history', observes Anthony King, 'have so many individuals and organisations been so comprehensively accountable to so many other individuals and organisations ... Where everyone is accountable to everyone else, it is always possible that no one is effectively accountable to anyone.'[36] In other words, despite all the developments in accountability, power is less directly 'come-at able' than it once was. This may seem a surprising claim, yet it becomes less surprising when set within the context of the changing character of government.

If accountability has become diffused, it is because government itself has been diffused. Power now sits in many different places – with the EU, with judges, with regulators and agencies, with corporations and markets – and governments have to explain their diminished role. Much of this is the product of a deliberate de-politicisation of decision-making. This makes it less surprising that there have been consequences for accountability. One response has been David Cameron's rejection of what he has described as 'bureaucratic accountability' and the embrace of individualised accountability in the form of a citizen army of 'armchair auditors'. However, another (and more pervasive) response has been a developing sense that

---

[33] M. Power, *The Audit Explosion* (London: Demos, 1994).
[34] O. O'Neill, *A Question of Trust* (Cambridge: Cambridge University Press, 2002).
[35] On this point, see T. Wright, 'What Kind of Accountability?' in Centre for Public Scrutiny, *The State of Accountability in 2013* (London: CFPS, 2013).
[36] A. King, *The British Constitution* (Oxford: Oxford University Press, 2007), 362.

power has escaped from democratic control. This may help to explain the political disengagement that has become a much-noticed trend across the advanced democracies. If politics can do less, then perhaps it can be attended to less.

It certainly helps to explain the paradox that the recent explosion of accountability in Britain has been accompanied by what can feel like a loss of direct political accountability. The challenge is to close this gap. It is a particular challenge for Parliament, if it really does want to sit at the apex of accountability. The task is to ensure that there is coherence in the accountability landscape; and that the multiplication of accountability mechanisms does result in more effective political accountability and not just in an unwieldy mess. It also means being serious about unaccountable private power, which (as the financial crash showed) seems to get a free ride while more accountabilities are being heaped upon the state. If governments are unable, or unwilling, to discipline all kinds of power in the public interest, then the reach of accountability is inevitably diminished.

The conclusion from all this is that accountability has indeed become the watchword of contemporary politics in Britain. This is reflected in the accountability explosion that has taken place, which has made itself felt politically on a wide range of fronts. The context in which this happened was a widespread recognition that executive power was insufficiently restrained and that an accountability deficit was the result. The remedy was therefore to put in place new accountability mechanisms of assorted kinds, or to strengthen existing ones. However the effect of doing this has been to produce new complaints; for example, that there is a loss of governing capacity, or that accountability is so diffused that direct political accountability is lost. An old accountability problem may have been solved, but (as is often the way) a new one has been created.

Further reading

N. Bamforth and P. Leyland (eds.), *Accountability in the Contemporary Constitution* (Oxford: Oxford University Press, 2013)

V. Bogdanor, *The New British Constitution* (Oxford: Hart Publishing, 2009)

T. Buck, R. Kirkham and B. Thompson, *The Ombudsman Enterprise and Administrative Justice*, Farnham: Ashgate, 2011)

M. Flinders, *The Politics of Accountability in the Modern State* (Aldershot: Ashgate, 2001)

J. Jowell and D. Oliver (eds.), *The Changing Constitution* (Oxford: Oxford University Press, 2015), 8th edn., particularly chapters 6 and 7

A. King, *The British Constitution* (Oxford: Oxford University Press, 2007)

P. Norton, *Parliament in British Politics* (Basingstoke: Palgrave Macmillan, 2013), 2nd edn.

T. Wright, *British Politics: A Very Short Introduction* (Oxford: Oxford University Press, 2013), 2nd edn.

6 Rights and democracy in UK public law

Aileen McHarg

Introduction

A central concern of contemporary constitutionalism is the protection and promotion of individual rights and freedoms. Drawing upon a natural law tradition which claims that people enjoy rights inherently, equally and inalienably by virtue of their humanity, rights are conceived as being prior to and foundational of, rather than derivative from, the constitutional and legal order. The archetypal constitutional form for the protection of rights is thus a bill or charter of fundamental rights, which acts as a set of guiding principles for, and – more importantly – judicially enforceable guarantees against, state action.

There is a long history of issuing declarations of traditional rights and freedoms in order to constrain tyrannous rulers – in the British constitutional tradition, for instance, Magna Carta (1215), the Petition of Right (1628), and the Bill of Rights/Claim of Right (1689). However, the notion of universal human rights as the foundation for constitutional government is a more recent phenomenon, first asserted during the American and French revolutions in the Declaration of Independence (1776) and the Declaration of the Rights of Man and the Citizen (1789), and in the writings of Jean Jacques Rousseau[1] and Thomas Paine.[2] The US Bill of Rights, adopted in 1791, is the first recognisably modern constitutional rights guarantee, in the sense of a legally binding and judicially enforceable document, hierarchically superior to other laws.[3] However, it was only in the twentieth century, and particularly after World War II, that rights came to occupy a central place in American constitutional law.[4] The post-war period also saw the proliferation of international and regional declarations of rights, and the widespread inclusion of judicially enforceable rights guarantees in

---

[1] *The Social Contract* (1762).   [2] *Rights of Man* (1791).
[3] *Marbury* v. *Madison* 5 US 137 (1803).
[4] M. Loughlin, *Foundations of Public Law* (Oxford: Oxford University Press, 2010), 358–59.

domestic constitutions. This rising 'rights consciousness' was both a reaction to the atrocities perpetrated by fascist dictatorships in the preceding decades, and an insurance against the post-war spread of totalitarian communism. Indeed, a clear connection was, and continues to be, drawn between democratic governance and respect for human rights. For example, the preamble to the European Convention on Human Rights ('ECHR' or 'the Convention') (1950) states that 'fundamental freedoms ... are best maintained on the one hand by an effective political democracy and on the other by a common understanding and observance of the Human Rights upon which they depend'.

Despite a strong tradition of respect for individual liberty, the UK has only belatedly joined the rights revolution. Although already bound in international law by various rights instruments – including, most significantly, the ECHR, which has its own judicial enforcement machinery – it was not until 1998 that it acquired a positive statement of justiciable rights as a matter of domestic law, when the Human Rights Act 1998 ('HRA') (and the devolution statutes)[5] partially incorporated the ECHR. For some, this was as a relatively minor change; simply a matter of providing better mechanisms for enforcing Convention rights, the important theoretical shifts having already been made in 1951 when the UK ratified the Convention and in 1966 when it accepted the right of individual petition to the European Court of Human Rights ('ECtHR') in Strasbourg.[6] In truth, though, the impact of the HRA on UK public law has been profound.

However, the HRA was, and remains, highly controversial. Paradoxically, much of the resistance to it is conducted in the name of democracy. There is a particularly strong strand of rights scepticism in British constitutional thinking, which sees fundamental rights and democracy as antagonistic, rather than mutually reinforcing, and regards political rather than judicial institutions as more appropriate and effective mechanisms for the elaboration and protection of individual rights.

The HRA was carefully crafted to respect the UK's democratic traditions, and is one variant of a so-called 'new commonwealth model' of constitutionalism which seeks to strike a more effective balance between

---

[5] Due to space constraints, this chapter does not deal with rights protection under the devolution statutes.

[6] See E. Wicks, *The Evolution of a Constitution: Eight Key Moments in British Constitutional History* (Oxford: Hart Publishing, 2006), 134. See also HM Government, *Rights Brought Home: the Human Rights Bill* (Cm 3782, 1997).

fundamental rights and democracy, and to harness *both* political and judicial institutions in the service of a new culture of rights protection.[7] It is, however, far from clear that it has done so successfully.

The aim of this chapter is thus to explore how the HRA has impacted upon UK public law. It examines, first, the UK's traditional approach to rights, and the case for and against enactment of the HRA. Second, it considers the impact of the Act on public law adjudication. Finally, it discusses the practical effects of the HRA, particularly its impact upon political support for the promotion of fundamental rights.

The UK's traditional approach to rights protection and the bill of rights debate

The UK's traditional approach to protecting the individual was a residual one. The focus was not upon rights, but upon liberty – understood as an undifferentiated mass, rather than an enumerated list[8] – and individual liberty was whatever was left over by the sum of legal restrictions on it. Fundamental or human rights were understood (if at all) merely as political claims;[9] *legal* rights were derivative not foundational, and were the product of political struggles enshrined in specific statutory or common law rules. Rights were therefore neither constitutive of, nor a constraint upon, political action. Instead, reliance was placed upon the force of public opinion acting through the sovereign Parliament, and on the vigilance of the judiciary in upholding the principle of legality,[10] to ensure that there was no excessive government interference with liberty. Whilst the best defence for the fundamental constitutional rule of parliamentary sovereignty undoubtedly lies in the principle of democracy,[11] which in turn entails a philosophical commitment to individual rights, the relationship between rights and legitimate state forms and behaviour was largely unexamined. The claim to parliamentary sovereignty was an institutional,

---

[7] See S. Gardbaum, *The New Commonwealth Model of Constitutionalism: Theory and Practice* (Cambridge: Cambridge University Press, 2013).

[8] D. Feldman, *Civil Liberties and Human Rights in England and Wales* (Oxford: Oxford University Press, 2002), 2nd edn., 70.

[9] J. A. G. Griffith, 'The Political Constitution' (1979) 42 *Modern Law Review* 1, 17.

[10] *Entick* v. *Carrington* (1765) 19 St Tr 1029, (1795) 95 ER 807.

[11] See *R. (Bancoult)* v. *Secretary of State for Foreign and Commonwealth Affairs (No. 2)* [2008] UKHL 61, [2009] 1 AC 453, [35], *per* Lord Hoffmann.

not a rights-based one, and the British public law tradition was deter-minedly positivistic.

This approach had three very important strengths. First, it embodied a presumption in favour of liberty. The burden of proof lay on those seeking to restrict freedom to show that encroachments were justifiable and legally authorised, without it first having to be established that a fundamental right was engaged. Secondly, there was no substantive hierarchy of rights. As Ewing puts it, 'one of the great virtues of the British constitution ... [was] its relative neutrality'.[12] It was for Parliament to decide which, how, and to what extent rights should be protected, which facilitated, broadly speaking, an expansive and responsive approach to the recognition and effective protection of rights.[13] Thirdly, it avoided any rigid public/private distinction, whereby the state was conceived *only as* a – and *as the only* – threat to liberty. Instead, state action could be regarded as a necessary precondition for the expansion of liberty, for example, through the crea-tion of social and economic rights, and as a bulwark against the abuse of private power, for instance by prohibiting discrimination in the provision of goods and services on grounds of race, sex and other characteristics. Certainly, it could not be argued that rights were necessarily better pro-tected *in practice* in countries with justiciable bills of rights than they were in the UK.

However, the traditional approach also had significant weaknesses. For one thing, the lack of legal constraints on parliamentary sovereignty meant that liberty – in particular that of unpopular minorities – was always vulnerable to erosion. Moreover, government dominance of the House of Commons, and the reduced power of the House of Lords after the Parliament Acts 1911–49, meant that Parliament's ability to control the executive was severely compromised – a situation famously described by Lord Hailsham as one of 'elective dictatorship'.[14] Writing in 1959, Sir Ivor Jennings acknowledged that, while

in normal times the free tradition is extremely strong in Great Britain ... [i]n wartime and other times of national hysteria, the dissident minority can expect

[12] K. D. Ewing, 'The Unbalanced Constitution' in T. Campbell, K. D. Ewing and A. Tomkins (eds.), *Sceptical Essays on Human Rights* (Oxford: Oxford University Press, 2001), 104.

[13] See K. D. Ewing, *Bonfire of the Liberties: New Labour, Human Rights and the Rule of Law* (Oxford: Oxford University Press, 2010), 267.

[14] Lord Hailsham, *The Dilemma of Democracy: Diagnosis and Prescription* (London: Collins, 1978).

no more mercy or toleration from the House of Commons than from the Government itself . . . In such exceptional times, the supremacy of Parliament is a very great danger, especially to minorities.[15]

A second weakness related to the role of the judiciary in policing the limits of interference with liberty. While judges could do little to resist an unambiguous parliamentary intention to override individual rights, they did nevertheless have an important part to play in defending liberty, through the process of statutory interpretation, via development of the common law, and through judicial review of administrative action. There were two problems here. One was a lack of judicial robustness in resisting encroachments upon rights.[16] Again, particularly in times of emergency, judges often proved to be 'more executive minded than the executive'.[17] The other was that, operating in the shadow of parliamentary sovereignty and with a formalistic understanding of the separation of powers, judges were not obliged to justify the assumptions they made about the nature, value and limits of rights.

Compared to countries with a tradition of constitutional adjudication, therefore, British constitutional law was thin gruel indeed. In particular, it had only a poorly developed sense of the state as a distinct legal entity which, by virtue of its governing functions, coercive power, and greater access to resources, ought to be subject to different rights and responsibilities to those of ordinary citizens. The classic illustration is *Malone* v. *Metropolitan Police Commissioner*,[18] which held that the government too could benefit from the principle that 'everything is permitted except what is expressly forbidden'. Accordingly, since its action did not interfere with any of the plaintiff's specific legal rights, the government was not acting unlawfully by authorising the tapping of his telephone, even though there was no express legal basis for doing so. In other words, by treating the government as legally equivalent to a citizen, the effectiveness of the presumption in favour of liberty as a protection for the individual against the state was significantly undermined. The lack of a clear and principled basis for judicial action to protect liberty also left judges open to accusations of political bias, in particular that they were more protective of

---

[15] Sir Ivor Jennings, *The Law and the Constitution* (London: University of London Press Ltd, 1959), 5th edn., 264–65.
[16] See, e.g., K. D. Ewing and C. A. Gearty, *The Struggle for Civil Liberties: Political Freedom and the Rule of Law in Britain, 1914–1945* (Oxford: Oxford University Press, 2000).
[17] *Liversidge* v. *Anderson* [1942] AC 206, 244, *per* Lord Atkin.   [18] [1979] Ch 344.

economic liberty than political liberty, and of the interests of the powerful over those of the powerless.[19]

This picture had changed somewhat by the time the HRA was enacted, with judges (at least in the English courts) already beginning to pay more explicit attention to fundamental rights, under the influence of both the ECHR and European Union law.[20] Nevertheless, the impact of fundamental rights was still relatively weak and limited in scope, and the choice of rights to be protected lacked a firm constitutional foundation.

From the late 1960s onwards there was an increasing loss of faith in the efficacy of the traditional approach to liberty and a growing campaign – dominated by lawyers and supported by a number of senior judges – to incorporate the ECHR into domestic law.[21] Influential factors included: the state's illiberal reaction to Northern Irish terrorism;[22] the use by the Thatcher governments of their strong parliamentary majority to roll back hard won social and economic rights and to curtail political liberties in the name of public order and national security;[23] and the impact of a stream of cases from Strasbourg finding the UK to be in violation of the Convention. By 2000, when the HRA came into force, violations had been found in sixty-four cases,[24] a significant figure bearing in mind that the ECHR had been ratified and the right to individual petition conceded only on the assumption that it would have no practical impact.[25] The key political development came in 1993 when, as part of its 'modernization' process, the Labour Party dropped its historic opposition to a bill of rights.[26] Following the 1997 election, it therefore fulfilled its manifesto commitment to incorporate the Convention by securing the enactment of the HRA.

[19] See in particular J. A. G. Griffith, *The Politics of the Judiciary* (London: Fontana Press, 1997), 5th edn.

[20] See, e.g., M. Hunt, *Using Human Rights Law in English Courts* (Oxford: Hart Publishing, 1997).

[21] See M. Zander, *A Bill of Rights?* (London: Sweet & Maxwell, 1996), 4th edn., ch. 1.

[22] See A. McColgan, 'Lessons from the Past? Northern Ireland, Terrorism Now and Then, and the Human Rights Act' in T. Campbell, K. D. Ewing and A. Tomkins (eds.), *The Legal Protection of Human Rights: Sceptical Essays* (Oxford: Oxford University Press, 2011).

[23] See K. D. Ewing and C. A. Gearty, *Freedom Under Thatcher: Civil Liberties in Modern Britain* (Oxford: Oxford University Press, 1990).

[24] A. W. Bradley and K. D. Ewing, *Constitutional and Administrative Law* (Harlow: Longman, 2011), 15th edn., 403.

[25] Wicks (n. 6), 119, 129–30.

[26] See K. D. Ewing, 'The Human Rights Act and Parliamentary Democracy' (1999) 62 *Modern Law Review* 79, 80–82.

However, the passage of the HRA could not be said to signify that the intellectual case for constitutional rights had been won. A strong objection to the constitutionalisation of rights remains, based on the lack of any objective or agreed foundation for making decisions about rights. The controversial questions which arise in relation to rights relate not merely to essentially factual questions or questions of judgment about whether particular decisions or policies breach particular rights, but more fundamentally about which rights are regarded as worthy of constitutional protection, about the meaning and scope of particular rights, about the priority to be given when rights conflict, and about how far rights may be restricted in order to secure public interest goals. For rights sceptics, these are intensely political questions, and they do not cease to be political merely by virtue of being made judicially enforceable.[27] While there is no bright line distinction between adjudication under a bill of rights and under ordinary statutory or common law rules, the effect of entrusting judges with the enforcement of fundamental rights is nevertheless substantially to increase their power to determine disputes about appropriate political values. Sceptics therefore ask why such matters should be entrusted to unelected (and socially unrepresentative) judges, rather than to democratically accountable politicians. Despite considerable efforts by constitutional scholars worldwide to provide a convincing answer to this question, it remains probably the single most contested issue in the whole of constitutional theory.

The force of the sceptics' argument has clearly influenced the design of the HRA. On the one hand, the Act seeks to strengthen the role of the judiciary in protecting fundamental rights against legislative and executive interference, by obliging the courts to interpret legislation, 'so far as it is possible to do so', in accordance with Convention rights,[28] and by making it unlawful for public authorities to act incompatibly with the Convention.[29] The Act thus confers democratic legitimacy on the courts' role in protecting rights, and structures the exercise of that role by requiring judges to have regard to Strasbourg jurisprudence in interpreting and applying Convention rights.[30]

---

[27] See, e.g., Griffith (n. 9); J. Waldron, 'A Rights-Based Critique of Constitutional Rights' (1993) 13 *Oxford Journal of Legal Studies* 118; J. Waldron, *Law and Disagreement* (Oxford: Clarendon Press, 1999); J. Waldron, *The Dignity of Legislation* (Cambridge: Cambridge University Press, 1999).

[28] HRA, s. 3.   [29] HRA, s. 4.   [30] HRA, s. 2.

On the other hand, the courts have no power to strike down primary legislation which cannot be interpreted compatibly with the Convention. At most, they may issue a declaration of incompatibility,[31] which does not affect the validity of the legislation. As a matter of domestic law, Parliament, not the judges, thus retains the 'last word' on what the law is, and may continue to legislate in breach of the Convention – although this is subject to the continued right of disappointed litigants to petition the ECtHR which may, if it agrees that the Convention has been breached, create an obligation in international law to remove the incompatibility. The Act also attempts to engage politicians in the process of reviewing legislation for compatibility with fundamental rights, via the requirement on ministers when proposing legislation to issue a statement about whether or not the Bill is Convention-compliant.[32] This process has been enhanced by the establishment of the Joint (parliamentary) Committee on Human Rights ('JCHR'), and by the creation of the Equality and Human Rights Commission, which has the general function of promoting respect for and protection of human rights.[33] Finally, the HRA is not legally entrenched. As an Act of Parliament, it may be repealed or amended in the same way as any other statute (although, as a constitutional statute, it may not be subject to implied repeal).[34]

It would also be implausible to argue that the HRA is politically entrenched. Unlike the devolution statutes enacted at the same time, it was not subject to any special authorisation process. On the contrary, it was introduced as a manifesto bill, with no prior public consultation, and it was passed in the face of Conservative Party opposition. This lack of clear popular endorsement of the HRA – coupled with the absence of *any* public or parliamentary debate over the earlier decisions to ratify the ECHR and to recognise the right of individual petition (decisions which helped to create the impression that incorporation was inevitable) – further contributes to a deep ambiguity about the constitutional significance of the HRA. There is an important sense in which the rights revolution occurred in the UK by stealth, and, as we shall see, this presents a risk of divergence in legal and political attitudes to the constitutional protection of rights.

---

[31] HRA, s. 4.   [32] HRA, s. 19.   [33] Equality Act 2006, s. 3(b).
[34] *Thoburn* v. *Sunderland City Council* [2002] EWHC 195 (Admin), [2003] QB 151.

Public law adjudication and the Human Rights Act

The substantive impact of the HRA is not limited to public law. Both via the duty to interpret statutes compatibly with the Convention, and because courts are included within the definition of 'public authority', it also affects private law, criminal law and especially criminal procedure. In the public law sphere, however, the effect of the Act has not merely been to increase the number of cases in which human rights arguments can be raised, but more importantly to alter the constitutional role of the courts *vis-à-vis* Parliament and the executive both in controlling the content of legislation and in reviewing the exercise of administrative power. In so doing, it has significantly raised the profile of public law as a branch of the law.

As in other countries which have adopted bills of rights, the key effect of the Act has been to usher in a new 'culture of justification' in relation to human rights.[35] Thus, when interpreting statutes, Convention rights are no longer merely something that the courts *may* take into account in cases of ambiguity in seeking the (presumed) intention of Parliament. Rather, the HRA alters the primary rule of interpretation, such that judges *must* give a Convention-compatible interpretation where possible, even if it is clearly *not* what Parliament intended. Similarly, as regards administrative decisions, pre-HRA, whether a decision interfered unduly with fundamental rights was viewed as a question going to its merits rather than its legality. It could therefore only be struck down if it was *Wednesbury* unreasonable or irrational,[36] albeit the courts had latterly accepted that the rationality of decisions affecting rights would be subject to a heightened test of 'anxious scrutiny'.[37] Now, however, it is a question of legality, and decisions must comply with the Convention (unless interference is clearly required by primary legislation).[38]

The key structuring device for the assessment of Convention-compatibility is the proportionality test.[39] This requires the court to ask a series of questions:

[35] E. Mureinik, 'A Bridge to Where? Introducing the Interim Bill of Rights' (1994) 10 *South African Journal on Human Rights* 31, 32. See also A. L. Young, 'Accountability, Human Rights Adjudication and the Human Rights Act 1998' in N. Bamforth and P. Leyland (eds.), *Accountability in the Contemporary Constitution* (Oxford: Oxford University Press, 2013).

[36] *Associated Provincial Picture Houses* v. *Wednesbury Corporation* [1948] 1 KB 223; *Council of Civil Service Unions* v. *Minister for the Civil Service* [1985] AC 374.

[37] *R* v. *Ministry of Defence ex parte Smith* [1996] QB 517.   [38] HRA, s. 6(2).

[39] *R. (Daly)* v. *Secretary of State for the Home Department* [2001] UKHL 26, [2001] 2 AC 532.

1. Is a Convention right engaged?
2. Is the interference with the right in pursuit of a legitimate aim?
3. Is the interference authorised by law?
4. Is the decision suitable and necessary in order to achieve the aim?
5. Does it strike a fair balance between the right and the legitimate aim?

While the proportionality test does not necessarily produce different outcomes, it clearly does involve a more searching standard of review than in non-HRA cases.[40] In particular, whereas public law adjudication traditionally focused on the process by which decisions had been reached, rather than their substance, it has been emphasised that the role of the courts under the HRA is not merely to ascertain whether the decision-maker properly applied its mind to the balance to be struck between rights and other policy objectives, but rather *to decide the question of proportionality for itself*.[41] This means that more careful reasoning is required *both* from the initial decision-maker in seeking to defend its decision *and* from the court in justifying its assessment of Convention compatibility, thereby producing stronger and more nuanced legal control of public decision-making.

As Kavanagh argues, however, '[t]he climate of constitutional justification in which the law now operates, also requires justification of the exercise of judicial power'.[42] The key issues here concern, first, the limits of permissible Convention-compliant interpretation under s. 3 of the HRA, and the boundary between ss. 3 and 4, and secondly, the extent to which courts should show deference to legislative or executive judgments about the meaning of rights and assessments of proportionality. Both questions involve the constitutional separation of powers between the judicial and political branches of government. As with proportionality, we again see a general trend towards a stronger role for the courts, but also a more nuanced appreciation of when it is appropriate for judges to intervene in public decision-making.[43]

---

[40] *Daly* (n. 39), [27], *per* Lord Steyn.
[41] *R. (Begum)* v. *Denbigh High School Governors* [2006] UKHL 15, [2007] AC 100; *Miss Behavin' Ltd* v. *Belfast City Council* [2007] UKHL 19, [2007] 1 WLR 1420; *Huang* v. *Secretary of State for the Home Department* [2007] UKHL 11, [2007] 2 AC 167.
[42] A. Kavanagh, *Constitutional Review under the UK Human Rights Act* (Cambridge: Cambridge University Press, 2009), 3.
[43] See generally Kavanagh (n. 42), chs. 2–5, 7–9.

Thus, in relation to statutory interpretation, the courts have adopted an expansive approach to the use of section 3, treating a declaration of incompatibility as 'a measure of last resort'.[44] This permits the adoption of linguistically strained interpretations, plus extensive reading in and reading down of statutory words, provided that the interpretation does not go against the grain of the legislation or disturb a fundamental feature.[45] In place of a simplistic incantation of the distinction between interpretation and amendment,[46] it is clear that the choice whether to adopt a Convention-compatible interpretation or issue a declaration of incompatibility is not merely a question of what is linguistically possible, but rather involves a contextually sensitive assessment of the limits of acceptable judicial law-making in the particular circumstances of each case.[47] In relation to deference, similarly, a blanket approach to questions of justiciability, which placed certain areas of decision-making (such as national security) beyond judicial control, has been replaced by a more contextually sensitive analysis of the courts' institutional competence and legitimacy to make particular judgments about whether rights have been violated.

The correct approaches to questions of proportionality, the section 3/ section 4 boundary, and – especially – deference are all controversial matters which have generated substantial debate amongst academics and judges. For instance, in the *Nicklinson* case, concerning whether the statutory ban on assisted suicide in England and Wales breached Article 8 ECHR, nine Supreme Court Justices split three ways on whether, and to what extent, it was appropriate for them to defer to the legislature on this issue.[48] As Lord Hoffman pointed out in *Prolife Alliance*, the HRA 'appears to give the courts a great deal of scope to decide the limits of their own decision-making power'.[49] Accordingly, as rights sceptics would have predicted based on experience in other jurisdictions with constitutional bills of rights, there is still plenty of opportunity for judges to intervene or not in defence of rights, according to their personal views of the merits of cases and/or the likely political consequences of doing so. Nevertheless, the

---

[44] *Ghaidan* v. *Godin-Mendoza* [2004] UKHL 30, [2004] 2 AC 557, [39], [50], *per* Lord Steyn.

[45] *Ghaidan* (n. 44).

[46] See, e.g., *Duport Steels Ltd* v. *Sirs* [1980] 1 WLR 142, 157, *per* Lord Diplock.

[47] See Kavanagh (n. 42), 406.

[48] *R. (Nicklinson)* v. *Ministry of Justice* [2014] UKSC 38, [2014] 3 WLR 200.

[49] *R. (Prolife Alliance)* v. *British Broadcasting Corporation* [2003] UKHL 23, [2004] 1 AC 185.

general trend is towards greater judicial assertiveness, and confidence in their own ability to make legitimate and appropriate decisions about the scope and limits of fundamental rights. Again, this is a familiar pattern in other jurisdictions.

This growing judicial confidence is underlined by two recent, and related, developments in public law adjudication. The first is a changing attitude to the relationship between UK courts and the ECtHR. In 2004, in *Ullah*, Lord Bingham held that the obligation in s. 2 of the HRA means that domestic courts 'should, in the absence of some special circumstances, follow any clear and constant jurisprudence of the Strasbourg court. The duty of national courts is to keep pace with the Strasbourg jurisprudence as it evolves over time: *no more, but certainly no less.*'[50] However, more recent cases have been willing to depart from the *Ullah* principle, both to decline to follow Strasbourg, particularly where the judges consider that it has failed properly to understand domestic law,[51] and to go further than Strasbourg jurisprudence requires. For example, in *Nicklinson*, the Supreme Court held unanimously that, although the balance to be struck between the rights of people who required assistance to exercise their right to die and protection of the interests of vulnerable persons was within the UK's margin of appreciation under Article 8 ECHR, UK courts were nevertheless entitled *as a matter of domestic law* to hold that the statutory ban on assisted suicide was in breach of Article 8 (although on the facts, only two Justices actually did so).

The second recent development is an insistence that domestic law, not Convention rights, should be the starting point for analysis of public law protections against the state.[52] This serves as a useful reminder that domestic law may sometimes provide better protection for rights than the ECHR.[53] More importantly, however, it reflects a growing judicial insistence that the *common law* itself recognises fundamental rights which it

---

[50] *R. (Ullah)* v. *Special Adjudicator* [2004] UKHL 26, [2004] 2 AC 323, [20] (emphasis added).

[51] See, e.g., *R.* v. *Horncastle* [2009] UKSC 14, [2010] 2 AC 373; *Manchester City Council* v. *Pinnock* [2010] UKSC 45, [2011] 2 AC 104; and see R. Masterman, 'The Mirror Crack'd' (2013) *UK Constitutional Law Blog* (available at http://ukconstitutionallaw.org/2013/02/13/roger-masterman-the-mirror-crackd/).

[52] See *R. (Osborn)* v. *Parole Board* [2013] UKSC 61, [2013] 3 WLR 1020; *Kennedy* v. *Charity Commission* [2014] UKSC 20, [2014] 2 WLR 808; *A* v. *British Broadcasting Corporation* [2014] UKSC 25, [2014] 2 WLR 1243.

[53] See, e.g., *Kennedy*, above n. 47.

will protect against legislative encroachment.[54] It is not yet clear whether the courts will uphold common law rights only via the principle of legality – i.e. as a strong interpretive presumption that Parliament does not intend to legislate contrary to fundamental rights[55] – or as fundamental constitutional principles which take precedence even over unambiguous statutory words.[56] However, it does seem clear that the HRA, alongside devolution and EU membership, is fuelling a more profound constitutional revolution, in which the courts are reconceiving themselves as guardians of the constitution,[57] and in which human rights are increasingly playing a foundational role, cut loose from any democratic anchor.

The impact of the Human Rights Act

A focus on public law doctrine tells one story about the effects of the HRA, but consideration of its practical impact tells a different and more complex one. The question here is whether the Act has succeeded in fostering a culture in which human rights are more effectively protected, yet which still allows space for democratic articulation of their scope and limitations.

As regards the judicial record, there are no comprehensive and up-to-date statistics on the incidence or outcome of human rights cases. Nevertheless, the evidence suggests that the impact of the HRA has not been substantial, in terms of there being relatively few cases in which a violation of the Convention has been found and has changed the outcome.[58] According to Shah and Poole, their review of the use of the HRA in the House of Lords suggested that while 'the Law Lords are

---

[54] See T. Poole, 'Back to the Future? Unearthing the Theory of Common Law Constitutionalism' (2003) 23 *Oxford Journal of Legal Studies* 435.

[55] *R* v. *Secretary of State for the Home Department ex parte Simms* [2000] 2 AC 115, 131, *per* Lord Hoffmann.

[56] See *Jackson* v. *Attorney General* [2005] UKHL 56, [2006] 1 AC 262, *per* Lord Hope, Lord Steyn and Lady Hale; *AXA General Insurance Ltd* v. *Lord Advocate* [2011] UKSC 46, [2012] 1 AC 868, *per* Lord Hope.

[57] See R. Masterman and J. E. K. Murkens, 'Skirting Supremacy and Subordination: the Constitutional Authority of the United Kingdom Supreme Court' [2013] *Public Law* 800.

[58] See P. Greenhill *et al*, *The Use of Human Rights Legislation in Scottish Courts* (Edinburgh: Scottish Executive, 2004); Department for Constitutional Affairs, *Review of the Implementation of the Human Rights Act* (London: Department for Constitutional Affairs, 2006); S. Shah and T. Poole, 'The Impact of the Human Rights Act on the House of Lords' [2009] *Public Law* 347.

interested in *ruling* on human rights claims, they are not so sympathetic to the substance of [such] claims'.[59] The impact of the Act is further reduced by various factors including the limited range of rights it protects (being largely limited to civil and political rather than economic and social rights), the narrow interpretation given to the meaning of public authority,[60] which restricts the scope of protection, and the adoption of a narrow standing test, which means that cases can only be brought by the 'victims' of alleged rights violations.[61]

Nevertheless, the Equality and Human Rights Commission's 2009 review concluded that the Act had had a generally positive impact on public services.[62] Moreover, the HRA has clearly provided a channel for the articulation of rights claims by people who are genuinely excluded from the political process, such as convicted prisoners, asylum seekers, mental patients, and foreign terror suspects, as well as in circumstances where the democratic process has been manifestly deficient, such as the impending challenge to the controversial Data Retention and Investigatory Powers Act 2014, which passed through all its parliamentary stages in just four days.

However, a balanced assessment of the impact of the HRA must acknowledge that it cannot always be justified as compensating for democratic weaknesses. Convention rights have been used by the powerful, as well as by the powerless, to reopen debates that they have lost politically.[63] They have been used as an agenda-forcing device in relation to issues, such as assisted suicide, which have hardly been politically ignored.[64] The Act has also led to the substitution of judges' opinion for that of the legislature on highly contentious questions of conflicting rights, such as the right of rape defendants to subject rape victims to humiliating cross-examination on their previous sexual history.[65] More generally, the judicial preference for rewriting statutes under section 3 rather than issuing declarations of incompatibility under section 4 has reduced the scope for democratic

---

[59] Shah and Poole (n. 58), 369.

[60] *YL* v. *Birmingham City Council* [2007] UKHL 27, [2008] 1 AC 95.   [61] HRA, s. 7.

[62] Equality and Human Rights Commission, *Human Rights Inquiry* (London: EHRC, 2009), ch. 3. See also Department for Constitutional Affairs (n. 58).

[63] See, e.g., *R. (Countryside Alliance)* v. *Attorney General* [2007] UKHL 52, [2008] 1 AC 719; *AXA General Insurance Ltd* v. *Lord Advocate* [2011] UKSC 46, [2012] 1 AC 868; *Salvesen* v. *Riddell* [2013] UKSC 22.

[64] In *Nicklinson* (n. 48), three judges declined to issue a declaration of incompatibility only on condition that Parliament reconsiders the law.

[65] *R.* v. *A* [2001] UKHL 25, [2002] 1 AC 45.

choice over fundamental rights questions. In all these circumstances, judicial protection of human rights may be said to have violated the principle of political equality by privileging certain voices above others.[66]

Another line of criticism is that the HRA has proved to be insufficiently robust – some would say futile[67] – in the face of illiberal legislation and executive action, particularly in the area of terrorism. Despite the landmark ruling in the *Belmarsh* case,[68] in which the House of Lords declared the detention without trial of foreign terror suspects to be incompatible with Articles 5 and 14 of the ECHR, the overall judicial record in terrorism cases has been highly deferential, and arguably even counterproductive.[69] For instance, in response to the ruling in *Secretary of State for the Home Department* v. *JJ*[70] that control orders (the system of house arrest put in place following *Belmarsh*) of up to sixteen hours per day were compatible with the Convention, the government actually *increased* the length of some control orders, which had been shorter.[71] Indeed, the weakness of the domestic response has meant that there has continued to be a steady stream of ECtHR rulings finding the UK to be guilty of serious Convention violations.

In fact, this type of criticism points to the major paradox of the HRA, which is that it has coincided with a continued parliamentary assault on liberty, particularly in the wake of the 9/11 and 7/7 terrorist attacks.[72] Of course, there are still also instances in which Parliament has restrained or reversed restrictions on liberty, and has created or extended rights. However, there is little to suggest that the HRA has succeeded in inculcating a new *political* culture of respect for rights. Admittedly, on all but one occasion the law has been changed in response to a declaration of incompatibility, Ministers have only rarely certified legislation as being incompatible with the Convention under section 19, and the JCHR has been praised for its work in scrutinising legislation for compliance with

---

[66] But cf. Kavanagh (n. 42), ch. 13.

[67] K. D. Ewing, 'The Futility of the Human Rights Act' [2004] *Public Law* 829; K. D. Ewing and J.-C. Tham, 'The Continuing Futility of the Human Rights Act' [2008] *Public Law* 668; Ewing (n. 13).

[68] *A* v. *Secretary of State for the Home Department* [2004] UKHL 56, [2005] 2 AC 68.

[69] See generally C. Turpin and A. Tomkins, *British Government and the Constitution* (Cambridge: Cambridge University Press, 2011), 7th edn., 771–89.

[70] [2007] UKHL 45, [2008] 1 AC 385.   [71] Ewing and Tham (n. 67), 691.

[72] See in particular Ewing (n. 13).

human rights standards.[73] But the approach of both government and the JCHR has been highly legalistic, seeking to identify and avoid potential judicial challenges.[74] There is only limited evidence of politicians taking ownership of the HRA, and using Convention-based arguments in parliamentary debates[75] or initiating legal challenges, still less of the development of a 'culture of controversy', 'characterised not by deference to judicial interpretations of the Convention rights but rather by a desire to seize control of the very power to interpret rights, and to decide on the prioritisation between rights'.[76]

The failure to develop a robust human rights culture is problematic for two reasons. First, since very few decisions are ever challenged in court, the political environment in which public decision-making takes place is far more important in determining the level of human rights protection in practice than the attitudes of judges. Secondly, and more importantly, the political reaction to the HRA in some quarters has not been one of mere indifference, but rather active hostility. Encouraged by hostile and misleading media reporting, ministers in both the Labour and Coalition governments have attacked not only specific judgments, particularly in asylum and terrorism cases, but the HRA as a whole.[77] The most serious flashpoint has been prisoner votes – the one issue on which a declaration of incompatibility[78] has (so far) been ignored, and on which there have now been three adverse rulings against the UK by Strasbourg,[79] creating significant tensions in the UK's relationship with the Council of Europe.[80]

In fact, so serious is the political disenchantment with the HRA that the Conservative Party is committed to abolition of the Act and its replacement

---

[73] See J. Hiebert, 'Governing Like Judges?' in Campbell *et al* (n. 22).

[74] Hiebert (n. 73), 64; F. Klug and H. Wildbore, 'Breaking New Ground: The Joint Committee on Human Rights and the Role of Parliament in Human Rights Compliance' [2007] *European Human Rights Law Review* 231, 243.

[75] See M. Hunt, H. Hooper and P. Yowell, *Parliament and Human Rights: Redressing the Democratic Deficit* (London: Arts and Humanities Research Council, 2012).

[76] D. Nicol, 'The Human Rights Act and the Politicians' (2004) 24 *Legal Studies* 451, 454.

[77] See Nicol (n. 76); C. Gearty, 'Beyond the Human Rights Act' in Campbell *et al* (n. 22).

[78] *Smith* v. *Scott* [2007] SC 345.

[79] *Hirst* v. *UK (No. 2)* (2006) 42 EHRR 41; *Greens & MT* v. *UK* [2010] ECHR 1826; *Firth* v. *UK* [2014] All ER (D) 57.

[80] See P. Leach and A. Donald, 'Hostility to the European Court and the Risks of Contagion' (2013) *UK Human Rights Blog* (available at http://ukhumanrightsblog.com/2013/11/21/ hostility-to-the-european-court-and-the-risks-of-contagion-philip-leach-and-alice-donald/).

with a UK Bill of Rights, which would '[c]larify the Convention rights, to reflect a proper balance between rights and responsibilities'.[81] Having so far been prevented by their Liberal Democrat coalition partners from doing more than establishing a Commission to investigate the issue, the party is now promising to go even further by renegotiating the UK's obligations under the Convention so that ECtHR rulings are merely advisory rather than binding. Moreover, if this is not agreed, it is explicitly contemplating withdrawal from the Convention altogether.[82] While hostility to the Convention is no doubt partly attributable to a more general Euroscepticism, experience elsewhere seems to support the conclusion that the situations in which judicial protection of human rights is most defensible are the ones in which it generates the greatest political backlash.[83]

Conclusion

It is currently unclear whether the HRA will survive. It may be that it is simply suffering prolonged teething problems and will eventually overcome its legitimacy crisis to become an accepted part of both the legal and the political constitutional cultures. After all, many of the jurisprudential and practical objections which are made to the HRA are equally applicable to bills of rights in other constitutional systems which nevertheless enjoy strong popular and political support. There are in any case formidable barriers to the adoption of a UK Bill of Rights[84] and to withdrawal from the Convention, not least the implications for EU membership and the need for consent by devolved legislatures. But even if the HRA is abolished, it is unlikely to mean an end to judicial protection of human rights, whether in the form of a statutory UK Bill of Rights or fundamental rights at common law. It seems, therefore, that the HRA, whether it survives or not, will have effected a lasting shift in the conceptual basis of UK public law, and a significant empowerment of the judiciary.

[81] Conservative Party, *Protecting Human Rights in the UK* (London: Conservative Party, 2014), 5 (available at https://s3.amazonaws.com/s3.documentcloud.org/documents/1308198/protecting-human-rights-in-the-uk.pdf).

[82] Conservative Party (n. 81), 8.

[83] See, e.g., J. Fudge, 'The Canadian Charter of Rights: Recognition, Redistribution, and the Imperialism of the Courts' in Campbell *et al* (n. 12), 337.

[84] See Commission on a Bill of Rights, *A UK Bill of Rights? The Choice Before Us* (London: Commission on a Bill of Rights, 2012).

However, far from striking an effective balance between human rights protection and respect for democracy, the Act has highlighted the tensions between them. The adoption of a bill of rights represents a loss of faith in the power of democracy to control and guide the exercise of state power in a way that respects and enhances individual rights. But the enduring truth is that questions about rights do not cease to be political when they are entrusted to courts. On the contrary, constitutional protection of human rights means that courts are reconstituted as sites of political struggle. However, since they do not use political methods – relying on reason and authority rather than pressure, persuasion and mobilisation – this may turn out to be a source of resentment, perceived as allowing individuals unfairly to bypass or second-guess the political process. While the problem of protection of minority interests is undeniably a real one for democracies, victories for rights in the political process are ultimately more secure than victories through the courts.

Further reading

T. Campbell, K. D. Ewing and A. Tomkins (eds.), *Sceptical Essays on Human Rights* (Oxford: Oxford University Press, 2001)

T. Campbell, K. D. Ewing and A. Tomkins (eds.), *The Legal Protection of Human Rights: Sceptical Essays* (Oxford: Oxford University Press, 2011)

K. D. Ewing and C. A. Gearty, *The Struggle for Civil Liberties: Political Freedom and the Rule of Law in Britain, 1914–1945* (Oxford: Oxford University Press, 2000)

S. Gardbaum, *The New Commonwealth Model of Constitutionalism: Theory and Practice* (Cambridge: Cambridge University Press, 2013)

J. A. G. Griffith, 'The Political Constitution' (1979) 42 *Modern Law Review* 1

A. Kavanagh, *Constitutional Review under the UK Human Rights Act* (Cambridge: Cambridge University Press, 2009)

A. Stone Sweet, *Governing with Judges: Constitutional Politics in Europe* (Oxford: Oxford University Press, 2000)

J. Waldron, 'A Rights-Based Critique of Constitutional Rights' (1993) 13 *Oxford Journal of Legal Studies* 118

A. Young, *Parliamentary Sovereignty and the Human Rights Act* (Oxford: Hart Publishing, 2008)

7 Public law values in the common law

Mark Aronson*

A chapter on public law values in the common law is contingent at a number of junctures. 'Public law *values*' implies a separate 'public law', which is a term with no standardised meaning. Indeed, the very existence of a public–private divide is hotly debated, let alone whether it makes sense to talk of a single distinction, or multiple distinctions drawn for different purposes.[1] If one puts those debates to one side and accepts that it is sometimes useful to assign laws into 'public' or 'private' domains, one finds further debates about the nature and utility of identifying specifically public law 'values', as opposed, say, to public law *rights* or *political* values.

There are as many different definitions of public law as there are reasons for asking why we might want to categorise a law as public or private, and whether categorisation serves any purpose beyond the academy's convenience of designing workable curriculums. Certainly, most practitioners (even those expert in judicial review matters) would characterise their practices in ways other than 'public' or 'private' law – they might, for example, describe themselves as child welfare or migration lawyers. Practitioners frequently draw another distinction, describing judicial review applications as 'public law' and claims for damages for exactly the same underlying administrative action as 'private law'.[2]

Any choice between the 'public' and 'private' labels is important to the actual litigants only if its procedural or substantive consequences matter, and this chapter will note several serious consequences whose rationales are hard to defend. Ideally, what should count are the reasons for asking

---

* The author would like to thank Mark Elliott, Carol Harlow, David Feldman, Jason Varuhas and Greg Weeks for their assistance.
[1] On this point, see further D. Feldman, 'The Distinctiveness of Public Law' (Chapter 1 in this volume).
[2] For example, the Public Law Project ran a conference in March 2014 titled 'Private Law for Public Law Practitioners: Reaching the Injustices Other Public Law Remedies Cannot Reach' (see www.publiclawproject.org.uk).

why one might want to distinguish between public and private law, or between the values of public and private law.

This chapter will leave out of account laws that Parliament enacts for the public benefit, but that apply only to private sector actors or behaviour, obvious examples being the greater parts of statutory criminal law, and market competition law. Indeed, this chapter will deal with statutory law only so far as its underlying values have spilled over into the common law's public realms. Statutes are in one sense always enacted to advance a current perception of the public interest. Also omitted will be any discussion of what remains of the common law of crime and related police powers, although these have been classified as 'public' (but not necessarily 'public law') since Blackstone's time.[3] The discussion which follows will instead be confined to so much of the general or common law as treats public sector actors as special – either by giving them privileges not accorded to subjects, or by imposing higher standards or more restrictions upon them than would apply to people normally.

One of the components of Dicey's definition of the rule of law required that government officials be governed by the same common law liability rules as apply to everyone else.[4] That was and must remain an aspiration,[5] but there is an intuitive appeal to the concept of a 'level playing field'. It requires the common law to explain and justify its occasional exceptionalism – those instances where it treats government either more or less favourably than its subjects. That prompts some large questions.

Dicey's equality ideal was only ever intended to apply to money claims, and not even to all of those. Judicial review has always been subject to different rules, both procedural and substantive. Indeed, claims that there exists a distinctive set of public law values are on safest ground when they remain focused on judicial review. The first section of this chapter will

---

[3] See W. Blackstone, *Commentaries on the Laws of England* (London, 1803), 14th edn. with notes and additions by E. Christian, which treated torts as 'private wrongs' and crimes as 'public wrongs' (vols. 3 and 4 respectively). The relationship between governors and governed was for Blackstone the law of 'public relations', and the relationship between subjects was the law of 'private relations': vol. 1, ch. 2. He dealt with both categories in vol. 1, titled *Of the Rights of Persons*, a title that implied that Blackstone had no separate category for 'public law': J. Allison, *A Continental Distinction in the Common Law: A Historical and Comparative Perspective on English Public Law* (Oxford: Clarendon Press, 1996), 7–8.

[4] A. V. Dicey, *An Introduction to the Study of the Law of the Constitution* (London: Macmillan, 1959), 10th edn., 193–94.

[5] *Graham Barclay Oysters Pty Ltd* v. *Ryan* (2002) 211 CLR 540, [12], *per* Gleeson C.J.

therefore address judicial review's values, and, in particular, the values underlying the doctrine of procedural exclusivity. Procedural exclusivity tried to reduce 'collateral challenges' to the legality of government action, the assumption being that government deserved special procedural protections in any challenge (direct or indirect) to the legality of its conduct. Procedural exclusivity has changed shape, and is currently best described as a strong judicial discretion against collateral challenge where judicial review would have been at least as suitable. As discussed in the second section, procedural exclusivity's preferential treatment of government is now showing early signs of affecting the so-called 'private law' of tort. The third section will examine the ever-lengthening lists of values that public lawyers are claiming for their subject. The overall claim is that government must always act for the public interest, but the further one moves from the context of judicial review, the more difficult it becomes to validate this claim either descriptively or normatively. Tort law, for example, generally aims to treat public authority liability on the same basis as the liability of actors in the private sector. The fourth section of the chapter will then ask whether there might have been historical reasons behind the claims to a moral distinctiveness for public law.

The values underlying procedural exclusivity

If one were to confine one's reading to English decisions about the common law of judicial review of administrative action, one could be forgiven for equating 'public law' with 'judicial review'. That, however, is an elision reserved mainly for use by English practitioners. Academics tend to see judicial review as only a sub-set of a broader topic called either public or administrative law. The distinction becomes important here, because it appears that the claims for the moral distinctiveness of 'public law' seem to be on safest ground when confined to judicial review. The story seems to begin with judicial review, and although it branches out into much broader territory, the pull of judicial review upon the legal imagination resembles the gravitational pull of a black hole, constantly pulling the 'values debate' back into a tighter realm.

Judicial review has almost always been defined in terms of its remedies. Judicial review's principal remedies (its 'core remedies') used to be the prerogative writs of mandamus, prohibition and certiorari. These core remedies were supplemented by the injunction and the declaratory order. Although the substance of a judicial review matter is about the legality of government action, if that issue arises in a damages claim (for example, in a tort action for trespass), the legality issue is often said to arise 'collaterally' (or by way of 'collateral challenge').

Prerogative writ procedure was always special. Discovery and oral evidence were extremely rare, and although the court could make exceptions, the deadlines for initiating applications were generally somewhere between three and six months. The procedure itself required at least two hearings, the first being an undefended application for an order that the government party respond to the claimant's allegations, the idea being that vexatious or hopeless cases should be filtered out without bothering the government.

Determined claimants could outflank these pro-government restrictions fairly easily, because they applied only to the prerogative writs, judicial review's core remedies. Discovery and oral evidence were available for applications for injunctions and declarations, and if commenced at common law (instead of Equity), the declaration had a six-year limitation period. Neither remedy had a 'leave' filter. Collateral challenges (such as tort actions for false imprisonment) were also free of the prerogative writ restrictions, and were subject to the standard limitation periods.

The procedure remains essentially the same for the core remedies, although procedural reforms gradually removed some of the archaic nomenclature. 'Permission to proceed' now stands in place of 'show cause', which in its turn had replaced 'rule *nisi*'. Mandatory, quashing and prohibitory orders now stand in place of orders in the nature of the old prerogative writs, which had in the 1930s replaced the writs themselves. None of these procedural reforms was of any great consequence until the decision of the House of Lords in *O'Reilly* v. *Mackman*.[6] Faced with a new set of seemingly inconsequential court rules, that case ushered in a doctrine of 'procedural exclusivity', designed to put an end to the old strategies for outflanking the pro-government restrictions applying to the core remedies.

Largely condemned by the academy but defended by the judiciary, the doctrine has since been significantly diluted, but its essence was that

---

[6] [1983] 2 AC 237.

'public law' challenges could not be raised by way of 'private' actions – they had to be brought by application for judicial review. That created obvious difficulties in deciding when a party's claim (or defence) should be characterised as raising solely or even primarily a 'public law' concern. Those difficulties were never satisfactorily resolved, partly because the normative underpinning of 'procedural exclusivity' was descriptively inadequate and confused.

In the days of the former prerogative writs, no-one had paid much attention to justifying the existence of a special set of restrictive rules governing challenges to the legality of official decisions. That was an era focused more on procedure and remedies than on rights, and it seemed to go without saying that such challenges should be brought without delay, and that they should be brought only by those whose rights or legal interests were directly affected by decisions relating wholly or mainly to their particular situation. It is true that the courts had long claimed an ill-defined discretion to decline to issue the prerogative writs. However, this usually manifested as a discretion akin to the equitable discretion to refuse relief to those who had perfectly adequate remedies at common law,[7] or for reasons personal to the applicants (for example, that they had 'unclean hands').

Starting in the 1960s, judicial review began expanding both its reach and its content. It became accessible to public interest litigants with no larger rights or interests at stake than those of the community at large.[8] Its scope expanded beyond decision-making under statutes, to decision-making under prerogative or non-statutory powers.[9] Its subjects expanded beyond public officials, to private bodies exercising public powers or functions.[10] And perhaps above all, its 'grounds' for challenging the legality of administrative action expanded exponentially. Public officials had increasingly to satisfy judge-made requirements for reasonableness, procedural fairness, rationality, and even, on occasion, substantive

---

[7] One of the preconditions for mandamus used to be that the applicant had no other equally convenient, beneficial and effectual remedy. See, e.g., *R.* v. *Vice-Chancellor of Cambridge University* (1765) 3 Burr 1647, 1649; *R.* v. *Commissioners of Inland Revenue; Re Nathan* (1884) 12 QBD 461, 473; *R.* v. *Thomas* [1892] 1 QB 426, 429–31.

[8] *R.* v. *Inland Revenue Commissioners ex parte National Federation of Self-Employed and Small Businesses Ltd* [1982] AC 617.

[9] *R.* v. *Criminal Injuries Compensation Board ex parte Lain* [1967] 2 QB 864; *Council of Civil Service Unions* v. *Minister for the Civil Service* [1985] AC 374.

[10] *R.* v. *Panel on Take-overs and Mergers ex parte Datafin plc* [1987] QB 815.

fairness.[11] A fierce debate arose as to how one might justify these expansionary tendencies,[12] but the debate's premise was an increasingly abstract commitment to a 'higher purpose' for judicial review.

Judicial review has always taken itself seriously, but until recently, its moral claims rarely got much higher than holding government to the limits of legal power. Relatively recently, however, it has broadened its moral claims, leading to talk of its 'normative turn'.[13] The expansion of the *grounds* of review certainly means that its brief is no longer confined to policing the boundaries to the powers of official decision-makers. 'Boundaries' imply that action within them is unexaminable, and that action beyond them can be struck down for that reason alone. Under the new dispensation, the courts now check for 'abuse of power'[14] and 'unfairness',[15] and claim to be enforcing 'good administration'[16] and the rule of law.[17] The so-called normative turn might also reflect the moral underpinnings of human rights litigation, although the moral considerations in that context tend to be embedded within the definitions of the rights under protection, whose infractions require strong justification.

With public interest suits now allowed, and with such higher purposes claimed for judicial review, it was inevitable that there be a weakening of the formerly solid focus on the rights and obligations of individuals and on the powers of official decision-makers. With judicial review's job no

[11] Various labels have attached to substantive fairness review; for example, 'unreasonableness', and protection of 'legitimate expectations'. The doctrines and justifications for these and similar bases for substantive review are discussed in all leading texts on administrative law.

[12] E.g. C. F. Forsyth (ed.), *Judicial Review and the Constitution* (Oxford: Hart Publishing, 2000).

[13] D. Dyzenhaus, 'The Politics of the Question of Constituent Power' in M. Loughlin and N. Walker (eds.), *The Paradox of Constitutionalism: Constitutent Power and Constitutional Form* (Oxford: Oxford University Press, 2008), 135; T. Poole, 'The Reformation of English Administrative Law' (2009) 68 *Cambridge Law Journal* 142, 167; W. Lucy, 'Private and Public Law: Some Banalities About a Platitude' in C. MacAmhlaigh, C. Michelon and N. Walker (eds.), *After Public Law* (Oxford: Oxford University Press, 2013), 56, 82.

[14] *R.* v. *Secretary of State for Education ex parte Begbie* [2000] 1 WLR 1115, 1129; *R.* v. *North and East Devon Health Authority ex parte Coughlan* [2001] QB 213, 242, 245; *R. (Lumba)* v. *Secretary of State for the Home Department* [2011] UKSC 12, [2012] 1 AC 245, [69].

[15] *Coughlan* (n. 14), 245, 250; *R. (Bancoult)* v. *Secretary of State for Foreign and Commonwealth Affairs (No. 2)* [2008] UKHL 61, [2009] 1 AC 453, [135]; *Lumba* (n. 14), [69].

[16] *R. (Nadarajah)* v. *Secretary of State for the Home Department* [2005] EWCA Civ 1363, [67]–[68]; *Lumba* (n. 14), [311].

[17] *R. (Cart)* v. *Upper Tribunal* [2011] UKSC 28, [2012] 1 AC 663.

longer restricted to the protection of individual rights and interests, it acquired a 'public interest' dimension, which in turn required stronger antidotes than the old safeguards against undue delay or those whose behaviour warranted discretionary refusal of relief. Public interests favouring judicial intervention have now occasionally to be counter-balanced by public interests against it. Procedural exclusivity is a mechanism for ensuring adherence to judicial review's tighter deadlines and thresholds for arguable claims, but it is also much more than that. It is also a vehicle for safeguarding not just the government party, but the wider public interest.

Lord Woolf, an enthusiastic proponent of procedural exclusivity, argued that because public bodies act for the public at large, the law subjected them to 'higher ethical standards'[18] than those set for private bodies.[19] Public bodies defend claims against them regardless of whether the issue arises by way of judicial review or an action for damages. However, his Lordship was obviously concerned about collateral challenges, where the public body (and therefore the public at large) might not have separate representation because it might not be a party.[20] By implication, it would then fall to the courts to look after the public interest, and he maintained that the best way of doing that would be to force inherently 'public law' matters to proceed by way of judicial review. One of the functions of procedural exclusivity, therefore, was to require a procedure which invested the court with a discretion to refuse relief to applicants whose claims were good in law but 'unmeritorious'. That discretion, he argued, had counterparts in Equity but not in common law actions.[21]

Procedural exclusivity has weakened over time. It nevertheless made a significant contribution to judicial review's shift from a primarily rule-bound body of law focused on protecting the rights of individuals, to a body of law subject to huge swathes of judicial discretion based upon shifting judicial assessments of where the greater public interest might lie. The court has a 'public interest' discretion to hear judicial review challenges brought by people who are no more affected by government action than the public at large.[22] Some of the grounds of challenge

---

[18] H. Woolf, 'Public Law–Private Law: Why the Divide? A Personal View' [1986] *Public Law* 220, 223.

[19] Woolf (n. 18), 57.   [20] Woolf (n. 18), 60–65.   [21] Woolf (n. 18), 61.

[22] *National Federation* (n. 8); *AXA General Insurance Ltd* v. *HM Advocate* [2011] UKSC 46, [2012] 1 AC 868, [60]–[63], [167]–[171]; *Walton* v. *Scottish Ministers* [2012] UKSC 44, [2013] PTSR 51, [91]–[92], [103].

are themselves variable from case to case by reference to public interest considerations; the most obvious examples are challenges for unreasonableness,[23] disproportionality,[24] and breach of legitimate expectations.[25] And even if a claimant eventually establishes that the government acted beyond its lawful powers, the court has the discretionary power to refuse a remedy, if it thinks that the inconvenience or harm to third parties or to the broader public would clearly outweigh the benefits of granting a judicial review order.[26]

Equitable remedies (such as the injunction) are discretionary, but the discretions are cast more narrowly than the judicial discretions that abound in judicial review doctrine. The common law's private rights are *shaped* by a variety of policy considerations, including those relating to the interests of third parties or the public more generally, but once those rights are established, their material elements are not amenable to variation between individual cases by reference to wider public interest concerns. In short, judge-made private law is conceived as the domain of rights and obligations defined by rules, not judicial discretion, and generally impervious to government pleas for special (usually favourable) treatment. Its remedies are also conceived as rights defined by rules, not judicial discretion. Public law is seen as the opposite, or at least as trending to the opposite, as regards all of those features.

This account of a distinctively public law is at its strongest when confined to the field of judicial review – confined, in other words, to claims for mandatory, prohibitory, and quashing orders. In essence, however, those orders merely nullify government action, stripping it of such adverse legal consequences as might otherwise have applied to the claimant. Judicial

---

[23] *R.* v. *Ministry of Defence ex parte Smith* [1996] QB 517 introduced the language of 'anxious scrutiny' for an assessment of the reasonableness of entrenchment upon fundamental rights or freedoms. Its justification and precise meaning might be debated, but not its premise that a threat to fundamental public interests might heighten the intensity of judicial scrutiny.

[24] Public interest considerations are in play when considering the government party's reason for infringing upon a protected interest, and when considering whether the particular infringement at issue was normatively justified: see *R. (Daly)* v. *Secretary of State for the Home Department* [2001] UKHL 26, [2001] 2 AC 532; *Huang* v. *Secretary of State for the Home Department* [2007] UKHL 11, [2007] 2 AC 167, [19] –[20]. There remains a debate as to whether this ground is available in the UK in cases beyond the remit of the Human Rights Act 1998, or whether it merely informs an assessment of reasonableness: H. Woolf, J. Jowell, A. Le Sueur, C. Donnelly and I. Hare, *De Smith's Judicial Review* (London: Sweet and Maxwell, 2013), 7th edn., para. 11–084.

[25] E.g. *Coughlan* (n. 14).   [26] *Walton* (n. 22).

review's orders are minimally intrusive of government action. They do not compensate claimants for flawed government decisions, nor replace them with outcomes the court would prefer. Whilst judicial review's special protections for government parties might strike one as out of keeping with a Diceyan-style aspiration to the level playing field, it is worth remembering that it is a litigation process, a judge-made set of administrative standards, and a trio of distinctive remedies, that *can* only apply to government.

The diffusion of procedural exclusivity

Procedural exclusivity stood little chance of surviving in its original form. Its presumption that collateral challenges were an abuse of process quickly fell apart; the doctrine remains, but largely in the form of a broad judicial discretion.[27] This is partly because it was propounded in a country with a strong (and continuing) tradition of rejecting the creation of a separate judicial system for suing the government, with its consequent need for bright-line distinctions between public and private matters.[28] But it is also because legislation and court rules allowed (and continue to allow) damages claims to be tacked on to claims for the judicial review remedies where that is thought appropriate.[29] The resulting confusion of underlying values is evident in *R (Lumba)* v. *Secretary of State for the Home Department*,[30] in which a claim for judicial review had been joined to a damages claim for false imprisonment.

Mr Lumba was a non-citizen whose prison sentence was about to end. The Home Secretary had him transferred into immigration detention pending deportation, where he remained for roughly four and a half years. The court held that his detention may have lasted too long, and that it had in any event been unlawful at the outset. The Home Secretary had abused her discretionary powers by applying a blanket policy which she had sought to conceal whilst feigning adherence to a published policy. The

---

[27] See the discussion in *Trim* v. *North Dorset District Council* [2010] EWCA Civ 1446, [2011] 1 WLR 1901.

[28] J. Allison, *A Continental Distinction in the Common Law: A Historical and Comparative Perspective on English Public Law* (Oxford: Clarendon Press, 1996).

[29] Senior Courts Act 1981, s. 31(4); Civil Procedure Rules, part 54, r. 3(2).

[30] Above n. 14.

majority refused to say that a detention that was unlawful in public law could be lawful in tort law. The claim in false imprisonment therefore succeeded. However, the court awarded only nominal damages, because the Home Secretary would have ordered Mr Lumba's immigration detention even if she had applied her public policy. Mr Lumba had therefore lost no chance of dodging immigration detention. In no other case to that point had a court awarded only nominal damages for an extended period of unlawful imprisonment. In essence, the discretionary characteristics of judicial review's remedies (and, in particular, of the declaratory order) were transferred to the question of damages in tort law.

Lumba may be contrasted with *Adamson* v. *Paddico (267) Ltd*,[31] in which the Supreme Court allowed two separate landowners in joined appeals to seek rectification of the public registration of their lands as town or village greens. The Act made provision for rectification, and it appeared likely that the courts would require landowners to pursue this procedure rather than judicial review. Judicial review has presumptively tight deadlines, and the question was whether rectification applications should be informed by the general approach in judicial review, whose deadlines are underpinned by a statute that articulates three rationales.[32] The first is to protect non-parties from 'substantial hardship', and the second is to protect the 'rights' of non-parties from 'substantial prejudice'. The third is to avoid anything that 'would be detrimental to good administration', which rather puzzled the court, because 'good administration' should (at least, in most cases), conform to the law. In any event, *Adamson* held that the general approach should be more 'private' than 'public' in rectification matters, because the property rights of landowners were at stake. Opponents of rectification would be allowed to lead evidence that the local authority itself, or non-parties, had taken steps in reasonable reliance upon the validity of the public register, but the landowner's rights would be the proper starting point.

Claims for a morally distinctive public law

Procedural exclusivity's end point is the preferential treatment of government parties. Public law textbooks and other secondary literature, however,

---

[31] [2014] UKSC 7, [2014] AC 1072.   [32] Senior Courts Act 1981, s. 31(6).

devote relatively little attention to this aspect of their subject. *Lumba* treated government preferentially, but the standard public law textbooks generally focus on ways in which government must conform to *higher* standards than those applicable to subjects. Government bodies are said to have 'an obligation to act only in the public interest',[33] and there is some basis for that claim. The law requires public officials to put aside purely personal considerations, the most obvious being political allegiance, religious creed, personal enrichment, and convenience; these must all be put to one side when exercising legal power conferred upon them for a public purpose.

A leading administrative law textbook[34] famously distinguishes between the common law's default positions for 'private persons', who can act selfishly, malevolently, spitefully, and for revenge, and 'public authorities', who can do none of those things. These are default positions that Parliament can override, but their starting point is that those invested with public power are to exercise it only for the public good, or (more commonly) in accordance with the constraints and public purposes discernible from the relevant empowering Act.

Altruism, however, is not the sole preserve of government; nor must government always be other-regarding. Trustees, agents, solicitors, doctors, teachers, employees, airline pilots – all must prioritise the interests of others over their own. And government itself is allowed in some of its activities to act as selfishly as anyone else. The same contract law applies to a government entity's contract to purchase office equipment as would apply were a private sector organisation to be the purchaser. Public authorities are allowed private interests.

Public law's secondary literature, however, tends to focus on those circumstances in which government is held to higher standards. The literature commonly claims the following values for its subject: legality[35] (as opposed to the principle of legality);[36] good

---

[33] *Aston Cantlow Parochial Church Council* v. *Wallbank* [2003] UKHL 37, [2004] 1 AC 546, [7], *per* Lord Nicholls.

[34] H. W. R. Wade and C. F. Forsyth, *Administrative Law* (Oxford: Oxford University Press, 2014), 11th edn., 296.

[35] The most obvious public law value, but also, and rather curiously, the least celebrated in the secondary literature. Judicial supervision of government to ensure that public authorities comply with the law is a necessary (but scarcely sufficient) component of the rule of law.

[36] The 'principle of legality' is a relatively new label for a long-established practice of interpreting statutes restrictively where they might otherwise conflict with the common

faith;[37] the rule of law;[38] fairness (usually procedural, but occasionally[39] substantive); impartiality;[40] consistency;[41] rationality; stability of practice (in the absence of strict law, or where it is unclear);[42] accessibility of judicial and non-judicial grievance procedures; accountability; transparency;[43] and, of course, human rights. Michael Taggart compiled two lists which added further values, namely, independence, legitimacy, equity, and equality.[44] Harlow and Rawlings have a much smaller list, namely, 'transparency, participation and accountability'.[45] They explain that their focus is on the values of good administration (or 'good governance'), rather than on the values that good administration might be promoting. Australia's Chief Justice offers a slightly longer list[46] of 'themes and values'.[47]

A good many of these 'public law values' have their origins in statutory reforms, such as those establishing ombudsmen, merits review tribunals, legal aid for public interest suits, access to government documents, and audit mechanisms. Their statutory origins have not stopped them from spilling over into the common law, with ever-greater demands upon government.

More generally, the most remarkable feature of public law value catalogues such as those listed above is their proximity to judicial review. These

---

law's fundamental rights, freedoms or privileges. This interpretive principle is not so much a value in itself, as a mechanism for protecting other values.

[37] R. S. French, 'Administrative Law in Australia: Themes and Values Revisited' in M. Groves (ed.), *Modern Administrative Law in Australia: Concepts and Context* (Melbourne: Cambridge University Press, 2014), 37.

[38] A heavily contested term, but requiring at its minimum that government be restrained by laws, legal principles, and institutions that work in combination to avoid arbitrary and unrestrained power.

[39] As where the courts will protect people from unreasonable departures from government's non-contractual promises upon which people have relied: e.g. *Coughlan* (n. 14).

[40] A requirement not just of judges, but also of an apolitical Civil Service.

[41] *Lumba* (n. 14), [26], [190], [302]; *R. (Reilly)* v. *Secretary of State for Work and Pensions* [2013] UKSC 68, [2014] AC 453, [58]–[65].

[42] *Lumba* (n. 14), [26].

[43] One of the rulings in *Lumba* (n. 14) concerned the Minister's adherence to a 'secret' policy.

[44] M. Taggart, 'The Province of Administrative Law Determined?' in M. Taggart (ed.), *The Province of Administrative Law* (Oxford: Hart Publishing, 1997), 3; M. Taggart, 'The Nature and Functions of the State' in P. Cane and M. Tushnet (eds.), *The Oxford Handbook of Legal Studies* (Oxford: Oxford University Press, 2003), 103.

[45] C. Harlow and R. Rawlings, *Law and Administration* (Cambridge: Cambridge University Press, 2009), 3rd edn., 46.

[46] Namely, lawfulness, good faith, rationality, impartiality, and fair procedure.

[47] French (n. 37), 37.

public law values are almost self-evident where the context is the administration of statutory schemes or the process of governing, but they are far less obvious where the context involves liability claims for conduct that can be undertaken by government and private parties alike.

The Human Rights Act 1998 ('HRA') might well turn out to be a game-changer here, because its doctrinal content is heavily value-laden. Of course, at a strict doctrinal level, its protected rights are indeed *rights*, not just 'values', and its protections against torture, slavery and forced labour, and the death penalty, are not defeasible. Nevertheless, something as important as the HRA must also be viewed in contexts beyond its strict doctrinal reach. It was always intended to effect a culture change within the broader public sector, and it may well be acknowledged to have that effect in judicial doctrine and practice.

Lord Hoffmann claimed in the *Belmarsh* case that the values informing the HRA were

not some special doctrine of European law ... The United Kingdom subscribed to the [European] Convention [on Human Rights] because it set out the rights which British subjects enjoyed under the common law.[48]

Historically dubious,[49] his Lordship's claim has now been embellished with a claim that HRA's principles are stated at an extremely high level of abstraction, with domestic law (both legislative and judge-made) and practices (such as legal aid arrangements) providing the finer details.[50] Accordingly, domestic law and practice exemplify values which are stated in, but not confined to, the HRA; they 'permeate' the entire legal system.[51]

One might well have considerable reservations about transposing the values underlying a rights-based regime (where the judges have the last word) into judicial review more generally, where the judges have no power to replace administrative decisions with their own preferred outcomes.

---

[48] *A* v. *Secretary of State for the Home Department* [2004] UKHL 56, [2005] 2 AC 68, [88].

[49] See T. Poole, 'Harnessing the Power of the Past? Lord Hoffmann and the *Belmarsh Detainees* Case' (2005) 32 *Journal of Law and Society* 534; J. Allison, 'History to Understand, and History to Reform, English Public Law' (2013) 72 *Cambridge Law Journal* 526.

[50] *Osborn* v. *Parole Board* [2013] UKSC 61, [2014] AC 1115, [54]–[63].

[51] *Osborn* (n. 50), [55], *per* Lord Reed. *Osborn* also emphasised the dialogue nature of the UK judiciary's conversations with Strasbourg. The court again referred to the dialogue model in *R. (Chester)* v. *Secretary of State for Justice* [2013] UKSC 63, [2014] AC 271 at [27], which also acknowledged that the views of the Grand Chamber of the European Court of Human Rights will almost always prevail over those of a domestic court.

Nevertheless, the increasingly normative 'style' (if not exactly a 'normative turn')[52] of appellate judgments in judicial review is now clear. The HRA might not change judicial review's basic architecture where (as in most cases) protected rights are not at stake,[53] but it may well have narrowed the gap between proportionality review under the HRA and domestic law's *Wednesbury* reasonableness review.[54] More broadly, Lord Walker recently protested against any sharp distinction between HRA and so-called 'conventional judicial review grounds'. Where fundamental rights were at stake, his Lordship thought that the old 'conventions' had to go, with the HRA's principles being 'woven into the fabric of public law'.[55]

Putting judicial review to one side entirely, and turning to private rights of action, one would expect negligence law to weigh more heavily on public authorities than the private sector if it were *generally* true that government must observe higher standards. That, however, has not generally been the case. The common law of negligence has tried on several occasions to impose duties of care upon government where none would be imposed upon private actors, but these attempts have for the most part backfired, with the creation of liability exemptions for defendants *because* they are government authorities. Cases such as *Dorset Yacht*[56] (imposing liability for losses consequent upon failing to prevent a prison escape) and *Anns* v. *Merton*[57] (proposing public authority liability for such failures to protect the public as are founded in *ultra vires* decisions) are no longer representative. Police, for example, owe no general duty of care to potential victims of crime.[58] Although that is in line with the general proposition that negligence law rarely requires any defendant (public or private) to protect a claimant from harm inflicted by a third person, the principal

---

[52] See above, n. 13.

[53] For the contending views, see T. Poole, 'The Reformation of English Administrative Law' (2009) 68 *Cambridge Law Journal* 142; J. Varuhas, 'The Reformation of English Administrative Law? "Rights", Rhetoric and Reality' (2013) 72 *Cambridge Law Journal* 369.

[54] In some situations, 'it is not possible to see any daylight between the two tests': *Doherty* v. *Birmingham City Council* [2008] UKHL 57, [2009] 1 AC 367, [135], *per* Lord Mance, quoting an extra-judicial speech of Lord Hoffmann.

[55] *Doherty* (n. 54), [109].   [56] *Dorset Yacht Co Ltd* v. *Home Office* [1970] AC 1004.

[57] *Anns* v. *Merton London Borough Council* [1978] AC 728.

[58] See *Hill* v. *Chief Constable of West Yorkshire* [1989] AC 53; *Brooks* v. *Metropolitan Police Commissioner* [2005] UKHL 24, [2005] 1 WLR 1495; *Smith* v. *Chief Constable of Sussex Police* [2008] UKHL 50, [2009] 1 AC 225, [97]–[100]; *Smith* v. *Ministry of Defence* [2013] UKSC 41, [2014] AC 52, [167]–[170].

reasons that the cases actually offer for denying the existence of a duty of care are the fear of dampening police initiative and the inherent dangers in courts second-guessing policing priorities.

In England, tort law's exemplary damages are theoretically reserved largely for government defendants,[59] although the courts in Australia,[60] New Zealand[61] and Canada[62] have declined to accept that common law restriction. In all four countries, however, an award of exemplary damages is exceptional, and if *Lumba* is any portent, then they may become even more rare.[63] 'Misfeasance in public office' is the only tort aimed solely at government, and it is the only tort whose material elements require government to conform to higher standards, but not to *all* of judicial review's higher standards. To be liable, a public officer must have acted in bad faith. More specifically, he or she must have known that their actions were illegal or have been recklessly indifferent about that possibility. In addition, they must have intended to harm the claimant, or have foreseen harm, or have been recklessly indifferent to the risk of harm.[64] Misfeasance is still very much in the developmental stages,[65] but its strict mental elements mean, in effect, that it is a tort to redress 'conscious maladministration',[66] or 'the absence of an honest attempt to perform the functions of the office'.[67]

---

[59] Aside from specific statutory provision for exemplary damages, they may be awarded in England in only two situations. They are available where public officials have behaved oppressively, arbitrarily, or unconstitutionally. They are also available against public or private defendants who have cynically calculated that their profits will exceed a 'normal' compensatory award, but restitution principles may make that category redundant. See *Rookes* v. *Barnard* [1964] AC 1129; *Broome* v. *Cassell and Co Ltd* [1972] AC 1027.

[60] *Uren* v. *John Fairfax and Sons Pty Ltd* (1966) 117 CLR 118.

[61] *Taylor* v. *Beere* [1982] 1 NZLR 81, 89–91; *Couch* v. *Attorney General (NZ) (No. 2)* [2010] 3 NZLR 149.

[62] *Vorvis* v. *Insurance Corporation of British Columbia* [1989] 1 SCR 1085, 1107–08; *Whiten* v. *Pilot Insurance Co* [2002] 1 SCR 595, 613, 635.

[63] The Full Federal Court J. in *Fernando* v. *Commonwealth* (2014) 315ALR547 applied *Lumba* to award compensatory damages of only $1 (and no exemplary damages) to a man kept unlawfully in immigration detention for almost four years. Had the authorities been aware of the legal defect in the detention order, they would clearly have made another (and valid) detention order.

[64] *Three Rivers District Council* v. *Bank of England (No. 3)* [2001] UKHL 16, [2003] 2 AC 1.

[65] M. Aronson, 'Misfeasance in Public Office: a Very Peculiar Tort' (2011) 35 *Melbourne University Law Review* 1.

[66] *Pyrenees Shire Council* v. *Day* (1998) 192 CLR 330, [124], *per* Gummow J.

[67] *Northern Territory* v. *Mengel* (1995) 185 CLR 307, 357, *per* Brennan J.

The strategic case for moral distinctiveness

If altruism is not the sole preserve of public actors, and if other 'public' values (such as legality, fair process, rationality, and accountability) exist also in 'private' areas (such as the laws of insurance, banking, consumer protection, and voluntary associations),[68] then one might question the motives behind claims for public law's 'moral distinctiveness'.

When Prime Minister Thatcher's government commenced its attempts to reduce both the size and the functions of government, it turned to the market, privatising government-owned businesses, outsourcing the delivery of government services to the public, and generally downsizing the public sector. Government, however, did not always wholly vacate the areas it sold or outsourced; indeed, government controls and red tape seem in some areas to have multiplied,[69] and non-state regulation has also flourished.[70] Regulations, complex licensing arrangements, and regulatory contracts commonly replaced government ownership or employment as the conduits through which to pursue government policy objectives.

The swing to the market was rapid and dramatic. It had been fiercely debated not just politically and socially, but also in legal circles, where public lawyers were initially opposed to it for the most part.[71] The public lawyers proposed various forms of resistance. These included expanding the reach of judicial review to 'public functions' performed by private bodies,[72] and colonising some parts of the wholly private sector (for example, large corporations, sporting associations, private ombudsmen, and employees' unions) with public law's values (but not necessarily its

---

[68] See D. Oliver, *Common Values and the Public-Private Divide* (London: Butterworths, 1999), ch. 3, which contends for five 'key values' that are common to both private and public law. These are dignity, autonomy, respect, status (in the communitarian sense of social recognition of group memberships), and security.

[69] C. Harlow, 'The "Hidden Paw" of the State and the Publicisation of Private Law' in D. Dyzenhaus, M. Hunt and G. Huscroft (eds.), *A Simple Common Lawyer: Essays in Honour of Michael Taggart* (Oxford: Hart Publishing, 2009).

[70] C. Scott, 'Regulatory Governance and the Challenge of Constitutionalism', in D. Oliver, T. Prosser and R. Rawlings (eds.) *The Regulatory State: Constitutional Implications* (Oxford: Oxford University Press, 2010).

[71] Their opposition was the dominant concern of most of the essays in M. Taggart (ed.), *The Province of Administrative Law* (Oxford: Hart Publishing, 1997).

[72] *R v. Panel on Take-overs and Mergers ex parte Datafin plc* [1987] 1 QB 815.

procedures and remedies).[73] Perhaps predictably, the expansion of judicial review had very little practical effect.[74] The attempted public law takeover of private law was even less successful. Debates continue to this day as to the wisdom of privatisation and outsourcing, although any resistance from public lawyers is generally more nuanced.[75] The important point for present purposes, however, is that each strategy had a common normative underpinning. Each supposed a distinctively 'public' set of values belonging to a distinctively 'public' law. Michael Taggart suggested that the search for public law values started (perhaps he should have added 'and became *strategically* relevant') as part of the resistance to the market model in general and its theoretical underpinning of 'public choice theory'.[76]

Opposition to privatisation and outsourcing took many points, but perhaps the most pertinent for present purposes was what amounted to a claim of moral superiority. *Even if* (or, at least, even when) government services were usually less efficient, effective, and economical than their private sector counterparts, the general claim was that the state and its emanations had to conform to higher standards. 'Different and higher ethical standards' were said to apply to public bodies, unless they were engaged in purely commercial operations.[77] The argument for the state's moral superiority usually comes down to two propositions.

The first proposition is that the state is unlike any person or organisation in the private sector, because it cannot be bound by the profit motive. The state and its emanations does and often should put other (and often intangible) values ahead of a purely monetary calculus of profit and loss. Civil society has many charities and not-for-profits, but government-owned businesses have sometimes continued to operate in financial circumstances that would equate to insolvent trading if they were in the private sector. An 'implicit government guarantee' is a political reality, even where the relevant Act makes express provision to the contrary. And it is not just government *businesses* that transcend the profit motive – it is government itself, the argument being that there is a radical distinction

---

[73] H. Woolf, 'Public Law–Private Law: Why the Divide? A Personal View' [1986] *Public Law* 220, 224–25, 238; H. Woolf, '*Droit Public* – English Style' [1995] *Public Law* 57, 63–64.

[74] M Aronson, 'A Public Lawyer's Responses to Privatisation and Outsourcing' in M. Taggart (ed.), *The Province of Administrative Law* (Oxford: Hart Publishing, 1997).

[75] See A. Davies, 'Public Law and Privatisation' (Chapter 9 in this volume).

[76] M. Taggart, 'The Nature and Functions of the State' in P. Cane and M. Tushnet (eds.), *The Oxford Handbook of Legal Studies* (Oxford: Oxford University Press, 2003), 103.

[77] Woolf, 'Why the Divide?' (n. 73), 223.

between the state and its citizens (conceived broadly) on the one hand, and *any* company (even a charity) and its members, customers or clients on the other. Israel's Supreme Court accepted this line of reasoning in a ruling that invalidated a law designed to establish a privately run prison. Writing for the majority, Beinisch P. reasoned that even if such a prison were to be superior in its management and prisoner amenities, the concessionaire's profit motive would impermissibly degrade prisoner's human rights and dignity. It came down in the end to an 'essentially ... ethical test',[78] with the result that the state could not alienate such an inherently sovereign function.

This leads to the second proposition, which is that government is duty-bound to serve its public; it has no choice in the matter, whereas charities and other altruistic bodies are volunteers. That is a rather dubious proposition as a matter of law, because most of the state's general duties to the public at large are aspirational or 'target duties'[79] at best, rising no higher than Austin's 'laws of imperfect obligation'.[80] The political sense of duty is often (and understandably) stronger than its legal counterpart.

Conclusions

Most people accept that it would be wrong to equate public law with judicial review, but the lists of public law values currently attributed to English common law are on safest ground when confined to judicial review. Judicial review has no room for the Diceyan ideal of according government neither privileges nor disadvantages relative to the governed.

Judicial review does require government administration to act with procedural fairness, and in a manner that is reasonable, rational, altruistic, honest, and impartial. Similar obligations are sometimes imposed upon those in the private sector, but only government actors are said to be acting for the general public. In this sense, therefore, judicial review holds public officers to higher standards than those applying generally to those within the private sector. One might question how often those are higher *ethical*

---

[78] *Academic Center of Law and Business, Human Rights Division* v. *Minister of Finance* (2009) HCJ 2605/05, [53].

[79] *R (Ahmad)* v. *Newham London Borough Council* [2009] UKHL 14, [2009] P.T.S.R. 632, [13], *per* Lady Hale.

[80] J. Austin, *The Province of Jurisprudence Determined* (London: J. Murray, 1832) 23–25.

standards, as opposed to procedural standards, but they can certainly be very demanding, and their content appears to be expanding.

However, judicial review's requirements for public officials to conform to higher standards are kept in some sort of check by the doctrine of procedural exclusivity, which offers government parties substantial procedural protections, together with overarching (and very large) judicial discretions to protect the public interest.

The picture is less clear beyond the realm of judicial review. Government parties have been largely successful in resisting attempts to impose 'higher' common law duties upon them in the contexts of 'private' causes of action. They might, however, be gaining some traction in seeking to gain preferential treatment in those contexts. Conceived in terms of legal rights and obligations, 'private law' is antagonistic to the idea of an overarching judicial discretion to disapply the strict law for reasons of public interest. Public interest concerns, however, appear to be having some impact in tort law, and possibly beyond that, and the danger is that the Diceyan ideal will be gradually eroded, as government claims to protect the general public interest will be given more credence.

Further reading

J. Allison, *A Continental Distinction in the Common Law: a Historical and Comparative Perspective on English Public Law* (Oxford: Clarendon Press, 1996)

D. Oliver, *Common Values and the Public-Private Divide* (London: Butterworths, 1999)

T. Poole, 'The Reformation of English Administrative Law' (2009) 68 *Cambridge Law Journal* 142

M. Taggart (ed.), *The Province of Administrative Law* (Oxford: Hart Publishing, 1997)

J. Varuhas, 'The Reformation of English Administrative Law? "Rights", Rhetoric and Reality' (2013) 72 *Cambridge Law Journal* 369

H. Woolf, '*Droit Public* – English Style' [1995] *Public Law* 57

H. Woolf, 'Public Law – Private Law: Why the Divide? A Personal View' [1986] *Public Law* 220

Paul Craig*

This chapter is concerned with the extent to which we should think in terms of 'public law' or 'public laws'. The topic is perennial. There has been debate in relation to most legal subjects as to whether we should, for example, think in terms of a law of contract or laws of contract, the latter capturing the idea that there are different bodies of law applicable to contracts of sale, employment, shipping, hire purchase and the like. So too in the realm of public law, there has been discourse as to whether the subject should be perceived in functional terms, in recognition of subject matter as diverse as social welfare and planning, tax and asylum, and utilities regulation and mental health.

While the topic is thus perennial there is also a sense in which it is under-theorized, in relation to public law at least. This is because the very idea of 'functional' public law that betokens an element of diversity conceals a range of more distinct ideas that must be disaggregated for the sake of analytical and normative clarity. This chapter is not predicated on the assumption that there is only 'one' correct meaning to be ascribed to the idea of functional public law. It is, however, premised on the assumption that clarity as to the sense in which the term is being used is a condition precedent to reasoned analysis concerning its utility. The ensuing discussion therefore explores four different ways in which the idea of a functional public law is used.

Different subject matter rules

We can begin with the most straightforward and least controversial, and thus clear the ground. There is no doubt that we have a regime of

* I am grateful for helpful comments from Mark Aronson and David Feldman.

public laws insofar as this captures the idea that there are distinct subject matter rules in relation to mental health, education, housing, tax, asylum and the plethora of other areas that the state regulates. To make clear, the term 'subject matter rules' connotes here the detailed statutory provisions that regulate the relevant area, whether this concerns access to welfare benefits, tax liability, the conditions for seeking asylum, or the circumstances in which a person can be sectioned pursuant to mental health legislation. This is self-evidently so, and no one would deny it.

A somewhat less self-evident, but nonetheless simple point flows from this, which is that many public law cases turn almost entirely on points of statutory interpretation about whether or not the relevant statutory conditions have been met. They will often not be read by general public lawyers, because they raise no particular point about the application of public law doctrine, but they will be regarded as important by specialists in the field of planning, asylum or social welfare, insofar as the legal decision is significant for the application of that statutory schema. There is, as will be seen below, a duality in the meaning of the much-used phrase 'context is everything'. When it is used here it simply captures the legal reality that the case has turned on the meaning of a term that is specific to the particular subject matter area.

It should be recognized that this holds true for many if not all legal subjects. Public law is not special in this respect. Thus there will be many contract cases that turn either on the specific terms of contract, with no special relevance for contract doctrine, and/or which entail interpretation of statutory provisions relating to that type of contract, which will be of interest to specialists in, for example, shipping or hire-purchase, but will not make their way into general contract texts.

Different constitutional rules

There is also no doubt that we have a regime of public laws within the United Kingdom insofar as this connotes different constitutional rules for different parts of the UK. This has been especially marked since the passage of devolution legislation in the 1990s. The Conservative Government under Margaret Thatcher had no interest in devolution of power, but the return of a Labour Government in 1997 brought the possibility of devolution onto the Westminster political agenda.[1]

Devolution may be structured such that the central government devolves all its power to the other body, with the exception of reserved matters. It can, alternatively, be structured such that specified matters are devolved, with the corollary that all other matters remain within the power of the central authority. There is no *a priori* reason why the first method should be more favourable to the devolved body,[2] since so much turns on the list of reserved matters. This is readily apparent from comparison of the Government of Ireland Act 1920, and the Scotland Act 1998. The list of reserved powers contained in the former Act is relatively short, and relatively general. The list contained in the Scotland Act 1998 is very long, contains general reservations and a plethora of much more detailed specific reservations.

The Scottish Parliament is given the power to make primary laws, which are known as Acts of the Scottish Parliament. This does not formally affect the power of the Westminster Parliament to make laws for Scotland,[3] but it has been established by what is known as the Sewel Convention that the Westminster Parliament will not legislate on devolved matters without the consent of the Scottish Parliament. The legislative power of the Scottish Parliament is nonetheless limited in a number of ways: it cannot legislate, *inter alia*, in relation to reserved matters, or in a way that is incompatible with rights in the European Convention on Human Rights ('ECHR'), or with EU law.[4] The list of reserved matters is very extensive,[5] and the Scottish Parliament is prohibited from legislating if the legislation relates to such matters.

Whether this is so can be tested through the courts, although it has not been easy for claimants to convince the courts that Scottish legislation should be invalidated on this ground.[6] The courts have striven to interpret

---

[1] N. Walker, 'Constitutional Reform in a Cold Climate: Reflections on the White Paper & Referendum on Scotland's Parliament', in A. Tomkins (ed.), *Devolution and the British Constitution* (London: Key Haven, 1998).

[2] Constitution Unit, *Scotland's Parliament, Fundamentals for New Scotland Act* (London: Constitution Unit, 1996).

[3] Scotland Act 1998, s. 28(7).   [4] Scotland Act 1998, s. 29(2).

[5] Scotland Act 1998, Sch. 5.

[6] A. Poole, 'Recent Legislative Competence Challenges' [2011] SLT 127; C. Himsworth, 'Nothing Special about that? *Martin v HM Advocate* in the Supreme Court' (2010) 14 *Edinburgh Law Review* 487.

the reservations so as allow the contested Scottish legislation to be regarded as valid,[7] although there have been instances where legislation has been caught by the reservations.[8]

The Supreme Court in *AXA*[9] made it clear that while Scottish legislation, emanating from a non-sovereign body, was subject to the supervisory jurisdiction of the UK courts, it was nonetheless made by a body with plenary authority over its assigned area, subject to the limits in the Scotland Act 1998. The consequence was the legislation did not have to be made for a specific purpose, or with regard to particular considerations, and accountability lay primarily to the electorate rather than the courts. A further consequence was that common law tools of judicial review, such as irrationality, developed for review of administrative bodies, were constitutionally inappropriate when reviewing Scottish legislation, although the Supreme Court reserved the right to review on grounds other than those in s. 29 in exceptional instances where the challenged legislation abrogated fundamental rights or the rule of law.

The initial devolution settlement in relation to Wales was markedly different. The Government of Wales Act 1998 only provided for executive devolution, in the sense that the National Assembly for Wales assumed responsibilities hitherto exercised by the Secretary of State for Wales. In 2002 those exercising executive powers on behalf of the National Assembly adopted the title 'Welsh Assembly Government', and appointed a Commission under the chairmanship of Lord Richard to review the operation of devolution in Wales. The Richard Report recommended that the Assembly should be able to make primary legislation for Wales.[10] This was the catalyst for the White Paper on *Better Governance for Wales*,[11] which laid the foundations for the Government of Wales Act 2006, which

---

[7] *Martin v. HM Advocate* [2010] UKSC 10, 2010 SLT 412; *Imperial Tobacco Ltd, Petitioner* [2010] CSOH 134, 2010 SLT 1203.

[8] *Henderson v. HM Advocate* [2010] HCJAC 107, 2011 SLT 488. See also *Whaley v. Lord Watson of Invergowrie* 2000 SLT 475.

[9] *AXA General Insurance Ltd v. HM Advocate* [2011] UKSC 46, [2012] 1 AC 868.

[10] Commission on the Powers and Electoral Arrangements for the National Assembly for Wales, *Report of the Richard Commission* (2004) (available at http://webarchive.nationalarchives. gov.uk/20100410160947/http://www.richardcommission.gov.uk/content/template.asp? ID=/content/finalreport/index-e.asp); R. Rawlings, *Say Not the Struggle Naught Availeth: The Richard Commission and after* (Centre for Welsh Legal Affairs, University of Wales, 2004); T. Jones and J. Williams, 'The Legislative Future of Wales' (2005) 68 *Modern Law Review* 642.

[11] Cm 6582, 2005; R. Rawlings, 'Hastening Slowly: The Next Phase of Welsh Devolution' [2005] *Public Law* 824.

now provides the framework for Welsh devolution. Wales now has legislative power, although by way of contrast to the Scotland Act 1998, the Government of Wales Act 2006 defines the scope of the Assembly's legislative powers by listing the subjects in relation to which the Assembly can make law, rather than only listing those areas outside its legislative competence.

The relationship between Scotland, Wales and Westminster is ordered through a Memorandum of Understanding, and accompanying Concordats.[12] The Memorandum of Understanding is not legally binding, but it is of central importance for relations between the bodies to whom power has been devolved and Westminster.[13] The Memorandum of Understanding provides for communication and consultation between the different administrations, co-operation on areas of mutual interest, and exchange of information. A Joint Ministerial Committee was established to consider non-devolved matters that impinge on devolved responsibilities, and vice-versa, the respective treatment of devolved matters in different parts of the UK, and disputes between the administrations. The Joint Ministerial Committee meets in plenary session, with more frequent meetings for issues dealing with sectoral areas such as Health, the Knowledge Economy and the EU. The Memorandum of Understanding is supplemented by individual Concordats between the Scottish Government and UK government departments,[14] and between the National Assembly for Wales and such departments.

Differential application of public law doctrine

The issue of whether public law doctrine is applied differentially is more complex. It is certainly true that Scotland has distinctive public law

---

[12] R. Cornes, 'Intergovernmental Relations in a Devolved United Kingdom: Making Devolution Work' in R. Hazell (ed.), *Constitutional Futures, A History of the Next Ten Years* (Oxford University Press, 1999); R. Rawlings, 'Concordats of the Constitution' (2000) 116 *Law Quarterly Review* 257.

[13] Memorandum of Understanding and Supplementary Agreements between the United Kingdom Government, Scottish Ministers, the Cabinet of the National Assembly for Wales and the Northern Ireland Executive Committee (Cm 5240, 2001); Memorandum of Understanding and Supplementary Agreements between the United Kingdom Government, the Scottish Ministers, the Welsh Ministers and the Northern Ireland Committee Executive (2010).

[14] A list of such concordats is available at www.scotland.gov.uk/About/concordats.

doctrine, but over and beyond this the extent to which it does and should vary with context, and in that sense embodies a regime of public laws, warrants careful examination.

Application of doctrine: functionalism and reductionism

We can begin with the most obvious, but least interesting, sense in which doctrine is functional, which is that the precepts of judicial review will necessarily have to be applied to a particular statutory context. Thus if the courts decide that all errors of law are reviewable, they will then have to decide whether there has been such an error, given the wording of the relevant statute; if the courts establish criteria for mistake of fact, they will then determine whether such an error has occurred in the contested proceedings; and if the courts accord a meaning to improper purposes, they will then determine whether the public authority was guilty of a transgression. In doing so context may well be everything, but only in the reductionist sense that any legal norm must be applied to a particular set of circumstances, and this is as true of rules of contract, tort and restitution as it is of judicial review.

Differential application of doctrine: institutional expertise

There are instances of differential application of judicial doctrine, where the determinative functional criterion is expertise. This can be exemplified by developments concerning judicial review for error of law, where greater latitude has been accorded to tribunals in part because of their expertise.

The courts have acknowledged issues of relative institutional expertise,[15] and there are prominent instances where they have been respectful of tribunal findings because of the latter's expertise.[16] This came to the fore in Cart[17] and Eba,[18] where the Supreme Court's rationale for limiting judicial review of the Upper Tribunal under the Tribunals, Courts and Enforcement Act 2007 Act was based in part on its expertise, such that the reviewing

---

[15] R (CENTRO) v. Secretary of State for Transport [2007] EWHC 2729 (Admin).

[16] R (Wiles) v. Social Security Commissioners [2010] EWCA Civ 258.

[17] R (Cart) v. Upper Tribunal [2011] UKSC 28, [2012] 1 AC 663.

[18] Eba v. Advocate General for Scotland [2011] UKSC 2, [2011] PTSR 337. See also, R. (Khalil) v. Truro County Court [2011] EWHC 3335 (Admin); PR (Sri Lanka) v. Secretary of State for the Home Department [2011] EWCA Civ 988, [2012] 1 WLR 73.

court should be slow to interfere with its decisions, the result being that the test for review of error of law is now more limited than the general test established by *Page*.[19]

The Supreme Court in *Cart* held that judicial review was an artefact of the common law, the object being to ensure that insofar as possible, decisions were taken in accordance with the law, and in particular the governing statute in the particular area. The Supreme Court also acknowledged that neither tribunals nor courts were infallible and any judge might be wrong in law, with the consequence that there should always be the possibility that a second judge, with more experience or expertise than the judge who initially heard the case, could check for errors. If a decision of the Upper Tribunal to refuse permission to appeal to itself was never amenable to judicial review, there would, said the Supreme Court, be a real risk of the Upper Tribunal becoming the final arbiter of the law, even when it was wrong in law, so that errors of law of real significance could be perpetuated. There had therefore to be some possibility of judicial review. The Supreme Court was nonetheless mindful of the status of the new tribunal regime. This was reflected in the 'restrained' test adopted as to when the ordinary courts would review the Upper Tribunal: it was for the claimant to show that the proposed appeal raised some important point of principle or practice, or there was some other compelling reason for the appellate court to hear the appeal.

Judicial restraint in the application of review for error of law as it pertains to tribunals was evident once again in *Jones*.[20] The case concerned a claim before the Criminal Injuries Compensation Authority for compensation under the Criminal Injuries Compensation Scheme 2001. The operative legal issue was whether the claim was attributable to a 'crime of violence'. The Supreme Court held that where the interpretation and application of a specialized statutory scheme had been entrusted by Parliament to the new tribunal system, it was for the Upper Tribunal to develop structured guidance on terms that were central to the scheme, so as to reduce the risk of inconsistent results by different panels at the First-tier level. The development of such a consistent approach to the term 'crime of violence' was a task primarily for the tribunals, not the appellate courts. A pragmatic approach should therefore be taken to the divide between law

---

[19] *R.* v. *Hull University Visitor ex parte Page* [1993] AC 682.
[20] *R. (Jones)* v. *First-tier Tribunal (Social Entitlement Chamber)* [2013] UKSC 19, [2013] 2 AC 48.

and fact, so that the expertise of tribunals at the First-tier and that of the Upper Tribunal could be used to best effect. The consequence was that an appeal court should not venture too readily into this area by classifying as issues of law those that were best left for determination by the specialist appellate tribunals.[21]

Differential application of doctrine: importance of the right/interest

Differential application of judicial doctrine may also turn on assessment of the nature of the interest infringed. This is most readily apparent in the divide between proportionality and rationality as tests for review of discretion depending on whether the claimant can assert a Convention right. It is, however, also evident within these broad categories, as exemplified by the differing intensity with which proportionality review is applied even in rights-based cases.

This is exemplified by the *Countryside Alliance* case,[22] in which it was alleged that the Hunting Act 2004, which prohibited the hunting of wild mammals with dogs, infringed Convention rights. The House of Lords concluded that Article 1 of the First Protocol was engaged, since the 2004 Act limited the use that an owner could make of his land. It nonetheless held that the restriction was proportionate and in reaching this conclusion accorded the legislature a wide margin of discretionary judgment on a controversial matter of social policy. Lord Bingham was duly mindful of the dangers of subverting the democratic process if 'on a question of moral and political judgment, opponents of the Act achieve through the courts what they could not achieve in Parliament'.[23] In similar vein Baroness Hale made clear that the concept of what might be necessary in a democratic society had to take into account the comparative importance of the right infringed in the scale of rights protected, such that what might be a proportionate interference with a less important right might be a disproportionate interference with a more important right.[24]

---

[21] *Jones* (n. 20), [16], [32], [41], [47], [48]. See also, *Moyna* v. *Secretary of State for Work and Pensions* [2003] UKHL 44, [2003] 1 WLR 1929, [20]-[28]; *Lawson* v. *Serco* [2006] UKHL 3, [2006] I.C.R. 250, [34]; Sir Robert Carnwath, 'Tribunal Justice – A New Start' [2009] *Public Law* 48.

[22] *R (Countryside Alliance)* v. *Attorney General* [2007] UKHL 52, [2008] 1 AC 719. See also *Bank Mellat* v. *HM Treasury* [2013] UKSC 39, [2014] AC 700, [21], [74], [75].

[23] *Countryside Alliance* (n. 22), [45].   [24] *Countryside Alliance* (n. 22), [124].

The same point is evident albeit in a different way from *Animal Defenders*.[25] The case concerned free speech, but in deciding that a blanket ban on political advertising was compatible with Convention rights, Lord Bingham nonetheless held that the weight to be accorded to Parliament's judgment depended on the circumstances and the subject matter. He gave it significant weight in the instant case because: it was reasonable to expect that democratically elected politicians would be sensitive to measures necessary to safeguard the integrity of our democracy; Parliament had recognized that the prohibition of political advertising on television might infringe Article 10 ECHR, but nonetheless decided to proceed with the legislation and Parliament's judgment on this issue should not be lightly overridden; and legislation had to lay down general rules, which meant that a line must be drawn, and it was for Parliament to decide where.

The differing intensity of proportionality review will be affected not only by assessment of the importance of the right, but also by the determination as to how much respect/deference/weight should be given to the views of the primary decision-maker. Thus in *Roth* Laws LJ articulated four principles that would guide the courts:[26] greater deference would be paid to an Act of Parliament than to a decision of the executive or subordinate measure; there was more scope for deference where the Convention required a balance to be struck, much less so where the right was stated in unqualified terms, although even in the latter instance there could be room for differences of view as to how the requirements of a Convention right could be met; greater deference was due to the democratic powers where the subject-matter was peculiarly within their constitutional responsibility, such as defence of the realm, and less when it was more within the constitutional responsibility of the courts, which were concerned with maintenance of the rule of law; and greater or lesser deference would be due according to whether the subject-matter was more readily within the actual or potential expertise of the democratic powers or the courts.

The courts also take account of the importance of the interest infringed in cases outside the Human Rights Act 1998, in deciding that the

[25] *R. (Animal Defenders International)* v. *Secretary of State for Culture, Media and Sport* [2008] UKHL 15, [2008] 1 AC 1312, [33].

[26] *R. (International Transport Roth GmbH)* v. *Secretary of State for the Home Department* [2002] EWCA Civ 158, [2003] QB 728, [83]–[87].

particular interest infringed warrants anxious scrutiny.[27] This standard of review has been held applicable in asylum cases, irrespective of whether a Convention right is engaged on the facts of the case. The leading case of *WM* concerned two failed asylum applications, subsequent to which the applicants presented new material to the Secretary of State that were said to constitute 'fresh claims'.[28] The Secretary of State refused to accept the new evidence, and the applicants sought judicial review. Buxton LJ, giving judgment for the Court of Appeal, held that although the decision remained that of the Secretary of State, a decision would be irrational if it was not taken on the basis of anxious scrutiny of the material to ensure that the applicant had not been incorrectly exposed to persecution. In determining whether the evidence amounted to a fresh claim, the Secretary of State had to decide whether there was a realistic prospect that an adjudicator would think that the applicant would be exposed to a real risk of persecution on return. The task for the court was to determine whether the Secretary of State had asked himself that question, rather than substituting his own views as to whether the claim was a good one or should succeed. The court also had to determine whether the Secretary of State had satisfied the requirement for anxious scrutiny, but it was not for the court to take the decision itself rather than reviewing how the Secretary of State had taken his decision.

Buxton LJ made clear that 'since asylum is in issue the consideration of all the decision-makers, the Secretary of State, the adjudicator and the court, must be informed by the anxious scrutiny of the material that is axiomatic in decisions that if made incorrectly may lead to the applicant's exposure to persecution'.[29] This was reinforced throughout the judgment. Thus Buxton LJ emphasized that the Secretary of State must satisfy the requirements of anxious scrutiny.[30] So too must the court when exercising judicial review, and this took effect through more searching rationality review in order to determine whether the Secretary of State had asked himself the correct question, and whether the Secretary of State exercised anxious scrutiny in relation to evaluation of the facts and the legal conclusions to be drawn from them.[31]

---

[27] P. Craig, 'Judicial Review and Anxious Scrutiny: Foundations, Evolution and Application' [2015] *Public Law* 59.

[28] *WM (Democratic Republic of Congo)* v. *Secretary of State for the Home Department* [2006] EWCA Civ 1495, [2007] Imm AR 337.

[29] *WM* (n. 28), [7].   [30] *WM* (n. 28), [11].   [31] *WM* (n. 28), [10]–[11].

Differential application of doctrine: systemic functional differentiation

There is undoubtedly evidence for the differential application of public law doctrine in the two preceding senses, whereby the courts modify the application of such doctrine in the light of institutional expertise and in accord with the importance of the right or interest at stake in the particular case. It is, however, more difficult to discern what might be termed systemic functional differentiation, whereby all or many aspects of public law doctrine are applied differentially because of the nature of the subject matter or area concerned. This is not to say that it might not occur, but simply that it is not easily discernible.

There may moreover be good reasons to explain why it does not occur. Most obvious is the fact that the variables that affect the way in which doctrine is applied may well cut across each other, and pull in different directions, within a particular area. Thus the public body may have considerable institutional expertise over the subject matter, which might in accord with the preceding case law cause the courts to give it more leeway when construing issues of law. The same public body may, however, also exercise power in an area where important rights are at stake, which would incline the courts to more intense review when the claim is that such rights have been infringed.

Differential application of doctrine: functional considerations and doctrinal categories

The idea of a regime of public laws as opposed to public law is also manifest in a rather different way from that considered thus far. It finds expression in dissatisfaction with doctrinal categories, coupled with the desire to reach behind them in order to reveal the real considerations that influence courts when reaching their decisions. This mode of thinking is in certain respects akin to that considered in the preceding discussion, in the sense that institutional expertise and the importance of the right/interest affected are central to the application of certain doctrinal precepts. What distinguishes the mode of thought addressed here from that considered above is a matter of degree, but an important one nonetheless.

This is manifest in two related ways. There is a desire for greater particularization of the factors that impact on the application of doctrine.

This may then be coupled with scepticism as to the need for the doctrinal categories, the suggestion being that we dispense with them and simply rely on the functional considerations to give us the answer in any particular case. Viewed in this way this approach might be regarded as the ultimate vision of a regime of public laws, where everything turns on each occasion on the way in which the wide range of functional considerations plays out.

This approach is interesting, and the reality is that there has always been an ebb and flow between the desire to construct a doctrinal structure and the desire to emphasize the more particular issues that affect the application of the doctrinal structure in a particular case. Academic fashion changes over time, and this is manifest in altered preferences in this regard. Having said that, it should also be recognized that the desire to deconstruct the doctrinal categories and concentrate instead on the functional considerations that are felt to be the 'real deal' is subject to three limits or constraints: conceptual, pragmatic, and logical.

The conceptual constraint is that you simply pull the doctrinal house down and it is then replaced by another. So, the drive for dispensing with established doctrine and focusing instead on the functional considerations that explain its application leads to a new set of doctrinal or quasi-doctrinal categories formed from the aggregation of particular functional considerations that are felt to warrant a particular result in terms of judicial review. The 'set' of functional considerations are abstracted and generalized to form what is in effect a new doctrinal category. This demands, however, articulation of a range of contestable issues concerning the nature of the subject matter area to which the functionally calibrated criteria are applicable and the more precise delineation of those criteria.

The pragmatic constraint is judicial acceptance. The approach is driven by the belief that what we as academics perceive to be the functional considerations driving judicial decisions can straightforwardly translate into a method of resolving cases that judges are comfortable with. Thus the fact that we might particularize in great detail the functional considerations that we see as underpinning case law does not mean that courts or barristers would feel content with resolving cases in this manner, shorn of the doctrinal categories that frame the inquiry. There is, moreover, the issue of the judicial capacity to take account, within the confines of the adversarial system, of a very broad range of functional considerations, more especially given the limits on evidence considered by the court and the time constraints on adjudication.

The logical constraint bears on the relationship between the functional considerations and the doctrine that frames it. It is logically possible, subject to the conceptual and pragmatic constraints, to take account of a broader range of functional considerations when applying doctrine. It is not logically possible to dispense with the doctrinal categories in their entirety, unless something analogous replaces them. The reason is as follows. The functional considerations are designed to tell you how much leeway or not as the case may be should be accorded to the primary decision-maker. The answer crudely put may be a lot, none or some. This does not, however, tell you anything about the base from which this estimation is being conducted. Thus to accord the primary decision-maker considerable leeway where the base line is otherwise a test of correctness or substitution of judgment, is quite different from granting such leeway where the base line from which the assessment is made is reasonableness or proportionality. It might be argued that this issue will in some way form part of the matrix of functional considerations. Leaving aside the difficulty of divining what precisely this means, this would simply be importing through the back door in a less clear manner the doctrinal category that had hitherto framed the analysis.

Distinctive public law theory

The preceding discussion would be incomplete if it did not address the argument that there is a distinct 'functionalist' public law theory. This embodies a view as to the very nature of public law, which also has implications for the way in which it is applied in particular contexts. The nomenclature of 'functionalist' public law theory was coined by Martin Loughlin, who used it in contrast to what he termed 'normativist' theories, whether of a liberal or conservative persuasion.[32]

For Loughlin, normativist theories are said to be grounded in ideas about the separation of powers, the rule of law and the need to subject government to law, with the emphasis on adjudicative and control functions,

---

[32] M. Loughlin, *Public Law and Political Theory* (Oxford: Clarendon Press, 1992); M. Loughlin, 'The Functionalist Style in Public Law' (2005) 55 *University of Toronto Law Journal* 361.

coupled with an idea of the autonomy of law. Law is said to precede legislation, and rights to precede the state, the latter being conceived of in largely negative terms.[33]

Loughlin contrasts such theories with those of a functional nature, which embrace more sociological conceptions of law.[34] Law is said to be viewed as part of the apparatus of government, with the focus on an active role for the state and law's regulatory and facilitative functions. Legislation is said to be the highest embodiment of law, freedom is perceived in positive not merely negative terms, and the relationship between citizen and state is conceived in more organic and less atomistic terms. On this view, public law should be used for the purpose of promoting human improvement, a healthy body politic and social solidarity. Government is the subject of duties, and public law is concerned with their substantive realization. Public law must on this view be interpreted purposively, in the sense of with regard to its function. Rights are regarded as claims 'that are recognized and enforced only insofar as their recognition promotes the common good'.[35]

Martin Loughlin has shed valuable light on the constituent elements of what he terms the functional approach to public law, and on its philosophical foundations. The dichotomy between normativist and functionalist theory is nonetheless doubly problematic. It aggregates theories under the label 'normativist' that are very different in many respects. It disaggregates those theories from others that are regarded as 'functional' when the reality is that all theories of public law are irreducibly both normative and functional, and that is so irrespective of whether they are grounded on conservative, liberal or more collectivist/socialist foundations.

Consider first the normativist perspective. The approaches to public law that Loughlin identifies are explicitly predicated on certain political theories. That is self-evidently so in relation to what he terms conservative and liberal normativism. It is, however, equally true in relation to what he terms functionalism, since, as Loughlin readily acknowledges, many, albeit not all,[36] of the principal proponents had a socialist or left of centre

---

[33] Loughlin, *Public Law and Political Theory* (n. 32), 60–61.
[34] Loughlin, *Public Law and Political Theory* (n. 32), 60–61; Loughlin, 'Functionalist Style' (n. 32), 363–64.
[35] Loughlin, 'Functionalist Style' (n. 32), 363.
[36] J. N. Figgis, *Churches in the Modern State* (London: Longman, 1913).

political philosophy.[37] Political theories address a variety of issues, which include the nature of rights, conceptions of justice, the relationship between justice and other virtues, and the extent to which the state should seek to prescribe behaviour for its citizens. It is readily apparent that political theories such as liberalism, conservatism, republicanism, communitarianism and socialism give different answers to such issues. Indeed it is these very differences that render them distinct political theories. All such theories are normative, as that term is commonly used. They all seek to provide convincing arguments as to why certain answers ought to be given to the preceding issues, albeit based on certain factual assumptions.

This is equally true for those Loughlin regards as coming within the functionalist school, as for those of a more liberal or conservative persuasion. Thus when, for example, Fabians or New Liberals argued for greater protection of social and economic interests, this was clearly premised on normative arguments as to why such interests should be protected in the manner argued for. This was also true for those who argued in terms of social interdependence or social solidarity.[38] Proponents of these theories also had distinct views about the separation of powers and the rule of law, albeit different from those propounded by adherents of other political theories. It is precisely because all such theories are normative that classic or current works on liberalism, conservatism, republicanism and the like discuss such concepts without any addition of the word 'normativism' or 'normativist'.

It is, moreover, equally important to take care when arguing that certain visions of public law are wedded to particular normative precepts. Loughlin's running together of all liberal theories is especially problematic. Thus repeated assertions that liberals conceive of liberty in negative terms as the absence of external restraint, coupled with the idea that liberals regard government as repressive, conceal more than they reveal.[39] The statement may be true in relation to the liberalism of Hayek[40] or Nozick,[41]

---

[37] See, e.g., H. J. Laski, *Studies in the Problem of Sovereignty* (New Haven: Yale University Press, 1917); H. J. Laski, *Authority in the Modern State* (New Haven: Yale University Press, 1919); G. D. H. Cole, *Social Theory* (London: Methuen, 1920); G. D. H. Cole, *Guild Socialism Restated* (London: Parsons, 1920).

[38] See, e.g., L. Duguit, *Law in the Modern State*, trans. by F. and H. Laski (London: Allen & Unwin, 1921).

[39] Loughlin, *Public Law and Political Theory* (n. 32), 60, 61, 96.

[40] F. Hayek, *The Constitution of Liberty* (London: Routledge and Kegan Paul, 1960); F. Hayek, *Law, Legislation and Liberty, A New Statement of the Liberal Principles of Justice and Political Economy* (London: Routledge and Kegan Paul, 1982).

[41] R. Nozick, *Anarchy, State and Utopia* (New York: Basic Books, 1974).

but it is not so in relation to that of Rawls,[42] Dworkin[43] or Raz.[44] Similar difficulties attend broad assertions that normativists regard rights as preceding the state, whereas functionalists regard rights as emanating from legislation.[45] Political theories clearly differ concerning the way in which rights are conceptualized. This is a central normative issue for all political theories, but the answer provided by 'functionalists' is not necessarily so different from that given by, for example, liberal theories. Thus Laski regarded society as preceding the state and believed that individuals came to the state with rights that the state had a duty to protect.[46] This is without prejudice to a second order issue, which is whether to protect such rights through courts, legislation or an admixture of the two.

Consider now the functional dimension. The reality is that all political theories have a functional as well as a normative dimension. There is no reason why the term functional should be reserved for those theories that are more collective or socialist in orientation. Loughlin uses the term functional in a variety of ways, but none warrant the conclusion that only collectivist type theories have this dimension, or that it is lacking from liberal or conservative theories.

The term is used by Loughlin in part to capture the idea that those who subscribe to functionalist theories argue for legal norms and governmental action that will effectuate the desired ends. They seek ways to ensure that the machinery of the state attains these particular goals. This is, however, equally true in relation to all political theories. Thus, for example, libertarian or public choice theorists are also functional in this sense. They too wish to ensure that the relevant constitutional, legal and political machinery of the state is configured so as to attain the functions that they believe the state should be performing. They too believe that public law should be used to support a healthy body politic. They go to very considerable lengths to specify what this entails.[47] They can and do regard law as part of the

---

[42] J. Rawls, *A Theory of Justice* (Oxford: Oxford University Press, 1973).

[43] R. Dworkin, *Sovereign Virtue, The Theory and Practice of Equality* (Cambridge, Mass: Harvard University Press, 2000); R. Dworkin, *Freedom's Law: The Moral Reading of the American Constitution* (Oxford: Oxford University Press, 1996).

[44] J. Raz, *The Morality of Freedom* (Oxford: Clarendon Press, 1986).

[45] Loughlin, *Public Law and Political Theory* (n. 32), 60.

[46] H. J. Laski, *The Foundations of Sovereignty and Other Essays* (London: George Allen & Unwin, 1921); H. J. Laski, *Liberty in the Modern State* (London: George Allen & Unwin, 1948).

[47] See, e.g., J. M. Buchanan and G. Tullock, *The Calculus of Consent: Logical Foundations of Constitutional Democracy* (Ann Arbor: University of Michigan Press, 1962);

machinery of government. They too focus on law's regulatory and facilitative function. They just adopt a radically different view of what that is
as compared to those of a more socialist persuasion.

The term functionalism is also used by Loughlin in a different sense.
He contends that liberal normativists are committed to law being non-
purposive, in the sense that the state is meant to be neutral as between
differing conceptions of the good. Functionalists are by way of contrast
said not to be troubled by this attachment to neutrality, with the consequence that they can perceive of law as functionally serving broader
societal and governmental goals.[48] It is certainly true that deontological
liberal theory of the kind posited by Rawls[49] is premised on the assumption
that the state should be neutral as between conceptions of the good, in the
sense that it is not for the state to make choices between the value of a life
reading philosophy or playing sport. Liberals of this persuasion are not,
however, neutral about the principles of justice. Nor are they neutral about
legislation or adjudication that affects these principles. To the contrary,
they demand legislative, executive and judicial action that is purposive
insofar as it relates to such principles of justice, including, in this respect,
protection for civil and political liberties, and including also under a
Rawlsian theory action to alleviate the plight of the socially and economically disadvantaged. Liberals regard law as purposive and functional to
attain these ends. It is no answer to contend that some might prefer, for
example, more extensive social rights or greater economic redistribution.
This might well be so, but it has nothing to do with whether public law is
purposive or functional. It simply reflects disagreement as to the background political theory that underpins public law.

There is, moreover, a third sense of the term functional that appears in
Martin Loughlin's work, although it is less evident than the preceding two.
Thus the term is sometimes used to capture the positive or descriptive
dimension of a desired approach. There is a meaningful distinction to be
had between positive/descriptive aspects of political science and more
normative political theory, although values permeate the former as well

---

J. M. Buchanan, *The Limits of Liberty: Between Anarchy and Leviathan* (University of
Chicago Press, 1975); J. M. Buchanan, *Freedom in Constitutional Contract: Perspectives of
a Political Economist* (College Station: Texas A & M Press, 1977); G. Brennan and
J. M. Buchanan, *The Reason of Rules* (Cambridge: Cambridge University Press, 1985).

[48] Loughlin, *Public Law and Political Theory* (n. 32), 60, 93, 96, 102.

[49] Rawls (n. 42). Compare the perfectionist liberal approach in Raz (n. 44).

as the latter. The relevant point for present purposes is that the distinction between positive/descriptive political science and normative political theory is equally applicable to all types of political belief. Thus one might ask how far a society exhibits the features of republicanism, and then proceed to advocate the further development of such attributes on the ground that it is felt in theoretical terms to be the best way to order society. The same might equally be true in relation to liberalism, socialism, conservatism and communitarianism. The argumentation might take a different form, whereby the observer concludes in descriptive terms that the pattern of societal ordering conforms to a liberal stereotype, and then argues that this is undesirable because it is felt that a more socialist society would be preferable. All this is standard fare, and reflects much of the to and fro of political discourse. It offers no basis, however, for any distinction between normativist and functionalist theories, precisely because the descriptive and normative dimensions are applicable to all types of political belief, whether they be conservative, liberal, socialist or idealist.

Conclusion

This chapter has sought to shed light on the extent to which we have a system of public law as opposed to public laws. The issue is interesting and under-theorized, and the answer depends, not surprisingly, on more specific delineation of the nature of the inquiry. Thus it is clear that we have a system of public laws insofar as this connotes distinct statutory rules on subject matter as diverse as education, health, asylum and licensing. It is equally clear that we have a regime of public laws insofar as this captures the distinct constitutional rules that pertain in Scotland, Wales and Northern Ireland. The extent to which this is also true in relation to the application of public law doctrine is more complex, as the preceding discussion has revealed. Care is also required when considering whether it is meaningful to talk about a distinctive functional public law theory.

Further reading

P. Craig, 'Judicial Review and Anxious Scrutiny: Foundations, Evolution and Application' [2015] *Public Law* 59

M. Elliott, 'Proportionality and deference: the importance of a structured approach' in Christopher Forsyth et al. (eds), *Effective Judicial Review: A Cornerstone of Good Governance* (Oxford: Oxford University Press, 2010), ch. 16.

M. Loughlin, *Public Law and Political Theory* (Oxford: Clarendon Press, 1992).

J. Mitchell, *Devolution in the UK* (Manchester: Manchester University Press, 2009).

T. Mullen, 'A holistic approach to administrative justice?' in M. Adler (ed.), *Administrative Justice in Context* (Oxford: Hart Publishing, 2010), ch. 16.

9 Public law and privatisation

A.C.L. Davies

Introduction

Most political scientists agree on some core functions for government: for example, to ensure that citizens enjoy a reasonable level of security, both in terms of maintaining order domestically and protecting the state from external attack. But beyond this core, there is little agreement about what else the state should do. In the United Kingdom, the role of the state has varied over time. In the 1950s, there was considerable expansion as many industries were nationalised and the welfare state was created. The government's proper role was thought to include the running of key parts of the economy, and the provision of health and social care to citizens. In the 1980s, the state began to shrink again, with the 'privatisation' of significant parts of the public sector, such as manufacturing industry and the utilities. And, where functions remained within the public sector, like social care or rubbish collection, the government encouraged much greater use of private firms to provide the services on a day-to-day basis. On this view, the government's task was to supervise private providers, rather than to provide the services itself.

In simple terms, the transfer of a previously public activity to the private sector involves a retreat of public law. Since public law regulates public sector activities, its intervention in what is now a private activity is not required. However, matters are not so simple in the majority of 'privatisation' cases, since the government often retains some control over the activity, either through regulation or through its ongoing role as the purchaser of a service under a contract. Public law remains potentially applicable to these situations.

The discussion will proceed in five parts. First, we will define the concept of 'privatisation' more precisely. Second, we will examine the relationship between the subject-matter of this chapter and broader debates about the public/private divide. In the third section, we will turn to the role of public law in regulating the process of privatising or contracting out a public service. Fourth, we will examine the role of public law in regulating public services once they have been privatised or contracted out. And fifth, we will consider the implications of privatisation and contracting out for the role of government and for democracy more generally. The UK will be used as the main case study in this chapter because of its early and enthusiastic adoption of privatisation and contracting-out policies.

Privatisation defined

In this section, we will distinguish between two senses of the term 'privatisation': privatisation strictly so-called, and contracting out. We will examine some different forms of each.

Privatisation in the strict sense denotes a change in the ownership of a particular activity from public sector to private sector.[1] For example, the government might set up a company to perform a particular activity and then sell shares to private individuals and institutional investors, so that the company is transferred from public ownership to private ownership. When considering examples of privatisation in this sense, a key question to think about from a public law perspective is the extent to which the public sector remains involved in the industry, for example, through regulation. When the gas, water and electricity providers were privatised, for example, the government remained heavily involved because it created regulators to ensure that the markets were competitive and consumers were not overcharged. In other cases – coal and steel, for example – the industries once privatised were not subject to any special regulation.

Contracting out refers to the situation in which the government hires a non-public provider (either a private firm or a voluntary sector organisation) to provide a service under contract.[2] A key feature of contracting out is that the government's involvement remains central. It decides what service it wants to purchase, chooses a contractor, pays the contract price,

---

[1] See, generally, C. Graham and T. Prosser, *Privatizing Public Enterprises: Constitutions, the State, and Regulation in Comparative Perspective* (Oxford: Oxford University Press, 1991); D. Parker, *The Official History of Privatisation* (Abingdon: Routledge, 2009).

[2] See, generally, A. C. L. Davies, *The Public Law of Government Contracts* (Oxford: Oxford University Press, 2008).

and takes action if the provider fails to deliver in accordance with the contractually agreed standards. For example, a local authority might invite bids from private firms for recycling collection. It will then pay the successful bidder to provide the service to households. If there are complaints, the local authority may make deductions from the private firm's regular payments, or terminate the contract altogether and seek a new provider. An important distinction to bear in mind in contracting out situations is that the contractual relationship may be more or less long-term. Under the Private Finance Initiative ('PFI') or Public/Private Partnership ('PPP') schemes, the government uses private firms to build significant infrastructure (hospitals, for example). The private firm takes responsibility for maintaining the hospital and providing associated services (cleaning and catering, for example) and leases it back to the public sector over a thirty-year period. Other contracting-out relationships, like our recycling example, involve less investment and tend to be of shorter duration.

It may be helpful to distinguish privatisation and contracting out from other, similar, types of activity. One is basic public procurement. The government is not, and never has been, self-sufficient in terms of the goods and services it requires to perform its functions. The government might continue to perform a particular function in-house, but use private contractors for support. For example, tax collection remains a public activity, but office buildings, computer systems and so on are all bought from the private sector. There is no bright line between this type of activity and the contracting-out of public functions: the more support the government buys in, the more 'contracted-out' its activities might seem. However, when people talk about contracting out, they generally mean situations in which the contractor provides services *directly* to the public, rather than supporting the government in its provision of public services. Another related, but distinguishable, phenomenon is the creation of markets *within* public services like education or healthcare. Sometimes, the government tries to encourage public bodies to compete with each other for the 'custom' of citizens (school pupils or patients, for example) by creating 'internal markets' in which citizens can choose their preferred provider. Although these markets are sometimes accompanied by contracting out – in the sense that private providers can also compete for contracts – they are, strictly speaking, distinguishable where the activity remains in public hands.

Why do governments adopt privatisation or contracting-out policies? This chapter is not the place for a long discussion of this question, but it may be helpful to give a brief overview of the main arguments by way of background. Often, the reasons behind privatisation or contracting out policies are ideological. Parties of the 'right' tend to advocate 'small' government, and to prefer leaving a greater share of activities to the private sector, whereas parties of the 'left' are more comfortable with big government and higher levels of public provision. Whether a particular task – such as supplying clean water to households – should be performed by a public body or a private firm is, in large measure, a political question. On a more pragmatic level, advocates of privatisation and contracting out generally argue that private firms will provide better quality services at lower cost, because they face competitive pressure, forcing them to be efficient and to please their customers. Critics argue that private firms will be motivated by profit, leading them to cut corners and to 'cherry-pick' profitable elements of particular services to the detriment of the public good. This debate is difficult to resolve because, of course, there are good and bad examples of service provision by both public and private sector providers.

Privatisation, contracting out, and the public/private divide

The trend of privatising or contracting out public services is often regarded as having contributed to a crisis within public law about its scope of application. Some scholars, notably Oliver, have argued that it is becoming so difficult to determine the scope of public law – to draw the public/private divide – that we should abandon separate systems of public and private law altogether.[3] We cannot resolve this very big argument in this chapter, but it is worth saying something about the relationship between privatisation, contracting out, and the worry about the public/private divide.[4]

The phrase 'public/private divide' is a shorthand for a complex set of distinctions between public and private law. There are different substantive rules of law (procedural fairness, *Wednesbury* unreasonableness[5] and so

---

[3] D. Oliver, *Common Values and the Public-Private Divide* (London: Butterworths, 1999).

[4] See also D. Feldman, 'The Distinctiveness of Public Law' (Chapter 1 in this volume).

[5] *Associated Provincial Picture Houses Ltd* v. *Wednesbury Corporation* [1948] 1 KB 223.

on). These rules apply to bodies performing public functions. These bodies usually derive their power from a public source: they are public officials or government departments, for example. But private firms may perform public functions, and public bodies may enter into transactions governed largely by private law. Cases involving public law are usually heard in the Administrative Court by means of a special procedure with special remedies, the application for judicial review, but public law issues may also arise and be dealt with in ordinary litigation in the ordinary courts. The complexity of the public/private divide reflects the fact that, in English law, it is a relative newcomer and is not built into the system in a rigid way. The obvious contrast is with French law, in which there is a clear structural separation between public and private law and the courts responsible for each.[6]

Privatisation is not particularly problematic in terms of the application of the public/private divide, though it clearly reduces the scope of application of public law by shrinking the public sector. It replaces a public body governed by public law with a private firm governed by private law, sometimes subject to supervision by a regulator, which is usually a public body governed by public law. Of course, if the newly privatised firm continues to perform public functions, it may still be subject to public law some of the time, blurring the boundaries between the two spheres. The likelihood of this increases as the privatisation trend cuts deeper into the public sector. However, privatisation's real impact on the public/private divide debate is at a deeper level. It reminds us that there is no consensus about the nature of 'governmental' activity, so that the task of drawing the public/private divide inevitably involves making political choices. This is particularly troubling when the task falls to the judiciary in borderline cases.

Contracting out is more complex from the perspective of the public/ private divide. In a contracting-out situation, the status of the parties to the transaction is usually quite clear: there is a public purchaser and a private provider, and their relationship is governed by a contract. The relationship between service users and the private provider may or may not be contractual depending on the circumstances. For example, the user of a privately run toll road may enter into a contract when he or she pays

---

[6] J. W. F. Allison, *A Continental Distinction in the Common Law* (Oxford: Clarendon Press, 1996).

to use the road, whereas a householder whose rubbish is collected by a private firm pays for the service through his or her council tax and has no direct relationship with the provider. The big question – one we will explore in more detail below – is whether the private provider should be under any public law obligations when it is providing the public service. In other words, should it be treated 'as if' it were a public body, since it is performing tasks on behalf of the public body?

This is a difficult question, for several reasons. First, there is a risk of both over- and under-inclusiveness. It is probably unnecessary to subject every individual or firm entering into a contract with the government to public law obligations.[7] Equally, though, citizens would lose important protections if no government contractors were ever subject to public law obligations. Drawing an appropriate line somewhere in the middle is, inevitably, difficult. Second, the political nature of the public/private divide is a factor here too. Those who are hostile to contracting out for political reasons tend to argue for more extensive public law regulation as a way of discouraging the practice, whereas those who favour the policy tend to argue for reduced public law obligations in order to encourage private firms to get involved in providing public services. And third, because the government has (as we shall see) free rein to decide how and when to contract out a service, there has been very little opportunity for a full public debate about the issue of contractors' obligations.

Of course, it is important to remember that the debate about the public/private divide is not simply a debate about privatisation and contracting out. There are broader questions about, for example, the status of bodies with uncertain legal underpinnings, and about the human rights obligations of private actors in private contexts. However, it is useful to approach that debate with a more detailed knowledge of privatisation and contracting out.

Public law control over the privatisation and contracting out process

In this section, we will consider some of the procedural dimensions of privatising or contracting out public services. Taking the UK as a case

---

[7] Though cf P. Craig, 'Contracting Out, the Human Rights Act and the Scope of Judicial Review' (2002) 118 *Law Quarterly Review* 551.

study, we will examine the mechanisms by which the government can initiate a privatisation or a tendering exercise, and the (relatively limited) potential for aggrieved citizens or service users to challenge such decisions. And we will also consider whether public law has a role to play in regulating the process of inviting bids and choosing a contractor, and thus whether it offers any redress to disappointed bidders.

The constitutional framework

In most legal systems, there is very little public law regulation of the government's decision to adopt a policy of privatisation or contracting out in any particular situation.[8] Constitutional limits on privatisation are unusual.[9]

Privatisation in the UK generally requires an Act of Parliament.[10] Where the government continues to be involved in the newly privatised service, legislation may be needed to set up the regulator responsible for overseeing the service and protecting the interests of service users.[11] Provided that the government has a parliamentary majority, this should not be difficult to achieve.

Contracting out is slightly more complex. If the contractor needs special powers over and above those given to ordinary citizens, such as the power to detain people, legislation may be needed to facilitate contracting out. Private prisons operate under a special statutory regime, for example.[12] The Deregulation and Contracting Out Act 1994 creates a more general facilitative regime for contracting out, which allows ministers to delegate public powers to contractors where they could have been delegated to civil servants, and local authorities to delegate powers to contractors where they could have been delegated to officials.[13] This has a few exceptions – it

---

[8] M. Freedland, 'Public Law and Private Finance – Placing the Private Finance Initiative in a Public Frame' [1998] *Public Law* 288.

[9] See D. Feldman and F. Campbell, 'Constitutional Limitations on Privatisation' in J. Bridge (ed.), *Comparative Law Facing the 21st Century* (London: BIICL, 2001).

[10] See, for example, Electricity Act 1989. It seems likely that a devolved government wishing to privatise a service would also require legislative authority either from Westminster or the relevant devolved legislature.

[11] See, for example, Utilities Act 2000, s. 1.

[12] Criminal Justice Act 1991, s. 84 (as amended).

[13] Deregulation and Contracting Out Act 1994, ss. 69 and 70. For discussion, see C. M. Donnelly, *Delegation of Governmental Power to Private Parties: A Comparative Perspective* (Oxford: Oxford University Press, 2007), 197–209, and M. Freedland, 'Privatising *Carltona*: Part II of the Deregulation and Contracting Out Act 1994' [1995] *Public Law* 21.

cannot be used for judicial powers, for example[14] – but of course the government could always seek specific legislation to get around these exceptions. However, where the contractor does not have a clear-cut need of special statutory powers, the government can just contract a service out without any particular legislative authority.[15] Statutes do not normally require the government to provide a service directly.[16]

Possible challenges

There are a number of routes open to aggrieved citizens or service users who wish to seek judicial review in a contracting-out situation, though the prospects of success are, in most cases, limited.

One option may be to challenge the constitutionality of the privatisation. This is possible in Greece and, to a limited extent, Israel, but not the UK.[17] Another is to argue that the public authority has no power to enter into the contract: in other words, that it is acting *ultra vires*. However, this is quite difficult to do, since most public authorities have broadly framed contracting powers. The Crown has long had the same capacity to contract as a natural person,[18] and local authorities have recently been given such a power by statute.[19] The courts have only upheld *ultra vires* challenges in extreme cases.[20]

---

[14] Deregulation and Contracting Out Act 1994, s. 71.

[15] In the 1980s, some local authorities opposed contracting out so the government used legislation to force them to adopt the practice: see, generally, Local Government, Planning and Land Act 1980, Local Government Act 1988. Nowadays, contracting out may form part of a local authority's demonstration that it offers 'best value' to local people: Local Government Act 1999, as amended, Local Audit and Accountability Act 2014.

[16] A well-known example is the National Assistance Act 1948, ss. 21 and 26, placing local authorities under a duty to 'make arrangements' for the provision of accommodation.

[17] On Greece, see T. D. Antoniou, 'The Constitutional Restrictions of Privatisation' (1998) 51 *Revue hellénique de droit international* 277; on Israel, see HCJ 2605/05 *The Academic Center for Law and Business* v. *Minister of Finance* (19 November 2009), discussed by B. Medina, 'Constitutional Limits to Privatization: The Israeli Supreme Court Decision to Invalidate Prison Privatization' (2010) 8 *International Journal of Constitutional Law* 690.

[18] For a relatively recent discussion, see *Shrewsbury and Atcham Borough Council* v. *Secretary of State for Communities and Local Government* [2008] EWCA Civ 148, [2008] 3 All ER 548.

[19] Localism Act 2011, s. 1. See A. C. L. Davies, 'Beyond New Public Management: Problems of Accountability in the Modern Administrative State' in N. Bamforth and P. Leyland (eds.), *Accountability in the Contemporary Constitution* (Oxford: Oxford University Press, 2013).

[20] See, for example, *Hazell* v. *Hammersmith and Fulham London Borough Council* [1992] 2 AC 1, *Credit Suisse* v. *Allerdale Borough Council* [1997] QB 306, though a finding of

Another, more promising option is to argue that the public authority's contracting out decision is procedurally flawed because it did not consult those affected before pursuing the policy. A challenge of this kind was successful in principle in the case of *R. (Nash)* v. *Barnet London Borough Council*.[21] The council in that case adopted a policy of contracting out virtually all of its services. The claimant challenged the council's contract award decisions pursuant to this policy. The judge at first instance held that the council had breached its duty under s. 3 of the Local Government Act 1999 to consult taxpayers and service users on its plans to secure 'continuous improvement' in service provision, since it had failed to consult on the outsourcing policy. However, the claim failed on the facts because it should have been brought when the policy was adopted and was thus out of time. This highlights the importance of bringing this type of challenge at the earliest possible moment in a complex decision-making process.

A third option is to use the public sector equality duty ('PSED') under the Equality Act 2010, s. 149. This requires public authorities to 'have due regard to' the impact of their decisions on people with characteristics protected by the Act, such as people with different ethnic backgrounds. In general terms, a decision to contract a service out or to appoint a new contractor without changing the service itself does not raise any PSED issues. However, if the contracting out process involves a change in the nature of the service to be provided, the public body may be in breach of the PSED if it does not conduct and take into account an assessment of the equality impact of the change. For example, in *R. (RB)* v. *Devon County Council*, the public authority appointed a 'preferred bidder' for a contract to provide children's services on the basis of the proposed contract price.[22] It was found to have breached the PSED because it did not evaluate the bidder's proposed services in equality terms. However, the judge refused to quash the decisions because the public authority had subsequently completed the assessment and because to do so would disrupt the procurement process.

---

ultra vires only renders the contract void if the public body lacks capacity: *Charles Terence Estates Ltd* v. *Cornwall County Council* [2012] EWCA Civ 1439, [2013] 1 WLR 466.

[21] [2013] EWHC 1067 (Admin), [2013] BLGR 515; upheld [2013] EWCA Civ 1004, [2013] PTSR 1457.

[22] [2012] EWHC 3597 (Admin), [2013] Eq LR 113.

It is important to note that, even if aggrieved service users are able to get a decision quashed on procedural or PSED grounds, the public body might simply rectify the failure (by consulting or conducting an equality assessment) and then continue with its original plans, with the result that the practical impact of the court's ruling is limited.

Procedural protections for contractors

Privatisation is a one-off process in which the government sells off a particular industry, usually by setting up a company and selling its shares. Contracting out is rather more complex because the government must choose a particular contractor (and, usually, repeat that choice at regular intervals to ensure that it is still getting a good deal). When a private individual places a contract, it is up to him or her to choose a contracting partner and there is no duty to act fairly when selecting between competing bidders. Should the government be regarded any differently?

Not all government decisions are subject to judicial review.[23] Contract award decisions tend to fall into the non-reviewable category because the courts regard the government as acting commercially when awarding a contract. On this view, the government should seek the best deal and should not be constrained by public law obligations.[24] However, if there is a sufficient 'public element' in the contract, the courts will sometimes hold that the contract award decision is subject to judicial review on procedural fairness or even irrationality grounds.[25] This seems to apply where the courts consider that the contractor will be performing an important public function, though there is ample scope for judicial discretion because it is a matter of opinion when this requirement is fulfilled. Where judicial review is available, the disappointed bidder is able to argue, for example, that it was not treated in accordance with principles of procedural fairness.

---

[23] Review under the Human Rights Act 1998 ('HRA') is always available for government decisions – the government does not have a private life under the HRA as it does in judicial review – but it is difficult to see what right an unsuccessful bidder might invoke in order to bring a claim under the HRA.

[24] *R.* v. *Lord Chancellor ex parte Hibbit & Saunders* [1993] COD 326.

[25] *R.* v. *Legal Aid Board ex parte Donn & Co* [1996] 3 All ER 1. See also *R. (Law Society)* v. *Legal Services Commission* [2010] EWHC 2550 (Admin).

The contract award process is, however, heavily regulated by European Union law,[26] implemented in the UK via the Public Contracts Regulations 2006 ('PCR').[27] Contracts above a certain financial value must be advertised and awarded after a fair tendering process in which bidders are treated equally. The government may choose from a menu of different types of tendering process depending on the nature of the contract. The purpose of this is to open up government contracts to bidders from other EU Member States and to discourage governments from favouring their own national firms in the award of contracts. Even lower-value contracts are still subject to some basic obligations under the Treaty: to advertise them and to award the contracts after a transparent and non-discriminatory process.[28]

Remedies under the PCR are confined to disappointed bidders,[29] but it is possible in principle for interested third parties (service users or unions representing affected workers, for example) to seek judicial review of a public authority's breaches of the PCR.[30] However, as we saw above in relation to judicial review more generally, there are practical obstacles: for example, in the *UNISON* case, the claim failed for various reasons including delay and the potential for serious disruption to the procurement process.[31]

Conclusion

The decision to privatise or contract out a particular service is largely one for the government in the UK, as it is under most other Westminster-model constitutions and elsewhere. There is a very limited role for legal accountability for these decisions, in part because of the UK's constitutional

---

[26] The main source is Directive 2004/18/EC on the coordination of procedures for the award of public works contracts, public supply contracts and public service contracts. A revised Directive 2014/24/EU must be implemented by April 2016.

[27] Public Contracts Regulations 2006 (SI 2006/5). See generally S. Arrowsmith, *The Law of Public and Utilities Procurement* (London: Sweet and Maxwell, 2014), 3rd edn.

[28] See Commission Interpretative Communication on the Community law applicable to contract awards not or not fully subject to the provisions of the Public Procurement Directives (2006 OJ C 179/02).

[29] PCR 2006, r. 47.

[30] *R. (Chandler)* v. *Secretary of State for Children, Schools and Families* [2009] EWCA Civ 1011, [2010] 1 CMLR 19; *R (UNISON)* v. *NHS Wiltshire Primary Care Trust* [2012] EWHC 624 (Admin), [2012] ACD 84.

[31] *UNISON* (n. 30).

tradition and in part because the courts (while occasionally allowing judicial review in principle) are concerned to avoid disruption to the business of government. Although there is extensive EU intervention, this is designed to ensure the fair treatment of bidders regardless of their nationality, with more general fairness as a by-product. As Freedland has argued, public law in its 'constitutional' mode has little to say about the changing shape of the modern administrative state.[32]

Public law control during the life of the contract

Once a service has been contracted out, there are at least two actors involved in its delivery: the public body responsible for paying for the service, and the private firm (or firms) providing the service. In this section, we will consider what happens if a service user claims that his or her rights have been infringed, or wishes to seek judicial review of a decision taken about the service.[33] Is the contractor subject to judicial review, or to HRA review? And what effect does contracting out have on the reviewability of the public body's decisions? It will examine the accountability gap created by decisions such as *YL* v. *Birmingham*, and consider issues of risk and uncertainty for contractors.[34]

Privatisation strictly so called will not feature heavily in this section. Privatisation normally removes the possibility of judicial review or (in the UK) Human Rights Act 1998 ('HRA') review of the private firm's decisions, except to the extent that any private firm is potentially subject to public law norms through, for example, the 'horizontal' application of the HRA. Contracting out is challenging because of the continuing relationship between the public body and the private firm.

Review of the public body's decisions

We will begin by considering how contracting out affects the public body's liability under the HRA and in judicial review. This area of law is not generally well understood.

---

[32] Above n. 8.

[33] For a more detailed account of the issues in this section, see Davies (n. 2), ch. 8.

[34] *YL* v. *Birmingham City Council* [2007] UKHL 27, [2008] 1 AC 95.

If a claimant brings an application for judicial review or a HRA claim against a public body in respect of a contracted-out service, it is arguable that it is no defence for the public body to say that the service is contracted out.[35] In principle, the delegation of a task to another person does not involve transferring power to that person, but rather empowering him or her to act concurrently with the delegator. This is so even where a public body formally delegates power to a contractor under the Deregulation and Contracting Out Act 1994.[36] The public body remains liable for the delegate's actions as well as its own. As a result, public authorities ought to include suitable clauses in contracts with private providers requiring them to fulfil any public law or HRA obligations relevant to their role.

Given that the public authority remains liable, it is worth pausing to consider why claimants still find it desirable to bring proceedings against the contractor. One reason may simply be a general lack of awareness of public authorities' ongoing responsibility in contracting-out situations. The other relates to remedies. Many of the cases brought so far have concerned decisions to close care homes. The residents have sought injunctions to prevent closure, relying either on the doctrine of legitimate expectations or on Article 8 of the European Convention on Human Rights. If the care home belongs to the private firm, it would be difficult for the public authority to comply with an injunction to keep it open, so the appropriate defendant in this situation is the private provider.

Review of the contractor's decisions

The task of deciding whether government contractors are subject to judicial review or to the HRA has been left largely to the courts. They have adopted a relatively restrictive version of the 'middle way' in which contractors can be subject to review but only if quite strict conditions are met. The courts' approach to judicial review and the HRA is broadly similar but we will consider them separately because some judges have

---

[35] See *Poplar Housing and Regeneration Community Association Ltd* v. *Donoghue* [2001] EWCA Civ 595, [2002] QB 48, [60], *per* Lord Woolf, and P. Craig, *Administrative Law* (London: Sweet and Maxwell, 2012), 7th edn., 118–19. Importantly, though, the argument from delegation does not turn on the public authority's positive obligations to protect human rights. For the contrary view, cf Joint Committee on Human Rights, *The Meaning of Public Authority under the Human Rights Act* (Seventh Report of Session 2003–04), [83].

[36] Deregulation and Contracting Out Act 1994, s. 72(2).

doubted the precedential value of the judicial review case law in HRA claims.

The leading judicial review cases on contractor liability are *Servite*[37] and *Partnerships in Care*.[38] Both cases require the claimant to show something more than just the presence of a contract with a public body in order to bring the contractor's activities within the scope of public law. This is often expressed in the phrase 'statutory underpinning', derived from the *Datafin* case, which was concerned not with a contractor but with a body of uncertain legal status, the Takeover Panel.[39]

In *Servite*, Wandsworth LBC placed a contract with Servite, a housing association, to run a residential home for the elderly. Servite wished to close the home because it was not profitable. The residents sought judicial review of Servite for breach of their legitimate expectation that they could stay in the home for life. The court held that there was no 'statutory penetration' sufficient to make Servite a public body.[40] It was a private body acting under a 'private' contract with Wandsworth London Borough Council and thus was not amenable to judicial review.

In *Partnerships in Care*, by contrast, the firm was the provider of a hospital. The claimant was compulsorily detained under the Mental Health Act 1983 in the hospital while she received treatment for a personality disorder. It was accepted that the treatment for personality disorder differed from the treatment for mental illness, but managers at the hospital proposed to treat more mentally ill patients on the ward in which the claimant was being treated. This would have left the claimant without appropriate care. In this case, the hospital was under a direct statutory duty to provide adequate care. It was held that breaches of this duty could be challenged by the claimant through judicial review.[41]

As is well known, s. 6 of the HRA draws a distinction between 'pure' public authorities and bodies performing 'public functions'. The former are caught by the HRA in respect of all their activities. The latter are subject to the HRA in respect of their public functions only. Although they are sometimes referred to as 'hybrid' public bodies, this shorthand is unhelpful because we are not concerned with the public or private status of the

---

[37] *R.* v. *Servite Houses ex parte Goldsmith* (2001) 33 HLR 35.

[38] *R. (A)* v. *Partnerships in Care Ltd* [2002] EWHC 529 (Admin), [2002] 1 WLR 2610.

[39] *R.* v. *Panel on Takeovers and Mergers ex parte Datafin* [1987] QB 815, 824, *per* Sir John Donaldson MR.

[40] *Servite* (n. 37), [76], *per* Moses J.   [41] *Partnerships in Care* (n. 38), [24], *per* Keith J.

body – usually it is a private firm – but with the public or private nature of the functions it is performing. As in the judicial review decisions, the courts have taken the view that not all government contractors are hybrid public authorities and that some additional public element must be shown to make them so.

The leading decision is that of the House of Lords in the *YL* case.[42] Here, the claimant had been placed by Birmingham City Council in a privately run care home. She was threatened with eviction from her care home because the owner of the home took exception to her family's behaviour during visits. She sought to assert Article 8 rights against the private provider of the home. A majority in the House of Lords held that the private provider was not subject to the HRA. Their Lordships emphasised the fact that the care home had no special statutory powers and argued that the functions would not be regarded as 'governmental' in nature. They argued that the care was not 'publicly funded' because although it was paid for by the council, it was obtained by contract rather than by any more general subsidy of the care home's activities. They considered the argument that this created a gap in protection in that those who benefited from 'in-house' services were better protected than those who benefited from contracted-out services. But they rejected this, largely on the ground that to hold the care home liable under the HRA would create another kind of unfairness as between those whose care was paid for by the local council and those who could afford to pay for their own care.

However, there may be a sufficient 'public element' in some cases to bring the contractor within the scope of the HRA. In *Poplar Housing*, the claimant was seeking to challenge her eviction from social housing.[43] The housing was provided by Poplar, a housing association, under contract to a local authority. It was held that the housing association was subject to the HRA because it had played a major role in assessing the claimant's entitlements.[44] The housing association would not have been able to do what it was doing without exercising the local authority's public powers. This was enough to bring it within the scope of the HRA. The *Weaver* case, decided after *YL*, adopted similar reasoning.[45]

---

[42] *YL* v. *Birmingham City Council* [2007] UKHL 27, [2008] 1 AC 95. See also *R. (Heather)* v. *Leonard Cheshire Foundation* [2002] EWCA Civ 366, [2002] 2 All ER 936.

[43] *Poplar* (n. 35).   [44] *Poplar* (n. 35), 70, *per* Lord Woolf CJ.

[45] *R. (Weaver)* v. *London and Quadrant Housing Trust* [2009] EWCA Civ 587, [2010] 1 WLR 363.

Thus, there are obvious similarities between the HRA approach and the judicial review cases. Something more than just a contract with a public body is required. The contractor must itself be exercising public powers or performing public duties. Although the *YL* decision has since been reversed by statute in respect of care homes,[46] the general approach laid down in the case remains applicable to other fact situations.[47]

For the reasons given above, it seems appropriate to attempt to distinguish contractors engaged in the performance of public functions from contractors merely providing public authorities with the means of performing public functions. What is more questionable is the idea that this should be left to the courts to decide, without any real attempt by the government to clarify the matter when deciding to engage a contractor. The current approach leaves citizens uncertain as to their rights in the event of a dispute, and contractors unsure of their liabilities. It also forces the courts to make political choices: the 3–2 split in the House of Lords in *YL* reflected, in part at least, a difference of opinion about what contracting out was designed to achieve and how it should be regulated. This is reflected most obviously in Lord Neuberger's suggestion that contracting out might be intended to cut costs by removing certain services from the reach of the HRA.[48] I have argued elsewhere that the government should be required to specify in clear terms which public powers and duties it intends to delegate when placing a contract subject, of course, to judicial review of the specification.[49] This would bring much-needed transparency to the process for contractors and service users.

Conclusion

This discussion has highlighted some of the practical consequences of the absence of a constitutional framework for the policy of contracting out discussed earlier in the chapter. The government can entrust private firms with important public tasks whilst leaving those firms' concurrent liability under the HRA and in judicial review uncertain. Although the government itself remains liable, there may be practical limits to the utility of bringing

---

[46] Health and Social Care Act 2008, s. 145.
[47] For critique, see Joint Committee on Human Rights, *The Meaning of Public Authority under the Human Rights Act* (Ninth Report of Session 2006–07).
[48] *YL* (n. 42), [152], *per* Lord Neuberger.   [49] Davies (n. 2), ch. 8

an action against the government in respect of a contracted-out service. In terms of legal accountability, then, there is a potentially significant gap when services are contracted out.

The commissioning state

In this section, we will focus on the impact of privatisation and contracting out on the government itself.[50] These policies have altered the government's role, reducing the emphasis on the direct provision of services and encouraging it to focus instead on regulating private firms (in the case of privatisation) and on deciding what services are required, selecting contractors and supervising their activities (in the case of contracting out). We will examine the impact of these changes from the perspective of political accountability.

Privatisation

Privatisation has two important consequences for the government's political accountability. First, it can give rise to confusion about the government's ongoing responsibility for a particular industry. Second, it is a difficult policy to reverse, making it one of the more 'permanent' decisions a government can take.

The privatisation of a particular activity can, as we saw above, involve either a full or a partial retreat of the state from that activity, depending on whether the newly privatised firm is subject to a special regulatory regime. The regulatory arrangements themselves may vary, giving ministers more or less control over a particular sector. For example, in the UK Ofgem (the gas and electricity regulator) is a non-ministerial department governed by the Gas and Electricity Markets Authority ('GEMA'), whose members are appointed by the Secretary of State. It operates under a detailed statutory framework setting out its objectives.[51] It has a reasonable degree of day-to-day independence from government, though the Secretary of State has a range of specific direction-making powers in

---

[50] For more detail, see Davies (n. 19).
[51] The statutory framework is complex but the main provisions are found in the Gas Act 1986, the Electricity Act 1989 and the Utilities Act 2000.

relation to it.[52] This generates considerable complexity in relation to public and political accountability. On the one hand, the government can quite justifiably assert that it does not control the consumer energy market. On the other hand, the sector remains politically controversial and ministers regularly respond to parliamentary and media questions about it.

A second point worth noting is that privatisation is a difficult policy to reverse. Although it would be perfectly possible to re-nationalise a privatised activity by legislation, the government would probably be forced to pay compensation to affected investors.[53] A simpler option is just to buy back the shares, though this obviously requires a significant investment of resources. One of the UK's few re-nationalisations of recent years, the acquisition of Railtrack by Network Rail, occurred when Railtrack was in financial difficulties affecting its value, but the government faced litigation from shareholders who lost money in the deal.[54] Thus, a privatisation policy may change the shape of the state for the foreseeable future. Although a government is unlikely to be able to sneak a privatisation Bill through Parliament without anyone noticing, the UK constitutional tradition does not offer any special scrutiny for important changes of this kind.

Contracting out

Two of the leading advocates of contracting out, Osborne and Gaebler, argued that the government's role should be to 'steer' rather than to 'row'.[55] The government should focus on deciding what services are required, selecting the most suitable contractor and monitoring that contractor's performance, rather than engaging in direct service provision itself. But how can we hold a 'steering' state to account?

One problem, much discussed in the literature, is the opportunity created by contracting out – just like privatisation – for the government to deny responsibility for service failures by blaming the contractor. To take a hypothetical example, imagine that the government contracts out the task of transporting prisoners to and from court. It awards the contract to

---

[52] For example, on social and environmental matters under ss. 10 and 14 of the Utilities Act 2000.

[53] Expropriation is likely to raise issues under Article 1 Protocol 1 ECHR.

[54] See, for example, *Weir* v. *Secretary of State for Transport (No. 2)* [2005] EWHC 2192 (Ch). The claim failed.

[55] D. Osborne and T. Gaebler, *Reinventing Government: How the Entrepreneurial Spirit is Transforming the Public Sector* (Wokingham: Addison-Wesley, 1993).

the bidder offering the lowest price. To provide the service within the agreed price, the contractor only assigns one member of staff for every ten prisoners being transported, with the result that some prisoners escape. On one view, this is the contractor's fault for bidding too low and providing an inadequate service. On another view, the government shares some of the blame for failing to scrutinise the contractor's bid or to set expectations about staffing levels. In terms of the traditional mechanisms of political accountability – scrutiny through parliamentary questions, for example – the introduction of a contractor blurs the 'line' of accountability from those delivering the service to the ministers or councillors in charge of that service.

Another problem, less frequently discussed but perhaps more important, is that the 'steering' state may find it difficult to change direction.[56] Continuing our scenario, imagine that a newly elected government wishes to re-nationalise the prisoner transport operation. Its capacity to do this will depend on the terms of the contract with the current provider, and the financial resources it has available. It may be prohibitively expensive to bring the contract to an end prematurely. The government could fall back on the rule against the fettering of discretion in order to argue that the contract is *ultra vires* and not binding, but (even if a court were persuaded by this argument) the government might find that there were significant long-term disadvantages in making contractors feel that the government is not a reliable contracting partner.[57] Thus, although politicians might promise to 'do something about' contracted-out public services, they may find that they lack the flexibility to make the necessary changes. This has serious implications for politicians' democratic accountability because it limits their capacity to fulfil the promises they have made to the electorate.

Those who favour contracting out would dismiss these concerns. It is often argued that, even if contracting out does reduce or constrain political accountability, this does not matter, for two reasons. First, political accountability is a weak form of accountability for reasons that are well known. Ministers or councillors cannot plausibly supervise every aspect of a complex public service, so they are unlikely to accept blame when things go wrong, and newly elected politicians often find, on taking up office, that their choices are constrained in various ways. Second, contracting out

---

[56] For a recent example of this in relation to contracts, see the facts of *R. (Essex County Council)* v. *Secretary of State for Education* [2014] EWHC 2424 (Admin).

[57] See Davies (n. 2), ch. 6.

gives rise to new and more effective forms of accountability. For example, contractors are accountable for the cost of service provision because they are expected to compete in the market for the contract, thus forcing them to keep their costs down. And they are accountable in several different ways for the quality of the services they provide. The contract may contain quality standards, with the possibility that the public body may make deductions from the contract price for breaches, and where the provider must compete for the 'custom' of service users, it has a strong incentive to maintain high standards. Whether these alternative mechanisms of accountability are an appropriate substitute for traditional political mechanisms is a matter of debate.[58]

Conclusion

This chapter set out to explore the impact of privatisation and contracting out on public law. The choice of this objective is, in itself, significant. Normally, we would expect public law to have an impact on the conduct of government. But in relation to privatisation and contracting out, the reverse is true.

Privatisation reduces the scope of application of public law by transferring activities from the public sector to the private sector. Any remaining public involvement takes place through special regulatory regimes. Very few legal systems have any constitutional controls over what can or cannot be privatised. And privatisation is difficult to reverse, because of the need to compensate private investors. Contracting out is similar to privatisation in some respects but significantly different in others. Again, there are few controls over what can be contracted out. The policy is difficult to reverse, at least in the short term. But there is more potential for public law mechanisms of accountability to be used against both the government and the service provider during the provision of the service: the government, because of its ongoing involvement, and the provider, because of its participation in the performance of public functions. However, the courts have been slow to recognise this potential and have allowed an accountability gap to emerge.

---

[58] See T. Wright, 'The Politics of Accountability' (Chapter. 5 in this volume).

Nowadays, most people think of public law as enjoying a period of expansion, with the enactment of the HRA and the ongoing development of the grounds of judicial review, but in relation to privatisation and contracting out, there is a very different story to tell.

Further reading

S. Arrowsmith, *The Law of Public and Utilities Procurement* (London: Sweet and Maxwell, 2014), 3rd edn

P. Craig, 'Contracting Out, the Human Rights Act and the Scope of Judicial Review' (2002) 118 *Law Quarterly Review* 551

A. C. L. Davies, *The Public Law of Government Contracts* (Oxford: Oxford University Press, 2008)

A. C. L. Davies, 'Beyond new public management: problems of accountability in the modern administrative state' in N. Bamforth and P. Leyland (eds.), *Accountability in the Contemporary Constitution* (Oxford: Oxford University Press, 2013)

C. M. Donnelly, *Delegation of Governmental Power to Private Parties: A Comparative Perspective* (Oxford: Oxford University Press, 2007)

M. Freedland, 'Public Law and Private Finance – Placing the Private Finance Initiative in a Public Frame' [1998] *Public Law* 288

C. Graham and T. Prosser, *Privatizing Public Enterprises: Constitutions, the State, and Regulation in Comparative Perspective* (Oxford: Oxford University Press, 1991)

P. Vincent-Jones, *The New Public Contracting: Regulation, Responsiveness, Relationality* (Oxford: Oxford University Press, 2006)

State architecture: subsidiarity, devolution, federalism and independence 10

Christopher McCrudden*

Introduction

The 'architecture' of the United Kingdom state seems quite straightforward.[1] Each of its *parts* is immensely complicated, of course, but the overall *structure* is clear, is it not? Governmental power is primarily exercised through a sovereign Parliament sitting at Westminster.[2] A government is formed that is able to command the support of the first chamber (the House of Commons). Parliament has agreed to delegate its sovereign powers both upwards and downwards, with some powers being exercised by European institutions, and other powers distributed (the term used is 'devolved') among the nations[3] of the United Kingdom (Scotland, Wales and Northern Ireland[4]). So, too, other powers are delegated to regional and local communities through a patchwork of local and municipal government. It is a liberal parliamentary democracy, with the first chamber and each of the other forms of government (national, regional and local) being elected by universal franchise. Judicial oversight seeks to ensure that public

---

* I am grateful to Christine Bell, Anne Davies, Mark Elliott and Brendan O'Leary for their extensive comments on earlier drafts, and to Brendan O'Leary and Rick Hills for providing copious references to relevant political science scholarship.

[1] For earlier political science accounts, see P. Dunleavy, 'The Architecture of the British Central State: Part I, Framework for analysis' (1989) 67 *Public Administration* 249; P. Dunleavy, 'The Architecture of the British Central State: Part II, Empirical findings' (1989) 67 *Public Administration* 391.

[2] On parliamentary sovereignty, see M. Elliott, 'Legislative Supremacy in a Multidimensional Constitution' (Chapter 4 in this volume).

[3] For a discussion of what constitutes a nation, see J. W. Friend, *Stateless Nations: Western European Regional Nationalities and the Old Nations* (Basingstoke: Palgrave Macmillan, 2012), 2–3.

[4] Referring to Northern Ireland as one of the four 'nations' that make up the United Kingdom, alongside England, Scotland, and Wales, is controversial. Purists will object that only part of the Irish 'nation' is included the United Kingdom. With this clarification, I shall continue to use the term 'nation' to refer to Northern Ireland.

bodies (with the notable exception of Parliament) obey the law, which includes protections for civil and political rights.

Looked at this way, the United Kingdom is best described as being a classic unitary state, i.e. a state with a system of government that involves the country being governed as a single entity, with the central government in Westminster being supreme, and with the other tiers of government exercising only those powers that the central government (defined to include legislature, executive and courts) has allowed them to exercise. These tiers of government, whether supranational or devolved, are ultimately the creatures of the central government, and will be created and abolished, and their powers broadened and narrowed, by the central government. A unitary state, like the United Kingdom, can be contrasted with a federal state, such as the United States or Germany, in which the sovereign power is shared between the federal government and the states. Unlike several continental European states, like France, the United Kingdom did not arise out of the Jacobin model stemming from the French Revolution and Napoleon, and is thus not based on a strong ideology.

That, at least, is the constitutional narrative as told in London, but the way in which at least one element of this structure is viewed, how governmental power is distributed 'downwards' among the nations of the United Kingdom, is seen somewhat differently in Cardiff, Belfast, Edinburgh, and Dublin (leaving aside how Brussels and Strasbourg view delegation 'upwards' to European institutions). The idea of the unitary state that the United Kingdom is traditionally thought to be (with power radiating from Westminster) is now subject to pressures to adapt to reflect these different understandings. A wide range of possibilities is being considered, from independence for some parts of the state (particularly popular among nationalists in Northern Ireland and Scotland), to increased devolution of powers to Scotland, Wales, Northern Ireland, and England.

How should we understand these developments? We might take a normative approach, in which (for example) we assess whether a unitary state or devolution or independence is to be preferred on the basis of which best conforms to democratic principles, or which is more likely to achieve preferred normative outcomes such as social justice.[5] This is not the approach adopted here. Instead, we shall be concerned with the task of establishing a framework for explaining how the current patterns of

---

[5] See, e.g. D. Miller, *Citizenship and National Identity* (Cambridge: Polity Press, 2005), ch. 7.

power distribution across the nations of the United Kingdom can best be explained, and may change in the future. In this chapter, there is no attempt to describe the existing pattern, however, and so it is more in the nature of a prolegomenon.

The period between the 1860s and the 1920s seems the closest 'domestic' analogy to the constitutional drama currently underway, at least in terms of the intellectual debates involved. During that period, from the perspective of British constitutional law, what became independent Ireland moved from being governed as part of the unitary state of the United Kingdom, then to Dominion status in 1921–1922, and then to being recognized as a Republic in 1948. By contrast, Northern Ireland, ironically that part of Ireland that had most resisted devolution, was established with a devolved parliament and government, separated from the rest of the island because the majority of its inhabitants opposed Ireland's independence. Many of the alternative models of government that currently occupy political debate were considered at that time,[6] from devolution (then called 'home rule') through to federalism, and independence, amid a flurry of scholarly and academic attention.[7] It is time for some of these debates to be brought back into consideration by public lawyers in the United Kingdom, for they provide a useful insight into some of the dilemmas we now face, although in other respects, of course, the context has changed beyond recognition, a point to which we shall return.

The rise and fall of imperial federalism

One of the more intriguing ideas of the late nineteenth century that never came to fruition was the proposal that there should be a new state established consisting of several of the Dominions (Canada, Australia, New Zealand) and the United Kingdom.[8] The new state would be organized on a federal basis, with separate local parliaments for each of the Dominions and for each of the four nations of the United Kingdom. There would, in

[6] A. J. Ward, *Irish Constitutional Tradition: Responsible Government and Modern Ireland, 1782–1992* (Blackrock: Irish Academic Press, 1994).

[7] T. Dunne, 'La Trahison des Clercs: British Intellectuals and the First Home-Rule Crisis' (1982) 90 *Irish Historical Studies* 134.

[8] J. Kendle, *Ireland and the Federal Solution: The Debate Over the United Kingdom Constitution, 1870–1921* (Kingston: McGill-Queen's University Press, 1989); J. Kendle, *Federal Britain: A History* (New York: Routledge, 1997).

addition, be an Imperial Parliament, with representation from each of the states making up the federation. Like the federal structure of the United States, each of these legislatures would be sovereign within their own sphere of allocated powers but none would have plenary and unrestricted power of the type that the United Kingdom Parliament claims. For some, this model had particular attraction as a way of dealing with the Irish home rule crisis.

Had the proposals for an Imperial Federation been accepted, the idea of the United Kingdom as a unitary state would have disappeared, along with parliamentary sovereignty, and the Westminster model. The collapse of the idea also had considerable significance in another way. The failure of Imperial Federalism meant that Albert Venn Dicey's view became the new orthodoxy. Dicey was confirmed as the high priest of the unitary-state view of the United Kingdom, which, together with the sovereignty of the Westminster Parliament, 'he elevated into ... dogma in 1886',[9] with the publication of *An Introduction to the Study of the Law of the Constitution*. We sometimes forget quite how comparatively recently this understanding of the central foundations of the British constitution became accepted wisdom.

James Bryce, A.V. Dicey, and Irish Home Rule

History has not been particularly kind to Dicey's old adversary in the Home Rule Crisis, James Bryce. Except in the United States, Bryce's reputation has suffered from comparison with Dicey, his contemporary and friend. Bryce is known mostly for his magisterial study of the United States constitution and system of government, *The American Commonwealth*, first published in 1888, which soon became a classic. In the British constitutional context, he is perhaps best known for the distinction he drew between flexible and inflexible constitutions, with the British constitution being classified as a representative of the former rather than the latter. Beyond that, British public lawyers pay him little attention.

---

[9] C. Harvie, 'Bryce, James, Viscount Bryce (1838–1922)' in *Oxford Dictionary of National Biography* (Oxford: Oxford University Press, 2004) (available at http://ezproxy-prd.bod leian.ox.ac.uk:2167/view/article/32141) (hereafter 'Bryce, DNB').

Bryce was a qualified supporter of the devolution of power to Ireland (though not to Scotland), whilst Dicey had become an ardent opponent of Home Rule and a strong unionist, as supporters of the unitary state were called. The fact that students of constitutional law in Britain now mostly read Dicey rather than Bryce is a testament to the grip that unionism has exercised on constitutional law in the United Kingdom, at least since 1922, when Ireland could be safely excised from the canon of British constitutional history, leaving the way for unionism to emerge as the dominant constitutional discourse. There were dissenting voices in Scotland and Ireland even after 1922, which claimed that Dicey's unionism was but one narrative among many.[10] These voices were drowned out, however, by the increasingly hegemonic (and English) understanding of the United Kingdom as a unitary state with a sovereign Parliament. Michael Burgess observes how Dicey's *Introduction* 'established a narrow legalistic conception of federation' that 'effectively excluded an important option for British constitutional reform up until quite recently'. Dicey's misunderstanding and confusion of the concept 'produced the phobia that has been a characteristic hallmark of British political culture'.[11] The authority of Dicey's *Introduction*, particularly in its rejection of federalism in favour of a unitary state, left future generations of lawyers, academics and practitioners alike singularly ill-equipped to deal with the events that were about to unfold, domestically and in Europe.

During the 1970s, significant political changes occurred in Scotland, Wales, and Northern Ireland that would challenge the Diceyan intellectual hegemony. Irish nationalism and militant republicanism reasserted themselves in Northern Ireland. In Wales, *Plaid Cymru*, a Welsh nationalist party committed to Welsh independence, increased its share of the vote from 4.5 per cent in 1966 to 11.5 per cent in the 1970 Westminster election. The Scottish National Party, committed to Scottish independence, polled almost a third of all votes in Scotland in the general election to the Westminster Parliament in October 1974. Although both the Scots and Welsh parties lost much of this support later that decade, their relative

[10] J. D. B. Mitchell, 'Sovereignty of Parliament – Yet Again' (1963) 79 *Law Quarterly Review* 196; N. MacCormack, 'Reflections on *MacCormack v Lord Advocate*' (1978) 29 *Northern Ireland Legal Quarterly* 1; R.V.F. Heuston, *Essays in Constitutional Law* (London: Stevens, 1964), 2nd edn., 20–30; H. Calvert, *Constitutional Law in Northern Ireland: A Study in Regional Government* (London: Stevens, 1968), 11–29.

[11] See M. Burgess, *Comparative Federalism: Theory and Practice* (London: Routledge, 2006), 21.

success encouraged the then Labour government to establish the Kilbrandon Commission on the constitution[12] and, following its Report, to propose the establishment of a Scottish Parliament and a Welsh Assembly.[13] The onset of the 'Troubles', with Northern Ireland's descent into violent insurgency and counterinsurgency and its emergence as a foreign policy problem for the Westminster government, brought a separate, more urgent, source of constitutional negotiation and initiatives.

All these constitutional initiatives were initially unsuccessful, but the local politics of Northern Ireland, Scotland, and Wales had altered sufficiently by the mid-1990s for a new Labour Government elected in 1997 to support the most extensive internal constitutional restructuring that had been seen since 1922, with the establishment of a Scottish Parliament in Edinburgh, a Welsh Assembly in Cardiff, and the re-establishment of a devolved government in Belfast.[14] Although enacted under the common heading of 'devolution', each of the new settlements was different in significant respects. There has been, as a result of devolution, an outpouring of commentary by public intellectuals in all four jurisdictions re-examining the British unitary state, and the place of each of these jurisdictions within it. This has been most evident in Scotland. By 2012, with the Scottish National Party holding a majority of seats in the Scottish Parliament, agreement was reached with the government at Westminster for a referendum to be held on independence for Scotland. Wales and Northern Ireland looked on from the sidelines at the possibility that the United Kingdom would be reconfigured, as it had been after the establishment of the Irish Free State in 1922.

In September 2014, Scotland voted against becoming an independent country by 55 to 45 per cent. There was a huge turnout; over 84 per cent of those eligible actually voted. In the run-up to the vote, the leaders of the three main UK parties (Conservative, Labour and Liberal Democrats) pledged that, if Scotland voted against independence, more powers would be devolved to the Scottish Parliament. Following the 'no' vote, the Prime Minister appointed a Commission to oversee the implementation

---

[12] *Report of the Royal Commission on the Constitution 1969–1973*, vol. 1 (Cmnd 5460, 1973).

[13] *Democracy and Devolution: proposals for Scotland and Wales* (Cmnd 5732, 1974).

[14] A. J. Ward, 'Devolution: Labour's Strange Constitutional Design' in J. Jowell and D. Oliver (eds.), *The Changing Constitution* (Oxford: Oxford University Press, 2000), 4th edn., 111–36. Northern Ireland had a devolved government between 1922 and 1972.

of this pledge, with draft legislation due to be published early in 2015. Although there was agreement in principle on further devolution, reaching accord on the details, and on the implications for other parts of the United Kingdom, appeared likely to be difficult. In this new environment, in which Diceyan unionism seems out of step with the *zeitgeist*, a reconsideration of Bryce's understanding of constitutionalism has become long overdue.

Centrifugal and centripetal forces

A year before Dicey had 'elevated into . . . dogma' his view of the absolute sovereignty of the Westminster Parliament in a unitary state,[15] Bryce had taken a less ideological and more coolly analytical approach to the study of constitutions and constitutionalism.[16] He pointed to the utility of considering how political constitutions are exposed to two conflicting forces: centripetal forces which draw 'men or groups of men together into one organized community', and centrifugal forces which make 'men, or groups, break away and disperse'.[17] The theme of this chapter will be to show how the continuing (and, as Bryce argues, inevitable) tension between these centripetal and centrifugal forces can be usefully applied to power relations between the various nations of the United Kingdom. The distinction, and Bryce's analysis of it, provides a basis for analysing how these nations are drawn or impelled by some forces towards a centralized unitary polity, whilst at the same time other forces tend towards dispersion of power. The resulting pattern may initially be analysed along a spectrum[18] from centralization to independence, with subsidiarity, devolution and federalism being seen as weigh stations along the way, although ultimately the application of these distinctions to the current distribution of powers in the United Kingdom will be seen as problematic.

---

[15] Bryce, DNB (n. 9).

[16] The essay 'The Action of Centripetal and Centrifugal Forces on Political Constitutions' was composed in 1885, but was not published until 1901 in J. Bryce, *Studies in History and Jurisprudence*, vol. I (Oxford: Clarendon Press, 1901) (available at: http://oll.liberty fund.org/titles/2003) (hereafter, '*Studies*').

[17] *Studies* (n. 16), 217. Bryce was probably influenced by *Federalist Paper*, No. 15.

[18] W. Livingston, 'A Note on the Nature of Federalism' (1952) 67 *Political Science Quarterly* 81, 88.

Bryce suggested that there are essentially four factors (or 'forces') in play that determine whether a polity will keep together or fall apart. First, using his terminology, there is the force of 'Obedience', meaning 'the readiness to submit and follow';[19] second, the force of 'Individualism' meaning 'the desire to let each man's individuality have full scope';[20] third, the force of 'Interest' (which we might better characterize today as economic self-interest), under which he includes 'all those influences which belong to the sphere of Property, including of course Industry and Commerce as means of acquiring property';[21] and, fourth, the force of 'Sympathy', which includes 'the influences which flow not from calculation and the desire of gain, but from emotion or sentiment.'[22]

The head of Sympathy is the most capacious. It includes a range of factors which we would often consider as giving rise to national identity: the 'sense of community, whether of belief, or of intellectual conviction, or of taste, or of feeling (be it affection or aversion towards given persons or things)';[23] 'the recognition of a common ancestry; the use of a common speech; the enjoyment of a common literature'[24] (although their importance, he thinks, can often be exaggerated); and 'identity of traditions and historical recollections, and ... the possession of the materials for a common pride in past achievements'.[25] In addition to issues going to national identity, he highlights also 'the influence of Religion', which, he writes, 'touches the deepest chords of man's nature'.[26] In addition to national identity and religious faith, sympathy also includes 'a large and rather miscellaneous category of sources of sympathy' including '[t]raits of character, ideas, social customs, similarity of intellectual culture, of tastes, and even of the trivial usages of daily life'.[27]

Janus-faced nature of forces

A key element that Bryce brings to his analysis is that the elements of Obedience, Individualism, Interest, and Sympathy are capable of being *either* centripetal or centrifugal. Which they prove to be in practice 'depends upon whether they are at the moment giving their support

---

[19] *Studies* (n. 16), 222.   [20] *Studies* (n. 16), 222.   [21] *Studies* (n. 16), 222.
[22] *Studies* (n. 16), 224.   [23] *Studies* (n. 16), 224.   [24] *Studies* (n. 16), 224.
[25] *Studies* (n. 16), 225.   [26] *Studies* (n. 16), 225.   [27] *Studies* (n. 16), 226.

to, or are enlisted in the service of, the State as a whole, or are strengthening the group or groups inside the State which are seeking to assert either their rights within the State or their independence of it'.[28] This is because '[t]here are always two centres of attraction and two groupings to be considered, the larger, which we call the State, and the smaller, which may be either a subordinate community, such as a province, district or dependency, or only a party or faction. And the centripetal force which draws men to the smaller centre is a centrifugal force as regards the larger.'[29] As we shall see, Bryce's assumption of competition between only two centres of attraction will need to be adapted to apply to situations, like that in the contemporary United Kingdom, where there is a three-way interaction (European Union, unitary state, and the Nations).

That aside, Bryce's insight is practically important: each of the forces may be either centripetal or centrifugal. Thus, 'obedience . . . which might seem primarily a centripetal force, may be centrifugal as against the State if it leads the partisans of a particular recalcitrant group to surrender their wills to the leaders of that group'.[30] Individualism can be centrifugal, in so far as 'the keenest individualist desires to convert other men to his individualism, and forms a league for the purpose with others who are like-minded',[31] but may also be centripetal 'if it disposes men to revolt against the tyranny of a faction and maintain the rights and interests of the whole people against the attempts of that faction to have its own way'.[32] Interests are usually centripetal, 'disposing [the citizen] to desire the extension of the State and the strength of its central authority'[33] in order to reduce barriers to freedom of commerce, trade and investment but may, exceptionally, be centrifugal, where economic protectionism is seen as economically beneficial. Sympathy, too, may play either role; religion, for example, has been 'efficient in knitting factions and States together'[34] *and* at 'breaking them up and setting the parts of a State in fierce antagonism to one another'.[35] The close attention paid to, and the controversies surrounding, the use of the Scots, Welsh, and Irish languages is a modern case in point. *Claiming* language rights can act as a centrifugal force that can encourage separatist nationalist sentiment at

---

[28] *Studies* (n. 16), 222.   [29] *Studies* (n. 16), 222.   [30] *Studies* (n. 16), 222.
[31] *Studies* (n. 16), 221.   [32] *Studies* (n. 16), 222.   [33] *Studies* (n. 16), 223.
[34] *Studies* (n. 16), 225.   [35] *Studies* (n. 16), 225.

the periphery; *conceding* these claims can act as a centripetal force when it demonstrates wise statesmanship at the centre.[36]

Role of constitutional law

As well as being an active politician, and keenly interested in what we would now call political science, Bryce was also a distinguished constitutional *lawyer*. Why should a constitutional lawyer now be at all interested in this topic? Isn't the question of what keeps a polity together or splits it apart only an issue for political science or history, rather than one for public law? For Bryce, the answer was clearly in the negative. One of the objectives of a Constitution, he wrote, 'is to . . . strengthen the cohesiveness of the country by creating good machinery for connecting the outlying parts with the centre'.[37] In pursuing this objective, 'a constitution seeks to achieve *by means of legal provisions* that which in ruder times it was often necessary to accomplish by physical force'.[38] The question is how a constitution should be framed (and, we might add, interpreted and applied) 'in order to enable it to maintain and strengthen the unity of a State'.[39]

Although the question is initially for historians and students of politics to address, Bryce argued, the implications of their study are indubitably pertinent for constitutional lawyers, both academics and practitioners. Indeed, to be effective, the 'constitutional lawyer . . . must always, if he is to comprehend his subject and treat it fruitfully, be a historian as well as a lawyer',[40] and in particular 'must have his eye constantly fixed' on these centripetal and centrifugal forces.[41] He continues: 'Their action will preserve or destroy the Constitution, – preserve it, if it has given them due recognition and scope, destroy it, if its provisions turn out to be opposed to the sweep of irresistible currents.'[42] Effective constitutional lawyers are the ones who, in advising or in drafting, attempt to increase centripetal and decrease centrifugal forces, and have the knowledge, experience and

---

[36] Gaelic Language (Scotland) Act 2005, Welsh Language Measure 2011, and Welsh Language Act 1993. For the position in Northern Ireland, see V. Ní Dhrisceoil, 'Language Conflict in Northern Ireland: revisiting the Irish language rights debate' [2013] *Public Law* 693.

[37] *Studies* (n. 16), 230.   [38] *Studies* (n. 16), 230 (emphasis added).

[39] *Studies* (n. 16), 231.   [40] *Studies* (n. 16), 218.   [41] *Studies* (n. 16), 220.

[42] *Studies* (n. 16), 221.

judgement to know which is which in the context in which they are operating.

Constitutions may use centripetal forces to promote national unity. Bryce emphasizes three methods in particular. The first and 'most generally available of these centripetal tendencies is trade',[43] capitalizing on Interest. A Constitution, he continues, 'can render no greater service to the unity as well as to the material progress of a nation than by enabling the freest interchange of products to go on within its limits.[44] The second, capitalizing on Interests and, possibly, Individualism, 'is the establishment of a common law and a common system of courts'.[45] Where one legal system 'can, without exciting resentment, be extended over the whole of a country, it becomes a valuable unifying force'.[46] However, it is not an influence 'which can be reckoned on so invariably or confidently as can the influence of commerce'.[47] This is because 'any hasty attempt to change the law (whether customary or statutory) to which men are accustomed may provoke resistance and retard the growth of unity'.[48] An example was provided in 2011, when a Supreme Court's decision to change various aspects of the Scottish criminal justice system provoked controversy, with Alex Salmond, the First Minister of Scotland, accusing the court of 'aggressive' intervention in Scotland's separate legal system.[49] Third, capitalizing on Sympathy, Bryce identifies a common religion as a method of enhancing political cohesion, but (importantly for those in predominantly secular societies such as the United Kingdom is today) he considers that the 'same principle applies to beliefs which cannot be called religious, but which exert a similar power over men's emotions'.[50] He continues: 'Even where no question of the supernatural is involved, the holding in common of certain ideas deemed supremely valuable whether for the individual or for society, may operate as a centrifugal or centripetal force.'[51] And, of course, religion may at one time be a centripetal force and over time

---

[43] *Studies* (n. 16), 231.

[44] *Studies* (n. 16), 232. Here Bryce demonstrates his commitment to a liberal tradition rooted in Montesquieu and Adam Smith, see H. D. Forbes, *Ethnic Conflict: Commerce, Culture and the Contact Hypothesis* (New Haven: Yale University Press, 1997).

[45] *Studies* (n. 16), 232.   [46] *Studies* (n. 16), 233.   [47] *Studies* (n. 16), 232.

[48] *Studies* (n. 16), 233.

[49] *Fraser (Nat Gordon)* v. *HM Advocate* [2011] UKSC 24. See further, the report of the Review Group set up by the Scottish Government following this, *Examination of the Relationship between the High Court of Justiciary and the Supreme Court in Criminal Cases* (2011).

[50] *Studies* (n. 16), 235.   [51] *Studies* (n. 16), 235.

become centrifugal – think of the changing role of Christianity in England, and the role of an Established Church, from the nineteenth century to the twenty-first century.[52] Apart from religion, Bryce emphasizes the potential for those framing a Constitution to 'make it provide a system of education which will give the people common ideas and common aspirations'.[53] And, in that context, too, the Constitution itself may provide a common rallying point, binding the different groups together around a common set of values and aspirations.

Constitutions may also reduce, regulate or disarm the centrifugal forces that threaten national unity. Of these, the most important to address are the centrifugal forces that arise from Interest. According to Bryce, it is necessary to provide for the effective redress of grievances, particularly where these affect 'a particular province' or a 'particular section of the people', and where these generate 'a sentiment of dislike on the part of the disaffected section towards the rest of the nation, or else a belief that great material advantages will be obtained by separation'.[54] For Bryce, a significant problem is majoritarianism, where 'there is a risk that the Constitution which the will of a majority has established may leave a minority discontented and unrestful, and that such discontent and unrest may impede the working of the machinery and create an element of instability'.[55] Where this is the case, he advises, 'it may be the part of wisdom for the majority to yield something to the minority, modifying the Constitution, so far as it can safely be modified, in order to remove the obstacles to harmony'.[56]

The constitutional techniques he advocated are remarkably modern. One is to 'enact certain securities against oppression, whether by the executive or by the legislature, giving to such securities a specially solemn sanction, and thus reassuring the minds of the citizens'.[57] Another is to 'provide means for varying the general institutions or laws of the State in such a

---

[52] J. Garcia Oliva, 'Church, State and Establishment in the United Kingdom in the 21st century: anachronism or idiosyncrasy?' [2010] *Public Law* 482.

[53] *Studies* (n. 16), 236.   [54] *Studies* (n. 16), 238.   [55] *Studies* (n. 16), 228.

[56] *Studies* (n. 16), 229.

[57] *Studies* (n. 16), 243. Bryce's use of 'securities' may have been influenced by the earlier use of the term in a similar context by Bentham: J. Bentham, *Securities Against Misrule and Other Constitutional Writings for Tripoli and Greece* (Philip Schofield, ed.), *The Collected Works of Jeremy Bentham* (General Editor, F. Rosen) (Oxford: Oxford University Press, 1990). See further J. Elster, *Securities Against Misrule: Juries, Assemblies, Elections* (Cambridge: Cambridge University Press, 2013).

way as to exempt particular parts of the State from any legislation that might be opposed to their special interests or feelings'.[58] A third is to adopt a strategy of what today we might call 'subsidiarity', assigning 'certain administrative and, within limits, certain legislative functions also to the inhabitants of minor local areas, such as counties, empowering them to regulate their local affairs in their own way',[59] provided that the powers given to such localities are not such as to be themselves threatening to stability. But stating the issue is easier than resolving practical problems. So, for example, would the creation of a separate judicial system in Wales recognize local differences, or create instability?[60]

Although we may find the language in which Bryce describes his Elements rather dated, and sometimes reflecting what we would now consider the casual racism of his time,[61] his underlying principles are ones that have considerable resonance in contemporary attempts to understand what the factors are that bring political communities together and what pushes them apart, particularly in federations.[62] We can translate Obedience into the language of 'consent' to constitutional constraints on the exercise of individual or collective will only when provided under the agreed constitution.[63] We can see strong echoes in Bryce's Individualism in contemporary concerns with 'individual rights' and the 'rule of law'. In Bryce's idea of Interest we can identify concern with the economic constitution and the extent to which the creation and distribution of wealth and economic goods become constitutional issues. The recent debate over whether corporation tax should be devolved to Northern Ireland to enable it to introduce a lower rate of tax compared to the rest of the United Kingdom is a case in point.[64] Current interest in 'constitutional identity' has much in common with Bryce's Sympathy, focusing attention on issues of social cohesion, including particularly the role of ethnicity.

---

[58] *Studies* (n. 16), 243.   [59] *Studies* (n. 16), 244.

[60] D. C. Gardner, 'Public Law Challenges in Wales: the past and the present' [2013] *Public Law* 1.

[61] Cf. Bryce's memo on Ulster to Gladstone, 'The case of the Ulster Protestants', 12 March 1886, Gladstone Papers, Add. 56447.

[62] Michael Burgess, *Comparative Federalism: Theory and Practice* (London: Routledge, 2006), 17–18. See also Nancy Bermeo, 'The Import of Institutions' (2002) 13 *Journal of Democracy* 96.

[63] N. Walker, 'Beyond the Unitary Conception of the United Kingdom Constitution' [2000] *Public Law* 384, 397.

[64] Economic Advisory Group, *The Impact of Reducing Corporation Tax on the Northern Ireland Economy* (May 2011).

Bryce and the European Union

Bryce's analysis is not just of contemporary theoretical relevance in the analysis of national constitutions. In the practice of the European Union, we also see the playing out of each of these elements. The Union's authorities attempt to capitalize on centripetal forces. The need for Obedience stimulates attempts to increase the political legitimacy of the Union, reducing the democratic deficit by strengthening the role of the European Parliament; the recognition of the importance of Individualism leads to the EU Charter of Fundamental Rights; Interest has been seen as the primary driving force for economic integration, and the Four Freedoms are developed, alongside a strong European judiciary; attempts to build Sympathy lead to the sustained development of European symbols – the flag, the anthem, an emphasis on a common European culture, and educational exchanges. The EU has frequently also recognized the logic of Bryce's position, that when one Element's centripetal force is diminished or broken, then another Element needs to be brought to the fore. As Interest in the shape of free trade or free movement diminishes or becomes counter productive, Individualism is increased; as Obedience is challenged, Sympathy is given greater importance. And much of this is done using legal methods – the EU is quintessentially a legal institution – resulting in sustained constitutional engineering of the type that Bryce contemplated. It is no coincidence that one of the most thoughtful of legal commentators, David Edward, formerly of the European Court of Justice, has drawn on Bryce's analysis of centripetal and centrifugal forces in seeking to explain the development of the EU.[65]

The 'European effect' on devolution

Bryce's analysis is not only of use in analysing the EU, but also in considering the effect of European integration on devolution. We have seen earlier, however, that an additional layer needs to be added to Bryce's analysis, in order to accommodate it to the three (or more) levels

[65] D. Edward, 'The Community's Constitution – Rigid or Flexible? The Contemporary Relevance of the Constitutional Thinking of James Bryce' in D. Curtin and T. Heukels (eds.), *Institutional Dynamics of European Integration: Essays in Honour of Henry G Schermers*, vol. II (Dordrecht: Martinus Nijhoff), 58.

of government that currently exist in the United Kingdom (EU, Westminster, and the nations). A structural feature of the United Kingdom's constitution that is now of immense importance is that, unlike in Bryce's day, subsidiarity involves the transfer of powers from the unitary state to a supranational entity, the European Union, which has informal but direct relationships with the devolved governments, leading on occasion to the expansion or contraction of their powers, with the potential for the nations to weaken links with Westminster at the same time as strengthening links to Brussels.

Thus far, we have considered devolution of powers by London 'downwards' to Scotland, Wales, and Northern Ireland separately from the allocation of powers 'upwards' to the European institutions. It is now time to bring them together because, of course, they are intimately related. The United Kingdom's entry into Europe, by which I mean its accession to, and continued membership of, both the EU and the Council of Europe (and, in the latter case, accession to the European Convention on Human Rights) is the single most significant external development affecting the domestic British constitution since 1922, surpassing even decolonization and the end of Empire in its significance.[66] It would be surprising if it had not also affected the terms of engagement between the nations that make up the United Kingdom, and there are, indeed, three respects in which there have been tangible effects on that relationship.

The EU is perhaps the most palpable expression of economic globalization and economic rationality. When it was established, the European Economic Community (as it then was) adopted enthusiastically the idea, first institutionalized in the European Coal and Steel Community, that through economic integration the prospect of war between the western European states that made it up would become unthinkable, and political integration would follow, leading to an 'ever closer union'.[67] In being so clearly an expression of modernity,[68] however, the effect is to attract the animus of those who are alienated by those aspects of modernity that they

---

[66] On the domestic constitutional implications of the ECHR and, in particular, of the Human Rights Act 1998, see A. McHarg, 'Rights and Democracy in UK Public Law' (Chapter 6 in this volume).

[67] E. Haas, *The Uniting of Europe* (Stanford: Stanford University Press, 1968), 2nd edn.

[68] J. H. H. Weiler, 'To be a European Citizen – Eros and Civilization' in J. H. H. Weiler (ed.), *The Constitution of Europe* (Cambridge: Cambridge University Press, 1999), 330–32.

resist, or simply do not understand.[69] Sustained as the EU's attempts have been to use constitutional methods to entrench centripetal forces, Bryce's warning that these Elements may also have centrifugal effects is equally apparent, as Euro-sceptical political parties and governments recognize their utility as a way of reining in the expansion of EU powers.

One effect of the allocation of powers upwards has been, paradoxically perhaps, to stimulate a resurgence of nationalist feeling in some states, drawing heavily on Sympathy to provide a counter to the EU's emphasis on Interest.[70] One apparent effect, in the United Kingdom at least, of devolution downward and allocation upward to the EU has been to stimulate exactly the sense of English nationalism, the absence of which Dicey thought had contributed to the success of the Union between Scotland and England in the first place. We should not exaggerate the role of the EU in this; it is only a part of the picture, but it is not an insignificant part. The Institute for Public Policy Research, for example, presented opinion poll evidence in 2012 which suggested that a new kind of Anglo-British identity had emerged, in which the English component was increasingly the primary source of attachment for English people, with accompanying greater scepticism of the EU.[71] Here, again, Bryce was prescient, suggesting that centripetal tendencies could help lead to a centrifugal counter-reaction, where 'the life of the smaller group' was intensified. The effect of growing English and Scottish nationalism occurring at the same time is a growing apart of Scotland and England, and growing resentment by each of the other.

A second effect of the EU on the debate between the nations has been to emphasize Interest, particularly economic interests, and all parties have been keen to appeal to these interests in seeking to gain support for their particular cause. This is apparent in several respects. The question of whether Scotland would be able to remain a member of the EU were it to vote for independence was a significant issue in the two years of debate leading up to the referendum.[72] One of the reasons for the concern over continuing membership was that Scotland would otherwise risk losing

---

[69] I do not mean here to imply that Euro-scepticism is necessarily anti-modernity, only that those who oppose modernity are likely also to be Euro-sceptics.

[70] Burgess (n. 62), 18.

[71] R. Wyn Jones, G. Lodge, A. Henderson and D. Wincott, *The Dog that Finally Barked: England as an Emerging Political Community* (London: IPPR, 2012).

[72] HM Government, *Scotland Analysis: EU and international issues* (Cm 8765, 2014).

access to trading partners in continental Europe, but also in England (assuming that the United Kingdom minus Scotland remained a member). A second reason, however, was that Scottish nationalism's appeal to Interest was not just based on the generation of wealth, but also its distribution. The EU's much-vaunted 'social model' was much closer to the Scottish Government's vision of an independent Scotland than was that of a Conservative-dominated UK government, seen as essentially an exponent of free-market capitalism. A third reason based in Interest that appealed to nationalists was that Brussels has increasingly been recognized as competing with London as the most important place to be represented for a political community that wants to influence the policies that matter to it on a day-to-day basis. Put simply, it may be better to be at the centre in Europe as an independent state with direct access to and membership of the European Commission and the Council of Ministers than to have mere representation in the Westminster Parliament.

The third effect of the EU on the internal debate between the nations of the United Kingdom was that it introduced a much more nuanced idea of 'sovereignty' and 'citizenship' than before membership, and this has affected the way in which the current debate is conducted. Before membership of the EEC, the idea that the 'sovereignty of Parliament', in the Diceyan sense, was questionable seemed confined to Scottish and Irish nationalists and academics. After membership, however, parliamentary sovereignty, and the legal concept of national sovereignty itself, was much more questionable, and questioned. Sovereignty now was less spoken of in binary terms and more in terms of a spectrum. So, too, citizenship itself came to be something that was frequently plural. The EU, after all, introduced the concept of European citizenship, not as an alternative to citizenship of one of the member states of the EU (indeed, such membership is a necessary and sufficient condition for EU citizenship) but as an addition to national citizenship.[73]

The most telling example of how more complex notions of sovereignty came to be applied in the context of relations between the nations of the United Kingdom occurred as a result of the peace agreement in Northern Ireland. Under the Belfast/Good Friday Agreement, individuals born in Northern Ireland were recognized, under British law, as having dual citizenship with the Irish Republic, if they so chose, and it was accepted that

---

[73] On which see Weiler (n. 68), 350ff, and M. Elliott, 'Legislative sovereignty in a Multidimensional Constitution' (Chapter 4 in this volume).

there were two sets of national aspirations represented in that jurisdiction. Indeed, there is provision for referendums to be held that will determine whether Northern Ireland remains within the United Kingdom or leaves, an opportunity that few other states allow to their citizens. So, too, in various ways, another independent state, the Irish Republic, is given a potentially considerable role in the political institutions of Northern Ireland. And all this was achieved and legally underpinned by an international treaty in which the two governments maintain a standing intergovernmental conference.[74]

The fourth effect of the EU concerns the role of human rights in the national debate. The Human Rights Act 1998 was one element, along with devolution, of the Labour Government's constitutional reform package that it introduced in the late 1990s. This was based upon, indeed it was commonly seen as incorporating, the European Convention on Human Rights (ECHR), and was presented as setting out a set of values that all of the United Kingdom could accept and share. It seemed, therefore, to be an example of the integrative effects that appeals to Brycean Individualism could bring about. However, as human rights have become caught up with general English Euro-scepticism, there have been moves, particularly within the Conservative Party, to replace the ECHR with a 'UK (sic) Bill of Rights', leading to the establishment of a Commission on a Bill of Rights. Although presented in 'UK garb', the Commission soon discovered two important factors: first, that scepticism about the ECHR was primarily an English phenomenon and was much less prominent in Scotland, Wales or Northern Ireland; and second, that the Convention and the Human Rights Act had been incorporated into the devolution arrangements in Northern Ireland and Scotland in a way that made its repeal a matter of negotiation between the nations, and between the UK and Ireland, to an extent that had clearly not been fully appreciated before.[75]

---

[74] O'Leary claims that this demonstrates that there is a 'federacy' in the making: B. O'Leary, 'Complex Power-Sharing in and over Northern Ireland: A Self-Determination Agreement, a Treaty, a Consociation, a Federacy, Matching Confederal Institutions, Inter-Governmentalism and a Peace Process' in M. Weller, B. Metzger and N. Johnson, *Settling Self-Determination Disputes: Complex Power-Sharing in Theory and Practice* (Leiden, Boston: Martinus Nijhoff, 2008).

[75] Commission on a Bill of Rights, *A UK Bill of Rights? The Choice Before Us*, vol. 1 (2012), ch. 9. See L. Blom-Cooper, 'The Commission on a Bill of Rights: an English approach to a UK Bill of Rights' [2013] *Public Law* 209.

Subsidiarity, devolution, and federalism

The different nations that currently make up the United Kingdom are, therefore, drawn or impelled by some forces towards a centralized unitary polity, whilst at the same time other forces tend towards dispersion of power, as identified by Bryce. The continuing (and, as Bryce argues, inevitable) tension between these centripetal and centrifugal forces can be usefully applied to power relations between the various nations of the United Kingdom, and between the UK and Europe, providing a basis for analysing how the British Constitution has appeared to adopt a Diceyan ideology of the unitary state, whilst in practice adopting a significant dose of Brycean pragmatism, with the latter increasingly coming to the fore.

The resulting pattern is immensely complicated. The complexity is increased by two further features of the constitutional structure. The first is that the distinctions between the concepts adopted to designate these different types of constitutional relationships (such as the distinction between devolution and federalism) are much less clear-cut than politicians and academics sometimes like to pretend, and there is often significant play at the margins, with each of them allowing an important degree of flexibility in what constitutes devolution, or federalism, or confederalism. The second is that particular areas of the exercise of government power need to be plotted differently along the hazy spectrum from unitary to federal. Thus, how one would describe the relationship between the centre and the devolved administrations over Bryce's Interests (such as economic and trade issues) will differ significantly from how one would describe the relationship over issues of Sympathy (such as cultural and language issues).

Conclusion

Bryce identified several Elements in play, which can either operate centrifugally or centripetally, helping to stabilize or destabilize political systems, which some have described in architectural terms.[76] There is a danger

---

[76] For uses of the architectural metaphor in the UK context, see Dunleavy (n. 1) and, more generally, D. Treisman, *The Architecture of Government: Rethinking Political Decentralization* (Cambridge: Cambridge University Press, 2007).

that Bryce's analysis when combined with the metaphor can give rise to a lazy teleological reading of the constitutional history of the 'British Isles',[77] by which I mean a reading that views the current constitutional structure as in some sense the inevitable path-dependent outcome of Bryce's Elements operating together to produce a stable political system. Bryce and (to his credit) Dicey warned their readers against such historical teleology, arguing that the contingencies of history might well have led to very different institutions and constitutional structures. So, for example, if Britain had not been first off the block in the Industrial Revolution, would Scotland have become so enthused about the Union during the nineteenth century? Or, if the Arch-Duke Ferdinand had not been assassinated in Sarajevo in 1914, would Ireland now be a Republic? Or, if 9/11 had not happened, would the Northern Ireland peace process have been completed to the extent that it has, leading to the actual devolution in practice of powers envisaged in the Belfast/Good Friday Agreement? The role that contingency plays in determining constitutional structure means that there is nothing inevitable or pre-ordained about the current relationships discussed above. Bryce provides a framework rather than a theory; his framework is consistent with, indeed it predicts, very different outcomes depending on the context. If polities break apart, the fault 'is not in our stars, but in ourselves'.[78]

Given how complex the variations in the distribution of power between these nations and the centre have become over time, therefore, the construction of any static architectural blueprint of the British state is bound to be misleading. Indeed, the architectural metaphor, with its implications of teleology and stability, needs to be rethought. The models of devolution to which the UK has moved have been equipped with various mechanisms to re-calibrate what powers are devolved and what are not. We can now suggest, with some justification, that by 2015 and following

---

[77] As the archipelago comprising the islands of Britain and Ireland is sometimes commonly called. 'These Islands' is the preferred designation in Ireland and the term now generally used in official documents drawn up jointly by the United Kingdom and Irish Governments, although the official name of one of the institutions is the British-Irish Council. So, the Good Friday/Belfast Agreement, Strand 3, para 1, provides: 'A British-Irish Council (BIC) will be established under a new British-Irish Agreement to promote the harmonious and mutually beneficial development of the totality of relationships among the peoples of *these islands*.' (Emphasis added.) On the British–Irish Council, see www.britishirishcouncil.org/.

[78] Shakespeare, *Julius Caesar* (I, ii, 140–41).

the Scottish referendum, the ideological position of the British state is shifting ever more towards the Brycean position, and that the ideology of the unitary state is somewhat in retreat, although fighting a powerful rearguard action. So, in some ways, the type of constitutional readjustments that Bryce contemplated have come to fruition. In an important sense the British constitutional approach has bypassed the idea of a spectrum from unitary state to devolution to federalism to secession, and has created a much more fluid and moveable set of relationships, which change depending on what is thought to be necessary to achieve greater centripetalism. Neil Walker's suggestion that we are in a state of 'constitutional unsettlement' captures what I intend to convey.[79] And, as Walker notes, although the issues discussed in this chapter (devolution, relationship with the EU, human rights) are subject to 'continuous disputation with deeply uncertain long-term consequences',[80] this is not necessarily a cause for undue concern.

But it brings with it certain implications, if it is not to become pathological. Managing Bryce's Elements, in light of contingencies, is a constant task and demands a sophisticated appreciation of public law, since this now provides the mechanisms by which these challenges are considered and managed on a day-to-day basis, sometimes in courts,[81] but more often in the day-to-day negotiations and proffering of legal advice by competing sets of government lawyers in Belfast, Edinburgh, Cardiff and London, lawyering that is usually well below the political radar.[82] It also requires a high level of constitutional skills and good political judgment by politicians, drawing on comparative experience and empirical analysis. And, finally, it requires an appreciation that the constitutional changes that have come about may be viewed somewhat differently in the different nations of the Union, and that the system needs to be flexible enough to recognize and accommodate this constitutional pluralism. Given the

---

[79] N. Walker, 'Our Constitutional Unsettlement' [2014] *Public Law* 529.
[80] N. Walker, 'Our Constitutional Unsettlement' (working paper version, available at http://papers.ssrn.com/sol3/papers.cfm?abstract_id=2419437).
[81] Raising the question of how the devolution statutes should be interpreted, an issue that the courts have not yet fully resolved; compare *Robinson* v. *Secretary of State for Northern Ireland* [2002] UKHL 32, [2002] NI 390 with *Attorney General* v. *National Assembly for Wales Commission* [2012] UKSC 53, [2013] 1 AC 792 and *Imperial Tobacco Ltd* v. *Lord Advocate* [2012] UKSC 61, 2013 SLT 2.
[82] See, e.g., R. Rawlings, 'Concordats of the Constitution' (2000) 116 *Law Quarterly Review* 257.

results of the Scottish referendum, and its fall-out, it may be wise for all concerned to brush up on their Bryce, and skip the Dicey of English constitutional orthodoxy.[83]

Further reading

C. Bell, 'Constitutional Transitions: The Peculiarities of the British and the Politics of Comparison' [2014] *Public Law* 446

S. Choudhry and N. Hume, 'Federalism, devolution and secession: from classical to post-conflict federalism' in T. Ginsburg and R. Dixon, *Comparative Constitutional Law* (Cheltenham: Edward Elgar, 2011)

B. Hatfield, 'Devolution: a national conversation?' in J. Jowell and D. Oliver (eds.), *The Changing Constitution* (Oxford: Oxford University Press, 2007), 7th edn.

T. Mabry, J. McGarry, M. Moore, and B. O'Leary (eds.), *Divided Nations and European Integration* (Philadelphia: University of Pennsylvania Press, 2013)

N. MacCormack, *Questioning Sovereignty* (Oxford: Oxford University Press, 2001)

N. MacCormick, 'The English Constitution, the British State, and the Scottish Anomaly' (1998) 101 *Proceedings of the British Academy* 289

C. McCrudden, 'Northern Ireland and the British Constitution since the Belfast Agreement' in J. Jowell and D. Oliver (eds.), *The Changing Constitution* (Oxford: Oxford University Press, 2007), 6th edn.

C. McCrudden, 'Using Comparative Constitutionalism in Human Rights Discourse: Ireland's Past and Scotland's Future' (2013) 17 *Edinburgh Law Review* 314

---

[83] The historical Dicey was both more interesting and more conflicted on the issue of parliamentary sovereignty and the unitary state than the mythological Dicey of first-year constitutional law, as is now clear from careful analysis of his hitherto unpublished papers. J. W. F. Allison (ed.), *The Oxford Edition of Dicey* (Oxford: Oxford University Press, 2013), vol. 1.

Soft law never dies 11

Richard Rawlings

'Soft law' is a fact of public life. Cast in terms of competing demands for flexibility and responsiveness, and consistency and coherence, official business could not sensibly be carried on without, to adopt a generous working definition, rules of conduct or pointers and commitments which are not directly legally enforceable but which may be treated as binding in particular legal or institutional contexts.[1] While the phenomenon is commonly associated with international governance, it has increasingly resonated in public law scholarship if under different labels. An uncodified constitution, famous since Victorian times for conventions of the constitution bearing on the behaviour of, and relations between, principal organs of the State,[2] is a natural habitat.

Examining a range of usages, this chapter looks at soft law as an instrument for, and barometer of, constitutional and administrative development over the course of a lifetime. Reflecting and reinforcing the notion of legalisation in contemporary society,[3] commonly observed in terms of more legislation and more jurisprudence, as well as more lawyers, it pursues the idea of 'soft law abounding'. While naturally vulnerable to the growth of formal legal norms, soft law techniques are also apt to be stimulated by it, in part by way of supplement and/or experiment, in part by way of counter-reaction.

The pervasive sense of ambiguity, as also the broad spectrum of rules, agreements, communications, etc. familiarly in play, is the other main starting point. Putting to one side the simplistic view of polar opposites,

---

[1] In enlarging on rules of conduct while up-fronting legal or institutional relevance, this formulation is wider and stricter than the well-known definition from which it is adapted: F. Snyder, 'Soft Law and Institutional Practice in the European Community' in S. Martin (ed.), *The Construction of Europe* (Dordrecht: Kluwer Academic, 1994), 198.

[2] A. V. Dicey, *Introduction to the Study of the Law of the Constitution* (London: Macmillan, 1959), 10th edn.; G. Marshall, *Constitutional Conventions* (Oxford University Press, 1984).

[3] M. Galanter, 'Law Abounding: Legalisation around the North Atlantic' (1992) 55 *Modern Law Review* 1.

an influential institutionalist model references different dimensions to legalisation, whereby law is characterised as 'harder' or 'softer' according to the degree and precision of the obligations created, as well as the extent of involvement by a court or tribunal.[4] Factors which point in a particular direction, a strong demand for authoritative interpretation and/or the constitutional symbolism of formal law perhaps, or conversely a preference for experimentation or 'learning by doing', may then be identified in functionalist fashion.[5] It is well to remember, however, that while the choice of soft law technique will often be mundane, it may on occasion be a matter of significant political and/or legal dispute.

A chief theme of this chapter is the way in which in different periods and different policy contexts certain types of soft law take on a new importance. Normative concerns relating to the creation and deployment of soft law technique are raised accordingly. As well as the classic bureaucratic modalities of rule formulation and application, particular attention is paid to the need for co-operative and co-ordinating arrangements associated with latter-day dynamics of constitutional and administrative fragmentation and multi-level governance. While the United Kingdom is the chief focus, consideration must also be given to the European Union, where the use of soft law scales new heights.

Extended state

Going back forty years or so, we find public law scholars in the UK making determined efforts to rebalance the discipline with bottom-up perspectives. Taking inspiration from the United States,[6] this meant focusing on, in American terminology, 'bureaucratic law';[7] and, more particularly, on the division between 'rules', 'principles' and 'standards',[8] and the potential for better forms of rule-making. The twin-sided nature of internal guidance

---

[4] K. Abbott and D. Snidal, 'Hard and Soft Law in International Governance' (2000) 54 *International Organisation* 421.

[5] G. Shaffer and M. Pollack, 'Hard and Soft Law' in J. Dunoff and M. Pollack (eds.), *Interdisciplinary Perspectives on International Law and International Relations* (Cambridge University Press, 2013).

[6] K. Culp Davis, *Discretionary Justice* (Westport: Greenwood Press, 1969).

[7] J. Mashaw, *Bureaucratic Justice: Managing Social Security Claims* (New Haven: Yale University Press, 1983).

[8] J. Jowell, 'The Legal Control of Administrative Discretion' [1973] *Public Law* 178.

and policy instructions, low down in the formal legal hierarchy but typically the first port-of-call for officials, commanded close attention.[9] Intimately bound-up with demands for entitlements to public provision, emphasis was duly placed on structuring, confining and checking the exercise of official discretion. The less pleasant areas of the extended post-war administrative State were a major target: policing of course, and then on through the seeming vagaries of, for example, social security administration and immigration control.[10]

In fact, some relevant themes had already been identified. Take the close interplay of hard law in general, and delegated legislation in the form of statutory instruments in particular, with suitably Weberian or internal hierarchical exercises of control through instruction, advice and guidance. While noting that classification depended on which definition of law is adopted, an issue which has duly morphed into never-ending theoretical dispute wherever the label 'soft law' appears,[11] the first English administrative law text of the post-war period made the practical importance of bureaucratic rules abundantly clear. As this determinedly functionalist account explained, both the control of administrative authorities and the ways in which they exercised their powers were 'very often … more a matter of administrative practice'. Readers should beware 'the fallacy of forcing a contrast between law and practice at the point where the two meet'.[12]

Then there is the typically *ad hoc* and piecemeal nature of the development in the UK constitution, which bears directly on this functional mix. As a means of promoting efficiency and consistency in the administrative process, while avoiding technical language, and also the elements of cost, delay and rigidity associated even with statutory instruments, particular soft law usages often have much to commend them. On the other hand, as

---

[9] R. Lister, *Justice for the Claimant: A Study of Supplementary Benefit Appeal Tribunals* (London: Child Poverty Action Group, 1974).

[10] See, e.g., C. Harlow and R. Rawlings, *Law and Administration* (London: Weidenfeld and Nicolson, 1984), chs. 16–19.

[11] Not least in its early terminological home: M. Goldmann, 'We need to cut off the head of the king: past, present and future approaches to international soft law' (2012) 25 *Leiden Journal of International Law* 335. See also R. Creyke and J. McMillan, 'Soft Law v Hard Law' in L. Pearson, C. Harlow and M. Taggart (eds.), *Administrative Law in a Changing State* (Oxford: Hart Publishing, 2008).

[12] J. A. G. Griffith and H. Street, *Principles of Administrative Law* (London: Pitman, 1952), 6. See further C. Harlow and R. Rawlings, 'Administrative Law in Context: Restoring a Lost Connection' [2014] *Public Law* 28.

the inter-war Donoughmore Committee on Ministers' Powers lamented, 'constitutional practice' on the making (or otherwise) of delegated legislation had 'grown up gradually ... without any logical system'.[13] Part of, and inevitably reflected in, the mass of paper circulating in government offices, this was the ragbag of rules, regulations, orders, etc.

Although historically blighted by wild claims of 'administrative lawlessness',[14] a healthy scepticism about executive practices with law-like effects has deep roots in the common law. Bureaucratic rules bearing on the relation of the State and the individual are apt to court controversy and, not least on a 'thin' version of the rule of law, rightly so. Seemingly beneficent administrative practices may be objectionable on grounds of preferential treatment and, depending in part on the extent to which the judicial review system is geared to protection of the individual, be more difficult to challenge. Such themes reached the august pages of the *Law Quarterly Review* some seventy years ago.[15] 'Administrative quasi-legislation' was the phrase coined to point up the significance of extra-statutory arrangements such as tax concessions. The analysis was more prescient than the author might have imagined in that age of the card index. On from a world largely bounded by statutes, statutory devices and case law, 'administrative quasi-legislation' was part of 'an expanding universe' confronting the legal practitioner.

Codes and circulars, policy notes and guidance, official notices and practice statements, etc. – succeeding decades would indeed witness 'an exponential growth' of quasi-legislation 'in a plethora of forms'. The term itself became part of the English public law vocabulary.[16] And the more that was seen, the more blurred things looked. Just as statutes might acquire an official gloss by policy statements, so it was realised that soft law could have varying degrees of legal force short of direct enforceability through judicial proceedings. Or, as might now be said, 'steering' the behaviour of others through means such as interpretative guidance, designating relevant criteria, and evidence of good practice, is all part of the

---

[13] *Report of the Committee on Ministers' Powers* (Cmnd 4050, 1932), 16.

[14] Lord Hewart, *The New Despotism* (London: Ernest Benn, 1929).

[15] R. Megarry, 'Administrative Quasi-legislation' (1944) 60 *Law Quarterly Review* 125. See also C. K. Allen, *Law and Orders: An Inquiry into the Nature and Scope of Delegated Legislation and Executive Powers in England* (London: Stevens, 1945).

[16] G. Ganz, *Quasi-Legislation: Recent Developments in Secondary Legislation* (London: Sweet and Maxwell, 1987), 1. See also R. Baldwin and B. Houghton, 'Circular Arguments: The Status and Legitimacy of Administrative Rules' [1986] *Public Law* 239.

practical effects. In this age of freedom of information and information and communications technology ('ICT'), however, it is hard to convey how much digging was required from public lawyers in a UK polity typified by official secrecy. A chief normative concern informing bottom-up approaches was the inaccessibility of much soft law material. In turn, reflecting concerns familiarly bound up in many constitutional systems with separation of powers, this underscored the lack of legislative – democratic – control. Perhaps hopefully, a dose of 'government in the sunshine' might not only broaden horizons but also serve as a valuable discipline.[17]

Fitting with a broad post-war consensus over the welfare state and mixed economy,[18] much was still heard of 'voluntarism'. Take central-local government relations, where the commendable notion that voluntary acceptance of rules is preferable to legal enforcement or justiciability held much sway.[19] As an instrument for co-operation and co-ordination in a burgeoning sector, 'government by circular' was something of a leitmotif of British public administration in the mid-twentieth century. Across the broad spectrum of persuasion and compulsion, things could hardly remain static, however. As epitomised by the rise of statutory codes of practice, in particular delivering different government policies in the workplace, a trend developed of harder-edged forms of quasi-legislation. Evidently, trust was in increasingly short supply.

A muted role for the courts in the constitution had also benefited the many architects of quasi-legislation. There was the occasional judicial grump or expression of puzzlement about circulars for example,[20] but for many years little more than that. The totemic case of *British Oxygen*[21] furthered the cause of bureaucratic rules by confirming that statutory discretion included discretion to make them as an expression of policy. Provided, then, the official mind was not entirely closed to exceptional circumstance, coherent and consistent guidance for dealing with multiple

---

[17] Notwithstanding the absence in the UK of an American-style Administrative Procedure Act; see W. West, 'Administrative Rule-making: An Old and Emerging Literature' (2005) 65 *Public Administration Review* 655.

[18] A. Shonfield, *Modern Capitalism* (Oxford: Oxford University Press, 1965).

[19] J. Griffith, *Central Departments and Local Authorities* (London: Allen and Unwin, 1966).

[20] See e.g. *Blackpool Corporation* v. *Locker* [1948] 1 KB 349 and *Patchett* v. *Leatham* (1949) 65 TLR 69.

[21] *British Oxygen Co Ltd* v. *Ministry of Technology* [1971] AC 610.

applications passed judicial muster. This was welcome recognition of the practical realities of modern administration.

Shake-up time

It is during the long years of Conservative government from 1979 that the now standard vocabulary of 'soft law' replaces that of 'quasi-legislation'. No doubt this reflects a growing internationalisation of public law;[22] and, more particularly, the burgeoning forces in this period of European integration. Rendered against the backdrop of a more globalised economy, and pointing up important means for aiding processes of convergence, the determinedly ductile term thus became standard currency in these related spheres in the 1980s.[23] Further, however, it could encompass wider usages associated with the fashion for New Public Management ('NPM') and the 'hollowing out of the state'[24] or passage of central government functions sideways to agencies and business as well as upwards to the EU. Surprising as it may sound, soft law then was an important component of the 'Thatcher Revolution'.

Take the flagship enterprise of sharpening policy performance by carving out executive bodies from monolithic central departments. Originally formulated in terms of 'Next Steps agencies', in the long view it constituted a standard twin-track methodology of formalising administrative arrangements and, by denying a separate statutory base, avoiding justiciability. Behind this lies the rise of 'pseudo-contract', which denotes the use in public administration of contract-type arrangements which are not true contracts in the legal sense of agreements enforceable in the courts.[25] Another example of soft law as a means of modelling institutional relations, it is the realm of published framework documents establishing mandate, budget, targets, etc. Nor could the constitutional significance

[22]   D. Feldman, 'The Internationalization of Public Law and its Impact on the UK' in J. Jowell, D. Oliver and C. O' Cinneide (eds.), *The Changing Constitution* (Oxford University Press, 2015), 8th edn.

[23]   C. Chinkin, 'The Challenge of Soft Law: Development and Change in International Law' (1989) 38 *International and Comparative Law Quarterly* 850; K. Wellens and G. Borchart, 'Soft Law in EC Law' (1989) 14 *European Law Review* 267.

[24]   R. Rhodes, 'The Hollowing Out of the State: The Changing Nature of the Public Service in Britain' (1994) 65 *Political Quarterly* 138.

[25]   C. Harlow and R. Rawlings, *Law and Administration* (Cambridge: Cambridge University Press, 2006), 2nd edn., ch. 8. See further A. Davies, *Accountability: A Public Law Analysis of Government by Contract* (Oxford: Oxford University Press, 2001).

be gainsaid, as some sharp controversy about ministerial accountability in relation to these arm's length bodies demonstrates.[26] Predictably, the issue rumbles on in light of the UK constitutional fundamental of parliamentary government; and the more so, in view of newly assertive parliamentary committees.[27]

Alternatively, take privatisation and the establishment of the 'Ofdogs', a new breed of statutory agencies effectively tasked with light-touch regulation and/or promotion of competition for the utilities. There is again a dual dynamic: not only the challenge to pre-existing informal means of 'club government' in vital sectors of the economy,[28] but also an attempt to avoid the disruptive potential of litigation, even perhaps American-style 'adversarial legalism', in the regulatory process.[29] Designed against the backdrop of a strengthening role for judicial review in the constitution, the statutory template was highly permissive in character: broad mandate and bare statutory requirements on which it was difficult to hang claims of unlawfulness. Conditions then were ripe for a vigorous growth of soft law through the exercise of agency discretion to make procedural rules; in particular, when Ofdogs sought to bolster regulatory legitimacy by trumpeting good governance values of transparency, participation and accountability.[30] Nonetheless, concerns about a lack of firm and consistent process and insufficient accountability especially to Parliament continued to dog this highly personalised model of small agencies headed by a Director-General.[31] Chief vehicle of a strong market ideology, it could not survive the more rounded quest for 'better regulation' eventually inaugurated under New Labour, which notably included clarification of key duties and heightened process requirements.[32]

---

[26] Hansard, HC, 19 March 1997, cols 1046–1047.

[27] See, e.g., House of Lords Constitution Committee, *The Accountability of Civil Servants* (HL 61, 2012–13).

[28] M. Moran, *The British Regulatory State: High Modernism and Hyper-Innovation* (Oxford: Oxford University Press, 2004).

[29] R. Rawlings, 'Changed Conditions, Old Truths: Judicial Review in a Regulatory Laboratory' in D. Oliver, T Prosser and R Rawlings (eds.), *The Regulatory State: Constitutional Implications* (Oxford: Oxford University Press, 2010).

[30] C. Foster, *Natural Justice and the Process of National Monopoly Regulation* (London: Centre for the Study of Regulated Industries, 1994).

[31] *Report of the Commission on the Regulation of Privatised Utilities* (London: Hansard Society, 1996).

[32] T. Prosser, 'The Powers and Accountability of Agencies and Regulators' in D. Feldman (ed.), *English Public Law* (Oxford: Oxford University Press, 2009), 2nd edn.

Soft law as a barometer of institutional relations is further illustrated in the Conservatives' dealings with local government. On from voluntarism: just as market disciplines should be unleashed, so competing sources of political power were to be reined in. Though the transformation of persuasive guidelines into statutory provision was hardly new, the 1980s clearly mark a step-change in this assertion of central control, concentrated around, but not confined to, compulsory competitive tendering and local government finance.[33] A not insignificant part of the story, however, concerns the capacity of soft law to regenerate in different forms. In the light of ever more elaborate 'hard law' intervention, interpretive guidance, advice, and best practice statements abounded, further serving in the hands of the Audit Commission as a major conduit for the bracing functional values of efficiency, economy and effectiveness through the sector.[34] The intimate connection with the evaluative paraphernalia of benchmarking, performance indicators and league tables, which so shaped public service provision in this period,[35] is made apparent.

At one with broader dynamics of 'juridification', the discernible tendency to formalise and encapsulate social relations in terms of law,[36] it is also in this period that 'tertiary rules' become familiar in the public law lexicon.[37] Once more highlighting the grey zone beyond the exercise of secondary legislative power conferred under statute or prerogative, the usage testifies to a still-expanding range of soft law techniques with 'the purpose or effect of influencing bureaucratic decision-making in non-trivial fashion'.[38] This particular development fits with the premium placed on NPM methodology, very dependent on rules for measuring, evaluating and controlling the work of subordinates.[39]

---

[33] M. Loughlin, *Local Government in the Modern State* (London: Sweet and Maxwell, 1986).

[34] M. Radford, 'Auditing for Change: Local Government and the Audit Commission' (1991) 54 *Modern Law Review* 912.

[35] M. Power, *The Audit Explosion* (London: Demos, 1994).

[36] G. Teubner, 'Juridification: Concepts, Aspects, Limits, Solutions' in G. Teubner (ed.), *Juridification of Social Spheres* (Berlin: de Gruyter, 1988).

[37] R. Baldwin, *Rules and Government* (Oxford: Clarendon Press, 1995). See also C. McCrudden, 'Codes in a Cold Climate' (1988) 51 *Modern Law Review* 409.

[38] L. Sossin and C. Smith, 'Hard Choices and Soft Law: Ethical Codes, Policy Guidelines and the Role of Courts in Regulating Government' (2003) 40 *Alberta Law Rev* 867, 871.

[39] C. Hood and C. Scott, 'Bureaucratic Regulation and New Public Management in the United Kingdom: Mirror-image Developments?' (1996) 23 *Journal of Law and Society* 321.

Given an additional boost by the harnessing of self-regulatory systems, most obviously in the professions,[40] the trend of agencification is again relevant. Tertiary rule-making would be closely associated with the burgeoning range of bodies exercising statutory – public – power. Standing for specialisation grounded in multiple sources of rule-making authority, the process is indicative not only of great variety, but also heralds a leitmotif of our contemporary, commonly fragmented and less bounded, system of governance: inter-institutional soft law in the form of all those Memorandums of Understanding ('MoUs').

Leading authorities in the process of widening and deepening the ambit of judicial review, a duo of famous cases sees the House of Lords chipping away at executive freedom of action. Faced with a preferential use of soft law technique in the *National Federation* case,[41] the court was prepared to accept that a discretionary tax concession challenged by third parties was reasonable and realistic. Liberalising standing to sue in accordance with the public interest in administrative legality also sent the message of no blank cheque. The *GCHQ* case[42] is twice relevant. A prime site for soft law technique, prerogative power would no longer constitute an entire judicial no-go area.[43] Boosted, the doctrine of legitimate expectation would give some usages of soft law a harder edge. Indeed, when subsequently extended to substantive expectations of service delivery,[44] it would prove particularly troublesome for public administration because of an inchoate jurisprudence.[45] The judicial contribution, however, must be kept in perspective. Amid the tough use of statutory provision, central-local relations duly became a 'litigation hot-spot'. On the other hand, illustrating that much in the broad constitutional development passed the courts by, 'judge-proofing' the new modalities of regulation proved highly successful.

---

[40] R. Baggott, 'Regulatory Reform in Britain: The Changing Face of Self-regulation' (1989) 67 *Public Administration* 436.

[41] *Inland Revenue Commissioners* v. *National Federation of Self-Employed and Small Businesses* [1982] AC 617.

[42] *Council of Civil Service Unions* v. *Minister for the Civil Service* [1985] AC 374.

[43] *R. (Bancoult)* v. *Secretary of State for Foreign Affairs* [2008] UKHL 61, [2009] 1 AC 453 benchmarks the subsequent development.

[44] *R.* v. *North and East Devon Health Authority ex parte Coughlan* [2001] QB 213.

[45] Though see now *R. (Patel)* v. *General Medical Council* [2013] EWCA Civ 327, [2013] 1 WLR 2801.

Speeding on

By the beginning of the century, visualisations of 'soft law' were becoming more and more stretched; the 'expanding universe' sometimes appeared to have no outer limit! One well-known account referred, for example, to 'rules, manuals, directives, codes, guidelines, memoranda, correspondence, circulars, protocols, bulletins, employee handbooks and training materials'.[46] Practical effects yes, but not all of this documentation is quasi-legislation as previously conceived. Future historians will surely fasten on the fundamental changes in public decision-making and service delivery brought about by the introduction of ICT and the evolution of e-governance. On again from 'tertiary rules', such is the dizzying era of 'fourth generation legislation' in the form of computer programs or all those algorithms, decision-trees and checklists increasingly used in mass administrative systems.[47] Multiplying the problems of democratic – let alone judicial – control, the very precision denotes hard-edged forms of soft law. Computers, after all, speak the language of rules.

The seemingly unstoppable rise in public law of 'risk regulation'[48] is another main driver. Such is the logic of a wide-ranging methodology predicated on setting regulatory standards via an assessment of risks of particular sectors and ordering regulatory activities by reference to the risks which particular operators pose to an agency's goals. For confirmation, one need only look at the burgeoning websites of powerful public institutions like the Environment Agency and the Health and Safety Executive. In the guise of information for stakeholders, these are replete with examples of soft law ranging, along one axis, from the highly prescriptive to the indicative and voluntary; and, along another axis, from internal operational advice to guidance for the regulated and the public. Behind this lies the worldwide quest for so-called 'better' and/or 'smart' regulation,[49] founded on principles of proportionality, consistency and targeting, and transparency and accountability. Sometimes legislatively

---

[46] Sossin and Smith (n. 38), 871.

[47] R. de Mulder, 'The Digital Revolution: From Trias to Tetras Politica' in I. Snellen and W. van de Donk (eds.), *Public Administration in an Information Age* (Amsterdam: IOS Press, 1998).

[48] E. Fisher, *Risk Regulation and Administrative Constitutionalism* (Oxford: Hart Publishing, 2007).

[49] R. Baldwin, M. Cave and M. Lodge, *Understanding Regulation: Theory, Strategy and Practice* (Oxford: Oxford University Press, 2012), 2nd edn.

mandated, more often, as in the case of the legislative process, administratively so, impact assessment has rapidly emerged as a chief analytical device in the UK.[50] This is the stuff of templates geared to more or less expansively defined costs and benefits, as well as input and output processes of consultation, monitoring and compliance. Glossing over the functional limitations of measurement, impact assessment thus stands for a (pseudo-)scientific pursuit of rational policy development – one which epitomises the strong enabling role of soft law technique in administrative procedure.

Building on the foundations laid in the Thatcher years, techniques of contractual governance are today so mainstreamed in UK public administration that they frequently go unremarked. All the more reason to point up the way in which, as a repository for rules, principles and standards, contract-style technique functions as a major source of regulation.[51] The recent Supreme Court case of *New London College*[52] is a useful touchstone, concerning as it does private provision of international educational services regulated by a system of licensing that mandates much regulatory activity by the market actor. Again sanctioning the widespread use of soft law forms, the Court rejected the argument that published guidelines setting out the requirements for the retention and grant of licences required express legislative authority. In adopting a broad view of the minister's ancillary and incidental powers, the majority fastened on her general statutory responsibility to administer the system of immigration control. Perhaps more worryingly in terms of effective judicial protection, the majority did not rule out the existence of substantial, residual, executive power analogous to the power of natural persons to do that which is not prohibited.[53]

In reworking the relation of State and individual in open-ended and horizontal fashion, the Human Rights Act 1998 and the Equality Act 2010 neatly illustrate the propensity of particular types of statutory provision

---

[50] As in many other countries: *Building an Institutional Framework for Regulatory Impact Analysis: Guidance for Policy Makers* (OECD, 2008).

[51] C. Harlow and R. Rawlings, *Law and Administration* (Cambridge University Press, 2009), 3rd edn., ch. 8. See further C. McCrudden, *Buying Social Justice* (Oxford: Oxford University Press, 2007).

[52] *R. (New London College Ltd)* v. *Secretary of State for the Home Department* [2013] UKSC 51, [2013] 1 WLR 2358.

[53] See House of Lords Constitution Committee, *The pre-emption of Parliament* (HL 165, 2012–13), ch. 3.

to foster large growths of soft law. Such is the never-ending struggle to 'mainstream' principles and values in the administrative process, as initially by a 'human rights task force' with special responsibility for producing core guidance for public bodies,[54] and subsequently through the 'guidance for all' made available on the website of the Equality and Human Rights Commission. It is also in the nature of the enterprise that wide-ranging public sector duties on eliminating discrimination and promoting equality of opportunity give a particular push to bureaucratic rule-making. Conversely, we see how soft law technique takes on additional (political) salience as a means of combatting (concerns about) mistaken compliance: so-called 'myth-busting advice' on how rights should be balanced.[55]

Reflecting the great contemporary demand for transparency, and hence for writing things down, a further dynamic sees soft law technique gaining in prominence in terms of conventions and the place of the Executive in the constitution. First published in the 1990s, the UK Government Ministerial Code is a textbook example of soft law as a medium for constitutional continuity and change. Buttressing and elaborating conventions through an informal process of codification is of the essence of the enterprise.[56] At one and the same time, the ground rules of ministerial responsibility in the Westminster system are rendered more specific and detailed; and, with optional assistance from an independent adviser, the Prime Minister's position as 'ultimate judge' of ministerial behaviour is reasserted.[57] 'A guide to laws, conventions and rules on the operation of government', finalised in 2011, the UK Government Cabinet Manual suitably illustrates the often intricate interplay between different types of legal, political and administrative instruments in the constitution.[58] Highlighted by a controversial attempt to declare a convention on government formation, the Manual also serves to demonstrate the innate insider – Executive – advantages of soft law technique (and hence the particular importance

---

[54] Human Rights Task Force, *A New Era of Rights and Responsibilities: Core Guidance for Public Authorities* (London: Home Office, 2000).

[55] *Guidance on the Human Rights Act for Criminal Justice System Practitioners* (London: Ministry of Justice, 2007).

[56] N. Barber, 'Laws and Constitutional Conventions' (2009) 125 *Law Quarterly Review* 294. See further, D. Feldman, 'Constitutional Conventions' in M. Qvortrup (ed.), *The British Constitution: Continuity and Change* (Oxford: Hart Publishing, 2013).

[57] *Ministerial Code* (London: UK Cabinet Office, 2010), para. 1.

[58] *Cabinet Manual* (London: UK Cabinet Office, 2011).

of public consultation).[59] In seeking to provide an authoritative but necessarily brief sketch of the complex business of government, it further points up both the force and the descriptive limitations of soft law writing.

We are living through a crisis of trust, or so it is said.[60] Once more demonstrating the innate capacity of soft law technique for multi-tasking, one of the more attractive features of the contemporary constitutional landscape is the spread across the public sector of clearly articulated codes of behaviour – ethics – designed both to buttress institutional legitimacy and give public accountability a sharper cutting-edge. As one might expect, much in the development is events-driven, as notoriously in the case of parliamentarians. Key elements include the fact of multiple sources, older-established bodies like the Parliamentary Ombudsman,[61] as well as specially created ones such as the Committee on Standards in Public Life;[62] the mutually supportive use of overarching principles of objectivity, impartiality, integrity and honesty; and the evident scope for statutory underpinning as latterly in the case of the Civil Service.[63] If it goes too far to speak, as one leading commentator does, of a politics-free dimension to the Constitution,[64] this characteristically earnest development well illustrates the pioneering and colonising attributes of soft law technique.

Overshadowing everything in the UK constitution today is the troubled state of the Union. An 'Edinburgh Agreement'[65] positing a possible break-up was hardly what the architects of the 1998 'devolution settlement' had in mind. Against this backdrop, the heavy premium placed on soft law in intergovernmental relations is all the more noteworthy. Further illustrating how particular usages take on a new importance in changing constitutional and political climes, devolution to Scotland, Wales and Northern Ireland thus spawned another major species of 'pseudo-contract', so-called 'concordatry'.[66] In a typically pragmatic approach to

[59] House of Lords Constitution Committee, *The Cabinet Manual* (HL 107, 2010–11), ch. 3. See also A. McHarg, 'Reforming the United Kingdom Constitution: Law, Convention, Soft Law' (2008) 71 *Modern Law Review* 853.

[60] O. O'Neill, *A Question of Trust* (Cambridge University Press, 2002).

[61] Parliamentary and Health Service Ombudsman, *Principles of Good Administration* (2007).

[62] Committee for Standards in Public Life, *Seven Principles of Public Life* (Cmnd. 2850, 1995).

[63] Constitutional Reform and Governance Act 2010, ch. 1.

[64] D. Oliver, 'The Politics-Free Dimension to the UK Constitution' in Qvortrup (n. 56).

[65] *Agreement between the United Kingdom Government and the Scottish Government on an Independence Referendum for Scotland* (October 2012); and see A. Tomkins, 'Scotland's Choice, Britain's Future' (2014) 130 *Law Quarterly Review* 215.

[66] R. Rawlings, 'Concordats of the Constitution' (2000) 116 *Law Quarterly Review* 257.

constitutional development, the demand to maintain good working relationships finds expression in myriad documentation on principles, structures and processes. There is even a hierarchy of sorts: the principal MoU on basic desiderata of co-operation, consultation, co-ordination and respect for confidentiality and on essential political machinery (the Joint Ministerial Committee);[67] overarching concordats with large multilateral elements, most notably on EU policy co-ordination; and bilateral concordats between individual UK departments and their counterparts centred on functional policy issues. *Ad hoc* and piecemeal development, lack of transparency, organisational skews in favour of the UK Government: major concerns originally raised continue to be voiced.[68] Looking forward, the hard-fought campaign and eventual 'no' vote in the Scottish independence referendum heralds looser forms of Union and greater complexity of relationships, coupled with increased pressure forinstitutional adaptation at UK level, as more is devolved to the Celtic lands and, indeed, inside England.[69] Previously a low-lying feature in the UK constitutional landscape, but so familiar in many federal-type systems, the machinery of intergovernmental relations is destined in turn to take on greater significance.[70] Running alongside reworked legal frameworks of powers, new soft law instruments of intergovernmental co-operation are very much part of the future of this cluttered Isle. And, one is tempted to add in the light of so much international experience, in other forms again if the Union does not endure.

EU governance

The EU abounds in soft law instruments, ranging from declarations attached to treaties and high-level inter-institutional agreements to

---

[67] *Memorandum of Understanding and Supplementary Agreements Between the United Kingdom Government, the Scottish Ministers, the Welsh Ministers, and the Northern Ireland Executive Committee* (current version, October 2013). For the original version, see Cm. 4444, 1999.

[68] House of Lords Constitution Committee, *Inter-governmental relations in the United Kingdom* HL 146(2014–15).

[69] R. Rawlings, 'A Coalition Government in Westminister' in J. Jowell, D. Oliver, and C. O'Cinneide (eds.), *The Changing Constitution* (Oxford: Oxford University Press, 2015), 8th edn. See further, House of Commons Political and Constitutional Reform Committee, *The fututre of devolution after the Scottish referendum* HC 700 (2014–15).

[70] Institute for Government, *Governing in an Ever Looser Union* (2015).

influential Commission recommendations and opinions, and on through to the much 'softer' mass of internal guidelines and instructions. In fact many of the purposes remind one of national as well as international practice: hierarchical control of a bureaucracy, policy recommendations or guidelines, codes of practice for multiple actors, etc.[71] Changing patterns again command attention as particular usages are accentuated in different domains and, referencing the expanded competence, in the EU context at large.[72] Special mention must be made of attempts at the turn of the century to revivify the European project, associated with the Commission's famous White Paper on European Governance.[73] Representing a boost for soft law technique, much would be heard of an equally flexible rubric, 'new governance method', and hence the potential for ranging beyond an official 'Community method' premised on formal legislative procedures and institutional balance.[74]

The way in which soft law is shaped by situation is powerfully illustrated in the case of EU administration, which is to an unusual degree fragmented, not least in the light of Enlargement. A heavy premium is placed on so-called 'network governance'; committees to represent Member States, more or less informal arrangements of regulatory bodies and experts, and increasingly EU agencies, clutter the landscape. While apparent in all kinds of constitutional systems, the demand for effective means of communication, co-operation and co-ordination is magnified. Another luxuriant growth of soft law technique is identified, with, as a natural habitat, myriad forms of administrative procedure.[75] Again, there is no better example than the EU of the role of institutional politics. Take the question of hard law consultation requirements; transparently keen to impose them on Member States, the Commission unsurprisingly insists on the grave disadvantages of 'an overly-legalistic approach' in respect of its own procedures.[76]

---

[71] P. Craig, *EU Administrative Law* (Oxford University Press, 2011), 2nd edn., part 1.

[72] F. Terpon, 'Soft Law in the European Union-The Changing Nature of EU Law' (2015) *European Law Journal* 68.

[73] COM(2001) 428 final.

[74] J. Scott and D. Trubek (eds.), 'Law and New Approaches to Governance in Europe' (2002) 8 *European Law Journal* special issue.

[75] C. Harlow and R. Rawlings, *Process and Procedure in EU Administration* (Oxford: Hart Publishing, 2014).

[76] European Commission, *Towards a Reinforced Culture of Consultation and Dialogue*, COM(2002) 704 final, 10.

Duly pressed by the European Parliament,[77] the further question arises of introducing some kind of European Law of Administrative Procedure at Union level. Whether by way of compromise the Commission is tempted to accept a systematised set of 'Model Rules'[78] remains to be seen.

Normative debate over the uses and abuses of soft law technique has been particularly sharp in the EU context, and understandably so.[79] From the standpoint of the Commission, historically determinedly integrationist, soft governance forms hold out the prospect of avoiding legislative procedures it does not control, of pressing forward in areas of joint or limited competence, and, via procedural convergence and all that dissemination of best practice, working towards stronger forms of harmonisation. Conversely, for critics of the enterprise, there are clear and present dangers of disguised EU expansionism, coupled with major problems of democratic scrutiny, more especially for national parliaments. Then again, for those of us concerned to promote the values of pluralism and diversity in the European construction, soft law technique continues to offer solid advantages in terms of innate respect for difference in and among the Member States.

The Open Method of Coordination ('OMC') commands attention as a flagship of decentralised process. Officially hailed as 'a means of spreading best practice and achieving greater convergence towards the main EU goals', more particularly economic growth and social progress, OMC involves techniques familiar from NPM: benchmarks and performance indicators for the Member States, backed up with periodic monitoring, evaluation and peer review designed as mutual learning processes.[80] General objectives and guidelines for policy development and implementation underwrite this. As a way of 'learning by doing', and paying due respect to the principle of subsidiarity, OMC has much to commend it. Conversely, concerns about efficacy or practical results, as well as limited

---

[77] European Parliament Resolution of 15 January 2013 with recommendations to the Commission on a Law of Administrative Procedure of the EU.

[78] H. Hofmann *et al* (eds.), *Model Rules on EU Administrative Procedure* (Research Network on EU Administrative Law (ReNEUAL), 2014).

[79] For a sense of the wider discussion, see successively, T. Christiansen and S. Piattoni, (eds.), *Informal Governance in the European Union* (Cheltenham: Edward Elgar, 2003); and T. Christiansen and C. Neuhold (eds.), *International Handbook on Informal Governance* (Cheltenham: Edward Elgar, 2012).

[80] Lisbon European Council, Presidency Conclusions, 23–24 March 2000; and see E. Barcevičius, J. Weishaupt and J. Zeitlin (eds.), *Assessing the Open Method of Coordination* (Basingstoke: Palgrave Macmillan, 2014).

involvement by the Parliament and restricted participation by sub-state and non-state actors, are par for the course.[81]

Other important elements are highlighted here. The weak adjective cannot disguise the potentials for soft law with 'sticks' and 'carrots', for example through 'naming and shaming', or, more tangibly, financial resources. Beyond *imperium* or the formal command of law, we touch here on the great power of *dominium*: the deployment – or otherwise – of wealth in aid of policy objectives. Then there is the manifold scope for hybrids or mixes of forms: as, simply, when making guidelines is mandated. OMC has taken soft forms of governance to new heights; treaty articles and sector-specific legislation helped to provide a framework.[82] Not before time, EU literature increasingly emphasises the complementarity of 'new' modes of soft governance and formal legal methods.[83]

Major EU regulatory frameworks serve to illustrate significant soft law contributions. A thoroughgoing reform of competition procedures sees national bodies like the UK's new Competition and Markets Authority actively engaged in enforcement of EU rules, while the Commission concentrates on big cases. While naturally providing powers, procedures and sanctions, the governing legislation[84] cedes space to the European Competition Network ('ECN'). Stretching across Union and Member State levels,[85] and designed for efficient case allocation and exchange of information and evidence, this grouping of enforcement bodies is increasingly seen taking on policy issues and generally promoting a common competition culture. Operating through countless meetings and a secure intranet and database, it is grounded in a Commission notice; the ECN has no formal legal personality. Evaluation is typically mixed: high scores for efficiency and effectiveness; good governance concerns over lack of transparency and external accountability. In *France Telecom*,[86] the General Court resisted the temptation to interfere in internal workings. In establishing

---

[81] A Harcourt, 'Participatory Gains and Policy Effectiveness' (2013) 51 *Journal of Common Market Studies* 667.

[82] D. Trubek and L. Trubek, 'Hard and Soft Law in the Construction of Social Europe: The Role of the Open Method of Coordination' (2005) 11 *European Law Journal* 343.

[83] M. Dawson, 'Three Waves of New Governance in the European Union' (2011) 36 *European Law Review* 208.

[84] Council Regulation 1/2003/EC on the Implementation of the Rules on Competition OJ L 1 (04.01.03).

[85] D. Gerardin, 'Public Enforcement: The ECN' in I. Lianos and D. Gerardin (eds.), *Handbook on European Competition Law*, vol. II (Cheltenham: Edward Elgar, 2013).

[86] Case T-339/04, *France Telecom* v. *Commission* [2007] ECR II-521.

the criteria for case allocation, the notice properly excluded individual rights to have a particular national authority investigate.

Multiplying soft law guidance[87] is the natural concomitant of reform prioritising self-assessment, a feature underscored by the demand to explain the economic analysis now critical in competition enforcement. As against the adversarial legalism familiarly associated with antitrust, the Commission rightly prizes the potential of informal rules to 'enhance the efficiency of investigations and ensure a high degree of transparency and predictability'.[88] Procedural soft law has both innovative and defensive roles to play in a regulatory domain long associated with 'rights of the defence' in a jurisprudence now extending to the EU Charter of Fundamental Rights. Echoing and commonly expanding on the formal legal protection, Commission best practice has burgeoned, together with more in-house checks for testing proposed enforcement action.[89] In the leading case of *Schindler*,[90] the Court of Justice sensibly rejected a challenge to the Commission's fining guidelines, which structure the exercise of discretion through mathematical formulae geared to the gravity and duration of infringements. The Regulation provided the legal basis for sanctions; no Treaty provision prohibits an institution from adopting such 'rules of practice'. Nor, in view of the dose of clarity, was the fact of broad discretion inconsistent with the rule of law.

Alternatively, take the recent drive for 'Banking Union', the realm of the much-vaunted single supervisory mechanism ('SSM'), a complex set of institutional arrangements centred on the Eurozone. The European Central Bank ('ECB') has dual responsibility for supervising big banks and for the general health of the system, while national authorities supervise other institutions.[91] Testimony to the level of political concern, the governing legislation[92] is full of provision in favour of co-ordination and

---

[87] See further O. Stefan, *Soft Law in Court. Competition Law, State Aid and the Court of Justice of the European Union* (Dordrecht: Kluwer, 2013).

[88] European Commission, Best Practices for the Conduct of Proceedings Concerning Articles 101 and 102 TFEU C 308/06 (2011), [1].

[89] Harlow and Rawlings (n. 75), ch. 8.

[90] Case C-501/11, *Schindler Holding and Others* v. *Commission* (Judgment of 18 July 2013).

[91] E. Ferran, 'The European Single Supervisory Mechanism' (2013) 13 *Journal of Corporate Law Studies* 255.

[92] Regulation 1024/2013 conferring specific tasks on the European Central Bank relating to prudential supervision OJ L 287/63 (29 October 2013).

co-operation across the tiers; thick procedural forms of soft law will follow on naturally. Two usages stand out, however. The key constitutional issue of the ECB's accountability to the European Parliament for its new role is classic territory for an inter-institutional agreement.[93] Cast in terms of competing demands for confidentiality and transparency, it is certain to be tested. The UK, meanwhile, enjoying the biggest share of EU financial services business through the City of London, famously shows no intention of joining the Eurozone/SSM. Close co-operation between the ECB and the Bank of England will be vital for effective prudential supervision in the Single Market. Denoting the inconvenient truth of a dual supervisory system, this involve on MoUs.[94]

Conclusion

Enough has been said to show why public lawyers, or at least those interested in the real world of public power, should take soft law seriously. At one level, the day-to-day functioning of the constitutional and administrative law system can only properly be understood with reference to the broader mass of soft law usages. Notably, the scale and continuing importance of the soft law contribution in the UK gives the lie to the monochrome view of change from, in the language of that most familiar contemporary debate,[95] a 'political' to a 'legal' constitution. At another level, soft law technique can so easily put in issue good governance principles: the classic trio of transparency, participation, and accountability. This is especially troubling when, as is frequently the case with European integration, it is used in determinedly instrumentalist fashion. Self-serving usages by particular groups of actors or institutions, however, should not obscure major attributes of flexibility and responsiveness, institutional efficiency, and accommodation of difference. Context is by no means everything, but in the case of soft law it goes a long way! At another level again, soft law technique is a useful prism through which to

---

[93] European Parliament and ECB, Inter-Institutional Agreement on the cooperation on procedures related to the SSM (2013).

[94] Regulation 1024/2013, Art. 3; see further, Harlow and Rawlings (n. 75), ch. 11.

[95] G. Gee and G. Webber, 'What is a Political Constitution?' (2010) 30 *Oxford J Legal Studies* 273.

view the uses and – yes – functional limitations of standard hard law techniques. Amid the rich complexities of contemporary society, it is not only the efficacy of soft law methodology which is in issue.

While it does not do to ignore differences from directly enforceable legal rules, both in terms of legitimacy and practical effect, the many different forms of hard(er) and soft(er) law must not be overly compartmentalised. A recurring theme of the chapter is the scope for creative mixes of technique, sometimes as a functional necessity and on other occasions as part of a sophisticated governance framework or direction of travel. Soft law forms may now be said to demonstrate a strong kaleidoscopic quality: complex, dynamic, variegated. Ranging beyond the indelible association with internal administrative rules as part of the lifeblood of bureaucracy, a long but sometimes thin strand of public law scholarship has rightly engaged with external usages and effects, not least in terms of the challenges for traditional constitutional means of legislative and judicial control. Expanding on this, another key message of the chapter is the place of soft law as a chief vehicle for, and measure of, the changing relations of citizens with public authority, the burgeoning elements of regulatory and technocratic power, and the successive constructions of inter-institutional relations.

A major set of contemporary drivers for soft law technique is identified. As regards formal legal and regulatory usages, for example, specific factors include both the style and substance of legislation and recent fashions in 'better' or 'smart' regulation and audit. In somewhat paradoxical fashion, the evident demand to bolster transparency and public trust also sees soft law technique increasingly applied. Partly it is a matter of supply, where the digital revolution opens up whole new lines of soft law development. Constitutionally speaking, however, it is the twin drivers of devolution and European integration which command attention, as also diverse forms of agencification. In the form especially of pseudo-contract, soft law usages are shown taking on another lease of life in the cause of co-operation, co-ordination etc. Indeed, when viewed in historical perspective, the broad dynamics of soft law development show little sign of slackening: quite the reverse. It is the multiple capacities for regeneration, reinvention and reproduction displayed in different periods and policy contexts which shine through. Soft law always has tomorrow.

Further reading

R. Baldwin, *Rules and Government* (Oxford: Clarendon Press, 1995)

C. Chinkin, 'The Challenge of Soft Law: Development and Change in International Law' (1989) 38 *International and Comparative Law Quarterly* 850

R. Creyke and J. McMillan, 'Soft law v hard law' in L. Pearson, C. Harlow and M. Taggart (eds.), *Administrative Law in a Changing State* (Oxford: Hart Publishing, 2008)

G. Ganz, *Quasi-Legislation: Recent Developments in Secondary Legislation* (London: Sweet and Maxwell, 1987)

R. Rawlings, 'Concordats of the Constitution' (2000) 116 *Law Quarterly Review* 257

L. Sossin and C. Smith, 'Hard Choices and Soft Law: Ethical Codes, Policy Guidelines and the Role of Courts in Regulating Government' (2003) 40 *Alberta Law Review* 867

F. Terpan, 'Soft Law in the European Union-The Changing Nature of the European Union' (2015) 21 *European Law Journal* 68

D. Trubek and L. Trubek, 'Hard and Soft Law in the Construction of Social Europe: The Role of the Open Method of Coordination' (2005) 11 *European Law Journal* 343

12 The impact of public law litigation

Maurice Sunkin*

It is widely said that judicial review is a principal means for giving practical effect to the rule of law in the United Kingdom. In order to understand judicial review's contribution to the rule of law, however, we need to know something about the practical effects of judicial review itself. How do public authorities respond to legal challenges and react to judicial review more generally? What do those who bring judicial review proceedings achieve by doing so? This chapter considers the current state of knowledge on these matters and reflects on what this reveals about judicial review's contribution to the practical application of the rule of law in the UK.

The chapter is not directly concerned with the broader impacts of judicial review on social or policy change, or with exploring executive or parliamentary reactions to judicial review, important and interesting as these matters are.[1] Nonetheless, it is worth noting that the growth in the importance of judicial review is a notable feature of the recent history of public law. It has been said to amount 'to a major change in Britain's constitutional structure, a major rebalancing of its constitution';[2] and to have caused 'war' between government and the judges.[3] Such tensions have also fuelled significant debate amongst academic commentators, in particular between the legal constitutionalists who broadly

* I would like to thank Varda Bondy for reading and commenting on an earlier version of this chapter. Varda has been a co-researcher on several of the research projects which are discussed in the chapter. I also thank Christopher Luff, the Senior Research Officer in the Nuffield-funded research on the value and effect of judicial review which is referred to; and David Howarth and David Feldman for their helpful suggestions and comments.

[1] See J. King, *Judging Social Rights* (Cambridge: Cambridge University Press, 2012), ch. 3.

[2] A. King, *The British Constitution* (Oxford: Oxford University Press, 2007), 127.

[3] King (n. 2), 141. King cites the following comment of the Rt. Hon. David Blunkett MP, made as Home Secretary: 'Frankly, I'm personally fed up with having to deal with a situation where parliament debates issues and the judges then overturn them.' (BBC Radio 4, *World at One*, 20 February 2003.)

applaud the growing importance of judicial review[4] and the political constitutionalists who fear a dangerous shift of power to the courts and away from systems of political accountability rooted in Parliament.[5]

Seen from the perspective of judicial review's ability to control government, the change is famously reflected by two contrasting statements in earlier editions of what is now *De Smith's Judicial Review*. Until the fourth edition (published in 1980), judicial review was said to provide:

just one of a number of legal controls of administrative action and its role is inevitably sporadic and peripheral.[6]

In the fifth edition (published in 1995) a rather different observation was added:

[T]he effect of judicial review on the practical exercise of power has now become constant and central.[7]

There are a number of accounts of the practical implications of these developments for the way government was conducted during the final decades of the twentieth century.[8] Writing in the early 1990s Andrew Le Sueur and I observed, for example, that within central government the approach to judicial review had changed from being essentially reactive (in which government responded to individual challenges as and when they were made) to being more proactive and systemic, as government sought to improve its ability to respond to the prospect of legal challenge.[9] These

---

[4] See, e.g., J. Jowell, 'Beyond the Rule of Law: Towards Constitutional Judicial Review' [2000] *Public Law* 671; J. Jowell, 'Parliamentary Sovereignty under the New Constitutional Hypothesis' [2006] *Public Law* 562.

[5] J. A. G. Griffith, 'The Political Constitution' (1979) 42 *Modern Law Review* 1; A. Tomkins, *Our Republican Constitution* (Oxford: Hart Publishing, 2005); R. Bellamy, *Political Constitutionalism: A Republican Defence of the Constitutionality of Democracy* (Cambridge: Cambridge University Press, 2007).

[6] S. de Smith (ed. J. Evans), *De Smith's Judicial Review of Administrative Action* (London: Sweet and Maxwell, 1980), 4th edn., 3.

[7] S. de Smith, H. Woolf and J. Jowell, *Judicial Review of Administrative Action* (London: Sweet and Maxwell, 1995), 5th edn., vii.

[8] E.g. M. Kerry, 'Administrative Law and Judicial Review: The Practical Effects of Development over the Last Twenty-five Years on Administration in Central Government' (1986) 64 *Public Administration* 163; S. James, 'The Political Impact of Judicial Review' (1996) 74 *Public Administration* 613. Cf. D. Feldman, 'Judicial Review: A Way of Controlling Government?' (1988) 66 *Public Administration* 21.

[9] A. Le Sueur and M. Sunkin, 'Can Government Control Judicial Review?' (1991) 44 *Current Legal Problems* 161.

changes included such things as improving awareness of judicial review amongst officials, for instance by circulating the *Judge Over Your Shoulder*,[10] and involving lawyers at an earlier stage in decision-making. This, we suggested, involved a shift from 'risk assumption' to 'risk taking', by which we meant a change from making decisions largely unaware of the risks of challenge to a situation where ministers and officials were able to assess whether the risks of legal challenge were worth running.[11] It also involved the government aspiring to a more strategic approach to judicial review in order to try to shape the law. In the late 1990s, Terence Daintith and Alan Page commented that:

> [D]espite its almost daily appearance in court, central government has not in the past had anything that could be called a litigation strategy – a broad view of what it wanted to get out of fighting judicial review applications ... there is yet no obvious sign that the executive consciously seeks to choose the *best* cases to fight; to develop lines of argument which ... [might] ... make it easier to for the executive to cope with judicial review.[12]

Responding to the spirit of this observation, if not to the observation itself, Lord Goldsmith, when Attorney General, called upon government lawyers to do precisely what Daintith and Page said was not being done. For example, he said that government lawyers needed to take a more co-ordinated and strategic approach when arguing for the merits of judicial deference in public law and in human rights matters. Significantly in the context of this chapter, he also stressed that in making such arguments it is 'absolutely crucial' that government take an evidence-based approach: 'evidence is essential to bring to the court the complexity of the policy background, and the ramifications of unsettling policy decisions'.[13] In other words, he argued for the importance of knowing about the effects of judicial review decisions. Whether Goldsmith's calls for an

---

[10] Government Legal Service and Treasury Solicitor's Department, *The Judge Over Your Shoulder* (London, 2006), 4th edn.

[11] Even Margaret Thatcher was on occasion deterred from pursuing policies by the perceived threat of judicial review. She records how she was deterred from capping local authority budgets by the fear of judicial review: M. Thatcher, *The Downing Street Years* (London: HarperCollins, 1993), 665.

[12] T. Daintith and A. Page, *The Executive in the Constitution* (Oxford: Oxford University Press, 1999), 347.

[13] Lord Goldsmith, 'New Constitutional Boundaries' (paper delivered to the Government Legal Service Conference on Current Developments in Administrative Law, 22 March 2002, p. 15).

evidence-based approach were effective is unclear. Certainly, recent criticism of the government for lacking an evidence base for their reforms of judicial review suggest that government has yet to fully engage with the need for an evidence-based approach to reform, and one suspects the same may be true in relation to the effects of judicial review litigation.[14]

The issues in the above paragraphs go the heart of the constitutional system and the relationship between the courts, the executive and Parliament. They are clearly important to the potential relevance of the rule of law in high-level policy making; but what, if any, relevance do they have for matters which more immediately concern ordinary people in their everyday lives? For example, how, if at all, does judicial review touch 'street level' or routine decision-taking by officials working in local housing authorities dealing with homelessness cases or in social service departments or officials dealing with social welfare claims?

Judicial review and routine official decision-making

Several studies have examined the impacts of judicial review on routine official decision-making in housing and various aspects of the social security system.[15] Given the vast volume of routine decisions taken by street level officials and their importance to those affected, it is clearly valuable to know whether, and if so how, officials are influenced in their daily work by the requirements of, and principles and values enshrined in, judicial review. This, after all, would indicate whether the rule of law has practical effect at the point where people are likely to have most contact with government.

Much of the work of street-level officials is undertaken in accordance with internal guidance and they may be expected to meet efficiency as well as quality targets. Moreover, when decisions are questioned the matter is much more likely to be dealt with by internal reviews or appeals to the tribunal system. If judicial review is used, normally this will only be as a

---

[14] See especially the conclusions of the Joint Committee on Human Rights, *The implications for access to justice of the Government's proposals to reform judicial review* (HL 174, HC 868, 2013–14).

[15] For a survey of the research, see G. Richardson, 'Impact Studies in the United Kindgom' in M. Hertogh and S. Halliday (eds.), *Judicial Review and Bureaucratic Impact: International and Interdisciplinary Perspectives* (Cambridge: Cambridge University Press, 2004).

last resort when all other opportunities to question decisions have failed. All this means that few officials are likely to have more than occasional, if any, direct contact with judicial review itself. And if one of their decisions is challenged, it is likely that the matter would be dealt with at a managerial level with the involvement of lawyers. Judicial review, then, is likely to be a rather distant consideration for street-level decision-makers, even if they are required to adopt processes which lawyers would recognise as being rooted in judicial review concepts, such as the need to act fairly and to provide reasoned decisions.

It is therefore perhaps unsurprising that the prevailing message of much of the research on the impact of judicial review on public administration points to judicial review's 'limited ability ... to influence administrative decision-making'.[16] The findings appear to suggest, as Richardson puts it, 'that there is nothing particularly significant about judicial review; it is likely to be simply one of a number of factors' influencing decision makers'.[17]

Moreover, work on routine decision-making has found that where judicial review does exert an influence, this tends to be negative in various ways. For example, based on his work on local housing authority decision-making in the context of homelessness, Halliday suggests that increased exposure to judicial review reduces the extent to which organisations scrutinise themselves – and that, when such scrutiny is undertaken, it does not 'reflect the values of judicial review'.[18] Loveland's research, also on homelessness, similarly found that moves on the part of local authorities to comply with legal requirements were essentially defensive, being designed 'to safeguard decisions from legal challenge, not to improve routine decision-making in any real sense'.[19] Richardson comments that such findings illustrate 'the relatively low priority which can be given to juridical norms in the context of bureaucratic decision-making'.[20]

Not all research findings, however, are this negative and Jeff King draws attention to research which paints a 'rosier picture'. He argues that work of the type referred to above is limited in several respects. In particular, he

---

[16] Richardson (n. 15), 112.   [17] Richardson (n. 15), 114–15.

[18] S. Halliday 'The Influence of Judicial Review on Bureaucratic Decision-making' [2000] *Public Law* 110.

[19] Richardson (n. 15), 114, citing I. D. Loveland, *Housing Homeless Persons: Administrative Law and Administrative Process* (Oxford: Clarendon Press, 1995), ch. 11.

[20] Richardson (n. 15), 114.

says that research on routine decision-making in areas such as home-lessness 'might not be representative of the administrative justice field as a whole'. He also doubts 'whether these studies ... take adequate note of how practitioners themselves view the role of law', noting that the studies 'do not for the most part consider the value of individual redress'. Finally, he comments that the work is predominantly qualitative in nature and that in the absence of 'more quantitative data it is difficult to draw any conclusions about whether judicial review and legal accountability are marginal'.[21]

Judicial review and the quality of local government services

Certainly there is evidence indicating that beyond routine decision-making judicial review is capable of influencing public bodies in ways that are more mixed and potentially more positive. For example, a recent major Economic and Social Research Council ('ESRC') study used qualitative and quantitative techniques to examine the impact of judicial review on the quality of local government in England and Wales.[22]

The qualitative dimension included case studies based on judicial review decisions that were identified by officials as having had significant impacts on local authorities. The research examined why these cases were considered to be so important and how they impacted on local authorities. It is worth noting that the cases identified by the officials were identified precisely because they were not typical or routine. Nor were they well known as legal landmarks, reminding us that practical impact is not necessarily associated with legal notoriety. Two of the cases may be used to illustrate some of the issues revealed by this aspect of the research.

The Behre case

In *Behre*,[23] the London Borough of Hillingdon was held to have mistaken the scope of its duties to former unaccompanied asylum-seeking children

---

[21] King (n. 1), 70–76.

[22] L. Platt, M. Sunkin and K. Calvo, 'Judicial Review Litigation as an Incentive to Change in Local Authority Services in England and Wales' (2010) 20 *Journal of Public Administration Research and Theory* i243.

[23] *R. (Behre)* v. *Hillingdon London Borough Council* [2003] EWHC 2075, [2004] 1 FLR 439.

who had been 'looked after' by the local authority. Hillingdon had argued that its duty to the children was limited to providing general support to those in need under s. 17 of the Children Act 1989 and did not extend to having to provide accommodation or aftercare services. The court found against Hillingdon, holding that the authority had a duty to continue to provide aftercare services, including accommodation, until the claimants were 21 years old, or beyond if they stayed in full-time education.

At one level this was a straightforward case. As a result of the judgment the authority now knew both that it had not been doing what it should, and what the law required. In this sense, while critical of Hillingdon, the judgment clarified the law and had operational benefits for the authority, particularly for those officials directly responsible for making decisions affecting the claimants and others in their position. As one lawyer who advised the authority put it:

Certainly ... the people who were consulting me ... didn't see it as a big problem, they saw it as: 'right we're clear about that'.

Another interviewee in children's services echoed this:

[I]t's clarity. We know what our responsibilities are, we know how we're supposed to deal with these things.

Officials often identify the provision of clarity about the law as one of the positive consequences of litigation, including where clarity is provided by judgments which are decided against them.

However, while clarification of the law was helpful to the 'street level' officials, the decision was unhelpful to those higher in the system with responsibility for making decisions about budgets and resource allocation. The real issue was that the judgment challenged Hillingdon's decision to use its resources in the way it considered necessary. Hillingdon had taken a view about how its scarce resources should be used and the judgment now required it to change its approach. The problem was that funding to deliver the relevant services came from central government, and Hillingdon, like other authorities, believed that it had insufficient funds to meet the additional duties which the judgment said had to be met.[24] Hillingdon was not the only authority affected by the judgment. Despite the possibility of

---

[24] E. Free, *Local Authority Support to Unaccompanied Asylum-seeking Young People: Changes since the Hillingdon Judgment* (London: Save the Children, 2005); Refugee Council, *Ringing the Changes: The impact of guidance on the use of Sections 17 and 20 of*

being challenged, some authorities seem to have refused to implement the judgment, while others did so in purely formal terms, for example by listing claimants as falling under the relevant statutory provision but without significantly altering the level of service provided.[25]

The litigation drew attention to a real and important gap between the policy requirements as expressed in the legislation and the financial ability of local authorities to deliver the policy. Given the increase in the number of asylum seekers this gap was likely to grow. On one view it was the judgment that created the problem: the court could have recognised the difficulties faced by local authorities and interpreted the legislation in Hillingdon's favour and thereby enabled the system to work within the existing resource constraints. Instead the judgment created a situation which meant that the system could not work, unless local authorities altered their spending priorities or obtained additional funding from central government. The former possibility was politically unattractive as it meant shifting funds from other services to support asylum seekers. The latter required a campaign to get more central government money. Hillingdon, together with other similarly placed local authorities, preferred to try the latter approach and used the court decision to lobby central government. The councils were eventually at least partially successful in obtaining additional funding.

The Caerphilly case

In the *Caerphilly* case the council was held to have failed in its duties to a minor who had left a young offender institution.[26] The judge, Munby J (as he then was), was highly critical of the 'mindset' and 'culture' of local authorities that exclude families from decision-making concerning care plans for their children, in possible breach of Article 8 of the European Convention for the Protection of Human Rights. Observing that it is 'depressing to see' this 'attitude in the present case', he went on to spell out what authorities should do in the future: 'because the point is so

---

the Children Act 1989 to support unaccompanied asylum-seeking children (London: Refugee Council, 2005).

[25] *Safeguarding Children: The Second Joint Chief Inspectors' Report on Arrangements to Safeguard Children* (London: Commission for Social Care Inspection, 2005), 16.

[26] *R. (J)* v. *Caerphilly County Borough Council* [2005] EWHC 586 (Admin), [2005] 2 F.L.R. 860.

important, and a clear statement of what is required may assist not merely this but other local authorities'.[27]

His judgment, then, was highly critical of the approach taken by this and other local authorities and provided specific guidance as to what should be done to improve their approach to establishing care plans. Officials told researchers conducting the ESRC study that the decision 'came out of the blue' and was 'a shock'. An official spoke of the judgment's 'harshness'. Other officials doubted whether the judge really appreciated the problems they faced having to deal with a young person who has a long history of difficulties, and felt that they had done the best they could for someone who would not co-operate with them. From the point of view of the officials, the decision had clear negative effects both for them and for the wider reputation of the authority, and at first they found it difficult to respond constructively.

Eventually, however, the authority embarked on developing fresh approaches, which in effect called for social services to take a new, some might say more legally oriented, professional approach. Over time the decision came to be viewed much more positively. When asked whether, looking back, the judgment could be considered to have been helpful, officials said that: 'It's taken a long time to become helpful, yes … I think "yes".' With hindsight the judgment was considered to have had 'a massive effect', and to have contributed to improving services within Caerphilly, which became a model for others.

These cases illustrate the difficulties of generalising about the effects of judicial review. They each called for major changes, in *Hillingdon* principally affecting budget and service priorities, and in *Caerphilly* affecting professional practice and cultural attitudes within social services. They illustrate how judicial decisions concerned with the legality of particular decisions may come to have impacts beyond the individual case and beyond the purely legal. They illustrate how the implications of court decisions may vary across departments within the same authority, with street-level officials benefiting from the clarity and guidance they provide and budget holders and senior managers confronting the more complex challenges posed. And they illustrate the difficulty of generalising about whether the effects of judicial review are negative or positive. This is largely a matter of perspective and context, not least because the

---

[27] *Caerphilly* (n. 26), [34].

implications of judgments may change over time. Decisions which initially shock and threaten may become resources stimulating and enabling authorities to find ways to reconcile the pressures to meet general demand, driven perhaps by populist policies, while meeting the needs of individuals and less popular groups.

Judgments do not tell the whole story

The above illustrations focus on how specific judicial review judgments affected local authorities. Judgments are significant when assessing the impacts of judicial review, not least because it is by means of judgments that courts exert their greatest formal influence. However, it is well established that the process of litigation may have significant effects even when cases do not reach the judgment stage and irrespective of the court's decision.[28] This is significant given that only a relatively small number of public law disputes go to judgment. The vast majority of disputes do not materialise into claims that are issued in the Administrative Court[29] and the vast majority of those which are issued will be settled, refused permission, or withdrawn for other reasons.

The ESRC study on the impacts of judicial review on local authorities also investigated whether local authorities are affected by their experience of challenge, whether or not legal challenges get to final hearings. This aspect of the study used quantitative techniques to see whether there is a link between levels of challenge and the quality of local authority performance.

The research was based on all judicial reviews against local authorities in England and Wales issued in the Administrative Court during the years 2000 to 2005.[30] Two questions were asked: first, whether poorly performing authorities attracted higher levels of challenge than better performing ones; second, whether challenges led to improvements in the quality of

---

[28] R. Gambitta, 'Litigation, Judicial Deference and Policy Change' in R. Gambitta, M. May and J. Forster (eds.) *Governing Through Courts* (London: Sage, 1981).

[29] It has been estimated that for every ten threats of litigation, approximately six are resolved without the commencement of proceedings: V. Bondy and M. Sunkin, *The Dynamics of Judicial Review Litigation* (London: Public Law Project, 2009), 30.

[30] For more detail on the data collected and the methods used, see Platt, Sunkin and Calvo (n. 22). See also M. Sunkin, K. Calvo, L. Platt and T. Landman, 'Mapping the Use of Judicial Review to Challenge Local Authorities in England and Wales' [2007] *Public Law* 545.

local authority performance. For the purposes of the research, official indicators of 'quality' were employed, namely Comprehensive Performance Assessment ('CPA') scores, used by government to judge the quality of local authorities.

The study found there to be a statistically significant negative association between levels of challenge and CPA scores, controlling for type of authority and a range of other characteristics that might influence the quality of services, such as levels of deprivation. In other words, authorities with lower scores for quality were challenged more often than authorities with higher scores, all other things being equal.

It is interesting, but perhaps unsurprising, that poorly performing authorities attract more challenges than better performing ones. After all, we might expect one of the signs of poor performance to be high levels of dissatisfaction. Also, we were aware that the findings could reflect an element of reverse causation in the sense that judicial review litigation may be the reason why some local authorities were performing badly. It is plausible that judicial review was itself causing problems in local authority services by diverting resources from service provision, thereby resulting in poorer CPA scores and an increase in complaints.[31] This would be compatible with a view that judicial review litigation detracts from the quality of good government. While there may be some truth in this, this is a factor that should not be exaggerated.

The study also found the incidence of judicial review challenge to be closely correlated with levels of complaint to the local authority ombudsman. This does not eliminate the possibility that judicial review leads to poorer CPA scores, but it implies that the rates of challenge reflected a genuine level of dissatisfaction with services, rather than, for example, the dissatisfaction of individuals or the litigation strategies of particular lawyers.

In relation to the second of the questions asked, we found an increase in the level of challenge to be linked to improvements in performance, as measured by the CPA scores. In other words, we found that where local authorities experienced an increase in the incidence of judicial review challenge from the level they had normally experienced, their CPA scores

---

[31] When commenting on an earlier draft of the chapter, David Howarth recollected being a Council Leader and worrying that the CPA process itself would draw resources from service provision and increase potential vulnerability to legal challenge.

improved. This intriguing finding suggests that far from detracting from quality, growth in legal challenge may drive improvements in local authority performance, as measured by official indicators. It should be noted in passing that this finding does not necessarily imply greater compliance with the requirements of judicial review or that decision-making had become more 'just', as these matters are not specifically picked up by the CPA.

When interpreting these findings, there is clearly a need for caution. First, it is difficult to infer causality. We cannot assume there to be a causal link between changes in the rate of challenge and later improvements in quality. Second, the association between litigation and CPA score may be spurious in the sense that we may be seeing the impact of separate factors that are simultaneously driving the increase in litigation and the improvement in CPA score.

Nevertheless, these quantitative findings are highly suggestive and while they may stand to be refuted or refined in later research, they are consistent with the view that public law contributes to improvements in the quality of local authority performance. They certainly challenge the assumption that a growth in judicial review necessarily hinders the work of public bodies or leads to a decline in the quality of public services. In so doing they present a rather more positive picture of the instrumental effects of judicial review than that which informed the Coalition Government's programme of reforms intended to curtail the use of judicial review. However, at this stage we can only speculate as to how judicial review might have a positive effect on the quality of services. Some clues may be gleaned from the effects of decisions such as those in the *Behre* and *Caerphilly* cases. There we saw how the judgments forced the authorities to rethink their approaches and this in itself may be conducive to improving service provision. However, it is possible that the influence of judicial review is deeper than this. It is arguable, for example, that important connections exist between the values inherent in the requirements of judicial review and the ethos of public service, which encourages public officials to use fair, consistent and legitimate processes for allocating scarce resources.[32] Such an ethos may also encourage officials to comply

---

[32] See Platt, Sunkin and Calvo (n. 22). See also P. Hoggett, 'A Service to the Public: The Containment of Ethical and Moral Conflicts by Public Bureaucracies' in P. du Gay (ed.), *The Values of Bureaucracy* (Oxford: Oxford University Press, 2005).

with the law, not because they are coerced into doing so or because it is economically efficient to do so, but because it is the right thing to do. In our research it was striking that respondents who were engaged in judicial review at a variety of levels and in different ways, stressed their desire to do the 'right thing', which included doing their best to comply with the law, even if that was not easy. As one official put it:

[L]local authorities tend to respond ultimately to what the court orders them to do, because that's how local authorities operate.[33]

Moreover, court judgments may assist officials to reconcile tensions which lie at the heart of public administration between the demands of the many and the needs of the few, especially when the few are in groups widely considered to be undeserving, such as benefit claimants, the homeless, or asylum seekers.[34] Cases such as *Behre* and *Caerphilly* illustrate how the courts may oblige public authorities to meet the needs of those in such minority groups and they may also educate them as to the appropriate processes for doing so. In so doing, court decisions may enable authorities to find ways to reach more equitable or just outcomes, leading to improvements in the services they provide to the community at large.

What do claimants achieve?

So far the chapter has been considering the impact of judicial review from the point of view of public bodies and the quality of the services they provide. The focus now turns to consider what claimants achieve from judicial review litigation.

Individual redress and public interest claims

Most claims are brought by individuals seeking redress in relation to decisions which directly affect them. Having exhausted other avenues of redress, such claimants typically turn to judicial review in the hope that it will provide a remedy as a last resort. They are likely to measure the success or otherwise of judicial review primarily according to whether it provides redress and especially whether it leads to tangible benefits such as the

---

[33] Cited in Platt, Sunkin and Calvo (n. 22).   [34] Hoggett (n. 32).

provision of services which the authority had previously refused to pro-vide. This is the class of case I am primarily concerned with in this chapter as it enables us to assess the effectiveness or otherwise of judicial review in the provision of redress.

However, it is necessary to comment on the numerically smaller class of claim that concerns public interests beyond the claimant's particular circumstances. Typically, such cases fall into two types. One is where the claimant argues that their treatment gives rise to issues which directly affect them and to issues of wider concern. For example, a prisoner challenging a decision to refuse him a hearing before a parole board might argue that this calls into question the procedures used at such hearings more generally. Such claims inevitably involve a combination of individual and public interest issues. The other type of claim is purely concerned with public interest matters.[35] In such cases the success or otherwise of judicial review will not be measured against the tangible results for the claimant but according to whether the litigation leads to, or contributes to, legal or policy reform.

There is little doubt that judicial review can play a part in achieving policy change not least by contributing to other campaigning strategies.[36] However, research indicates that significant social or policy reforms are unlikely to be caused by judicial review alone. Despite the increase in the influence of the courts over the past thirty years or so, Tony Prosser's conclusion to his classic study of the use of judicial review to achieve reforms of social welfare law still rings true:

> ... in the field of social welfare the courts alone are most unlikely to be a useful vehicle for achieving social change ... if a successful challenge to an administrative policy was achieved, it was almost certain to be swiftly nullified by legislative action.[37]

---

[35] A classic example is *R. v. Secretary of State for Foreign Affairs ex parte World Development Movement Ltd.* [1995] 1 WLR 386. It is this class of case that the Government seemed to want to curtail when they proposed introducing a narrower test of standing: *Judicial Review: Proposals for Further Reform* (London: Ministry of Justice, 2013). This proposal was dropped following consultation. In most public interest cases the claimant will have a direct interest: e.g. in *Hurley & Moore* v. *Secretary of State for Business and Innovation and Skills* [2012] EWHC 201 (Admin), [2012] HRLR 13, where the claimants were sixth formers who challenged the legality of university fees.

[36] See e.g. King (n. 1), 68–69.

[37] T. Prosser, *Test Cases for the Poor* (London: Child Poverty Action Group, 1983), 83. See also C. Harlow, 'Administrative Reaction to Judicial Review' [1976] *Public Law* 116.

Procedural weaknesses

At first sight judicial review as it operates in England and Wales is ill equipped to provide effective redress for claimants dissatisfied with decisions or actions of public bodies. The shortcomings flow from the nature of the High Court's inherent supervisory jurisdiction and the procedure by which that jurisdiction is accessed.

From the perspective of individual redress, the procedural weaknesses appear clear, especially when compared with other court procedures.[38] Claimants face an extremely short limitation period; they must obtain permission in order to argue their case in court;[39] there is no automatic discovery of documents or cross examination; even if successful, all remedies are discretionary and their availability cannot be guaranteed; and damages are not normally available to compensate for losses caused by action falling short of the requirements of judicial review.

While these procedural characteristics undoubtedly limit the ability of the procedure to provide individual redress, in practice the picture is not inevitably bleak. For example, while the permission hurdle does not exist in other proceedings, its effects are not necessarily negative from the perspective of claimants. For instance, in our research on the dynamics of judicial review litigation,[40] Varda Bondy and I found that many solicitors who represent claimants approved of the procedure because it provides a relatively cheap and swift way of obtaining a judge's view of the merits of the claim, thereby potentially saving time and money. The permission stage also plays an important role in encouraging early settlement of cases. We found that 34 per cent of the 1,449 judicial review claims in our sample were withdrawn prior to the permission stage.[41] Significantly, our interviews with representatives of both claimants and defendants indicated that the 'vast majority of cases that settled did so in favour of claimants'.[42] Here then we can see how the process may enable claimants to obtain positive outcomes without the need for a final court hearing. Of course, such findings beg a number of questions, not least of which is the question whether cases could have been settled at an earlier stage, thereby obviating the need for the claimant to start proceedings.

---

[38] Civil Procedure Rules, part 54.
[39] And this may be something of a lottery: Bondy and Sunkin (n. 29).
[40] Bondy and Sunkin (n. 29).   [41] Bondy and Sunkin (n. 29), 37, n. 4.
[42] Bondy and Sunkin (n. 29), 39.

The nature of judicial review: the risk of Pyrrhic victories

The very nature of the supervisory jurisdiction may limit its effectiveness in providing individual redress. Even when the Administrative Court decides that a decision should not stand, the court will only very rarely go a stage further and replace the impugned decision with its own.[43] Normally the matter will be referred back to the body concerned so that their decision can be retaken in accordance with the judgment. It has been widely assumed that 'a successful judicial review . . . would most likely be followed by an agency remaking the same decision, though taking care to avoid the earlier legal error'.[44] While such an outcome might satisfy the requirements of legality, it would be unlikely to satisfy a successful claimant who litigates in order to obtain tangible benefits. If this assumption were correct in practice it would certainly confirm judicial review to be of much greater symbolic than tangible importance to those with legitimate grievances against public authorities.

Significantly, research in several jurisdictions suggests that it is incorrect to assume that judicial review is ineffective in securing tangible redress. In the United States, Peter Schuck and Donald Elliott found that remand of decisions back to US agencies resulted in 'major changes' in the petitioner's favour in 40 per cent of cases.[45] In Australia, Creyke and McMillan found that in about 60 per cent of the cases in which the Australian Federal Court set aside an agency's decision, the applicant ultimately obtained a favourable outcome.[46] Creyke and McMillan conclude that the belief that after being successfully challenged administrative bodies will routinely seek to re-make their original decision 'has been disproved'. They say that:

If theories are built upon facts, then the value of judicial review in producing a favourable outcome to an applicant has been demonstrated.[47]

The above findings are compatible with those emerging from recent research in England and Wales on the value and effects of judicial review.[48]

---

[43] When a quashing order is made the court may, if statute permits, substitute its own decision for the decision to which the claim relates: Civil Procedure Rules, part 54, r. 19.2(b).

[44] R. Creyke and J. McMillan, 'The Operation of Judicial Review in Australia' in Hertogh and Halliday (n. 15), 186.

[45] P. H. Schuck and E. D. Elliott, 'To the Chevron Station: An Empirical Study of Federal Administrative Law' [1990] *Duke Law Journal* 984, 1059–60.

[46] Creyke and McMillan (n. 44).   [47] Creyke and McMillan (n. 44), 186.

[48] The study, funded by the Nuffield Foundation, was undertaken by Varda Bondy and Maurice Sunkin for the Public Law Project and the University of Essex respectively.

The findings of that study indicate that where public bodies make fresh decisions following a successful challenge, the fresh decisions often favour the claimant. The study identified thirty-four cases where the Administrative Court had quashed decisions in relation to which information was available about the post-judgment outcomes. In only four of these did the public body appear to reach the same decision on the substance as it had originally. In the remaining thirty cases, the public body appeared ultimately to have reached a decision that was favourable to the claimant. The tangible outcomes across these cases concerned a wide spectrum of matters and included: the achievement of a fresh care plan with appropriate placement and increased budget; an increase in the budget for residential care and accommodation services for the elderly; release from detention pending deportation and grant of damages; the removal of days wrongly added to a prison sentence for disobeying rules; and access to education in prison.

A number of factors may account for the authorities' change of mind: the authority may have responded to clear indications given by the judge; it may have reconsidered the matter in the light of the arguments in court, new information, or changed circumstances; it may have decided to concede the matter in order to avoid future litigation or cost; or it may have simply decided that it had initially reached the wrong decision.

Whatever the particular factors, the following observations on these emerging findings can be offered. First, in these cases it appears clear that judicial review enabled claimants to achieve tangible redress that is unlikely to have been achieved but for the litigation. Second, in these cases judicial review affected the substantive outcome and its influence extended beyond process and was more than symbolic. Third, the public authorities appear to have genuinely engaged with the consequences of the litigation and there is no apparent evidence that the authorities responded in ways that were wholly negative or ritualistic. Fourth, given that judicial review is likely to have been used as a last resort, when no other means of legal redress was available, the findings reinforce the importance of access to the High Court's inherent supervisory jurisdiction

Christopher Luff was the Senior Research Officer. See www.nuffieldfoundation.org/value-judicial-review.

to the achievement of individual redress. Finally, although transposing research findings across jurisdictions can be risky,[49] the findings suggest that the conclusions drawn by Creyke and McMillan also apply in England and Wales, and possibly more so.

When claimants use judicial review to seek redress in their own case, obtaining a tangible benefit is likely to be the most favourable outcome. Participation in litigation can, however, have other consequences which are significant for the individuals concerned and for society as a whole, such as gaining a sense of empowerment as a result of participation in the process and confidence in the legal system. Such benefits may be more likely when claimants win than when they lose. However, the emerging findings of the research show that such non-tangible benefits also occur when claimants fail to succeed in court or where they win in court but fail to obtain the desired outcome. To take one example, a solicitor who was interviewed for the study on the value and effects of judicial review described his client's experience following the dismissal of his challenge in the following way:

He felt that the judicial review, despite losing, was a positive experience and gave him a sense of empowerment . . . [T]he case gave him the feeling of being listened to; the judge's comments, especially, gave him hope and increased confidence on the basis of that reasoning.

Such responses underscore the importance of access to justice and the value of ensuring that public administration is legally accountable for the way it operates.[50]

Conclusions

This chapter has provided something of an overview of the current state of knowledge about the effects of judicial review. It has looked in particular at recent research on how public authorities respond to judicial review and

---

[49] See P. Cane 'Understanding Judicial Review and its Impact' in Hertogh and Halliday (n. 15), 30–31.

[50] There is a huge literature on procedural justice. The work of Tom Tyler is of particular pertinence: e.g. T. R. Tyler, *Why People Obey the Law* (Princeton: Princeton University Press, 2006), 2nd edn.

what, if anything, claimants achieve when they bring judicial review proceedings.

This discussion has shown that generalisations about the effects of judicial review should be treated with caution. In particular, it warns against accepting a monochromic image of judicial review as an institution that threatens public administration, is abused by claimants intent on impeding the implementation of public policy, and which fails to provide a route to substantive redress.

Public bodies may not welcome judicial review and may find it inconvenient when their decisions are challenged, especially when this requires them to revisit budget priorities or alter habits of practice. However, evidence indicates that judicial review may lead to improvements in the quality of public services; that it may assist officials in their work by clarifying the law, setting standards for decision-making, and stimulating re-evaluation of services. Judicial review may also enable public bodies to better reconcile the demands of the many with particular needs, including the needs of those unfavoured by populist pressures.

The chapter also shows the potential effectiveness of judicial review as a means for obtaining individual redress. Claimants often achieve success as a result of settlements. When they achieve success in court, it cannot be assumed that this will have been an expensive and time-consuming Pyrrhic victory. On the contrary, emerging findings suggest that successful claimants often achieve tangible benefits.

Empirical evidence helps provide an understanding of the value and limits of judicial review. This chapter has pointed to the growing evidence base indicating judicial review's contribution to the practical application of the rule of law in the UK, a contribution the importance of which should not be underestimated.

Further reading

V. Bondy and M. Sunkin, *The Dynamics of Judicial Review Litigation* (London: Public Law Project, 2009) (available at www.publiclawproject.org.uk/data/resources/9/TheDynamicsofJudicialReviewLitigation.pdf)

S. Halliday *Judicial Review and Compliance with Administrative Law* (Oxford: Hart Publishing, 2004)

M. Hertogh and S. Halliday (eds.) *Judicial Review and Bureaucratic Impact: International and Interdisciplinary Perspectives* (Cambridge: Cambridge University Press, 2004)

J. King, *Judging Social Rights* (Cambridge: Cambridge University Press, 2012)

L. Platt, M. Sunkin and K. Calvo, 'Judicial Review Litigation as an Incentive to Change in Local Authority Services in England and Wales' (2010) 20 *Journal of Public Administration Research and Theory* i243

13 Designing and operating constitutions in global context

Cheryl Saunders

Introduction

The contemporary concept of a constitution can be traced to the instruments so named that came into effect in the United States and France at the end of the eighteenth century, in each case in the wake of revolution. Over the century that followed, a constitution became widely accepted as a single written document that prescribes the key elements of a system of government and that derives its authority from a sovereign people. In time, it became more clearly established that a constitution is superior law, distinguished from ordinary law by the manner in which it is made and changed. Over the course of the twentieth century, it became widely accepted that constitutions can be enforced through courts, even at the expense of ordinary law, although the arrangements for doing so varied significantly, in accordance with the differing logic that underpinned them.[1]

While these generalisations are broadly accurate, at least two caveats are necessary. The ideas inherent in the concept of a constitution were not born in a vacuum at the end of the eighteenth century but had a long gestation in Europe, prompted in part by constitutional developments in seventeenth-century Britain, with long roots in the ancient world. Nor do all states have constitutions that match all facets of the modern conception, even now. In the United Kingdom, the Constitution remains an accumulation of laws, principles and practices. In New Zealand, the Constitution Act 1986 can be altered in the same way as ordinary law. There is no judicial review of the constitutional validity of national legislation in, for example, the

---

[1] Accounts of the shift from the 'ancient' to the 'modern' constitution include M. Loughlin, *Foundations of Public Law* (Oxford University Press, 2010), ch. 10; D. Grimm, 'Types of Constitutions' in M. Rosenfeld and A. Sajo (eds.), *Oxford Handbook of Comparative Constitutional Law* (Oxford: Oxford University Press, 2012), 98–103; C. H. McIlwain, *Constitutionalism Ancient and Modern* (Ithaca: Cornell University Press, 1947), 1–16.

Netherlands, Ethiopia and Switzerland, although the alternatives and the rationales for them differ. Nevertheless, at least for the moment, the general features of a constitution are sufficiently settled to provide a standard by reference to which exceptional cases can be identified and explained. Constitutions broadly in this form spread across Europe and Latin America in the first part of the nineteenth century and reached parts of Africa, the Middle East, Asia and the Pacific by the end of the century. They continued to proliferate in the twentieth century, in line with the increase in the number of independent states. In the second decade of the twenty-first century, there are 193 member states of the United Nations, each of which claims a constitution of some kind. Almost 130 of these constitutions are new or have been renewed in the past 25 years.

Almost by definition, each constitution is linked with a particular state, its system of government and its people. It is a source, if not the source, of the public law of the state; it provides the legal framework for political action; it needs to be responsive to the context in which it is embedded, including the history, economy, geography and demography of the state. Comparative constitutional law is a challenging field for these reasons. Deep understanding of a constitution extends beyond its text to its meaning (however determined), its operation in practice, and the theories that inform and explain it.

The umbilical relationship between a constitution and its state, however, must be juxtaposed with another reality: that each Constitution also is subject to transnational influences, emanating from sources beyond the state's borders. This is by no means a new phenomenon. The early written constitutions were made in awareness of each other and built on a pre-existing transnational body of constitutional ideas. From these beginnings, constitutions spread around the world through processes of conquest, colonisation and emulation. The contemporary concept of a Constitution itself began as a transplant, although it is now taken for granted. Every constitution in the world has drawn on experience elsewhere, usually for multiple purposes and to a significant degree.

The twenty-first century famously is a time of globalisation, using the term loosely to encompass the entire complex network of dealings between states and between their peoples. Its significance should not be exaggerated to the point of understating the considerable influence of globalisation on constitutional development in earlier times. Nevertheless, the contemporary impact of globalisation is sufficiently profound to make the difference more than a matter of degree. The interdependence of all parts of the world is greater, in a wider range of respects. Communications are dramatically faster, more reliable, more effective and more difficult to constrain. International law and institutions have proliferated and matured to a point where they palpably affect what many states do, in areas that hitherto would have been considered matters of purely domestic concern.

The remainder of this chapter will identify and examine the tensions between the statist character of constitutions and the forces of globalisation, in relation to both constitutional design and the operation of constitutions. The division in some respects is artificial because design and operation are segments of a continuous process, but the nature of the impact of globalisation differs sufficiently between the two to make separate treatment worthwhile. In doing so, the chapter will show why the resolution of these tensions still hangs in the balance. The institution of the state has been weakened but it remains the most powerful force in an international system that is still evolving. Globalisation affects different states differently and the erosion of state authority in any event is not a linear process. Constitutions continue to play both symbolic and critical functional roles for states, while their relevance in the international sphere remains, at best, opaque. The substantial degree of constitutional convergence that is a product of globalisation has not eradicated difference, although in some cases it may serve to conceal it. It may be that in time globalisation will be seen to have altered the very nature of constitutions. At least from the standpoint of public law, however, that time is not yet here.

Designing constitutions

Scope of constitutional design

Constitutional design involves at least three distinct sets of decisions: about the status of the constitution, the process by which it will be made, and its substance. Status typically now is assumed in favour of the constitution as superior to other forms of domestic law. There is considerable variation in the relationship between constitutions and international, including supra-national, law, however, and the issue of status also involves important ancillary questions about the procedures for constitutional change and the scope and form of judicial review. Both the constitution-making process and the substance of the resulting constitution require decisions on which the effectiveness of the constitution ultimately may depend. The former raises a prior question about whether to maintain legal continuity by following the constitution alteration processes laid down in an existing constitution. In the absence of legal continuity, the constitution-making process bears the considerable burden of securing the legitimacy of a new constitution, at least in the short term. Constitutional substance involves choices in relation to, at least, the principal institutions of the state and the rights held by citizens against the state, with multiple variations on both themes. An unlimited range of other matters may be included as well, however. Common examples include a framework for devolution, prescription of relations between religion and the state, and specification of one or more official languages. Because constitutions play a symbolic, as well as a functional role, constitutional design also requires attention to nuance and style which are likely to include, while extending beyond, the wording of the constitutional preamble.

Impact of globalisation

Constitutional design is affected by transnational influences of several kinds. One is the substantial body of ideas that now form part of the global constitutional commons and that are likely to be assumed in the design of almost any constitution. The list is substantial and growing but certainly includes representative democracy, separation of powers, judicial independence and the rule of law. Proportionality may be a recent addition. As these examples suggest, however, shared ideas often are cast at the level of general principle. The understanding of particular principles may differ between states or constitutional traditions. In any event, each can be given effect in a variety of different ways. Commonality reduces extreme differences between systems of government but does not obviate constitutional choices.

Two other types of transnational influence, however, may have more specific effect. One comprises a vast array of international standards and comparative constitutional models and experiences. The most significant international standards also represent binding obligations in international law, from which they derive additional persuasive effect. The international bill of rights is a case in point, which has affected any constitution designed in the last twenty-five years, in some way and to some extent.[2] Even leaving international law aside, however, the experiences of other states in making constitutions and adopting substantive solutions to particular constitutional problems are a significant source for any new constitutional project. Information about both is readily available on-line, including through searchable data sets of various kinds. In consequence, techniques devised by particular states to meet the challenges of negotiating, drafting and approving new constitutions, often in fraught circumstances, frequently are adopted or adapted by others. Modes of popular participation; specialist representative or 'constituent' assemblies; the use of interim constitutions during transitional periods; and, as a recent addition, national dialogue processes, all have been used multiple times in different contexts as fashions in constitution-making rise and fall. Similarly, institutions, principles, procedures and even text tend to recur in successive constitutions in the same or modified form. Examples that presently are in favour include a specialist constitutional court along German lines; a limitations clause of the type found in the Canadian Charter of Rights and Freedoms; the use of three lists to divide legislative powers for federal purposes between the centre and the states, as in India;[3] semi-presidentialism, as in France; and provision for independent constitutional commissions, as in South Africa. These trends do not necessarily result in homogenous constitutions or constitution-making processes. Cross-fertilisation causes variations of its own; new ideas, mercifully, continue to emerge; and transplants between different contexts famously produce surprises. They nevertheless reflect the processes of globalisation.

   A second type of influence, reinforcing the first, comprises a diverse range of people and institutions, drawn from what may loosely be described as the 'international community', which participate in constitution-making exercises around the globe. International involvement is likely where constitution-making follows a period of violent conflict to which new constitutional arrangements are seen to be a partial solution. A peace

---

[2] The international bill of rights comprises the Universal Declaration of Human Rights (1948), the International Covenant on Civil and Political Rights (1966), the International Covenant on Economic, Social and Cultural Rights (1966) and the Protocols to the two Covenants.

[3] The lists deal with the powers assigned exclusively to the Union, powers assigned exclusively to the states, and concurrent or shared powers: Indian Constitution, Part XI.

agreement may, effectively, prescribe a constitution, as the still relatively rare case of Bosnia Herzegovina shows. More commonly, intervening states or the United Nations itself influence the manner and/or direction of change in some way as in, to take some very different examples, Iraq, South Sudan, Kenya and Yemen. If, as arguably occurred in Namibia, a Security Council resolution approves aspects of the constitutional settlement, it may indirectly give the settlement binding force. Even in the absence of continuing violent conflict, however, constitutional design in developing countries often attracts assistance from United Nations agencies, international non-governmental organisations ('NGOs'), or wealthier states in the form of aid as in, for example, Timor Leste, Zimbabwe and Nepal. These international actors contribute to the diffusion of international standards and comparative experience, often drawing on a melange of constitutional ideas.

Transnational influence on constitutional design is not necessarily global in source and effect. Often, perhaps increasingly, it is regional or sub-regional, operating either through formal institutional arrangements or through less formal interaction between neighbours with shared problems and cultural instincts. Europe illustrates the potential for regional arrangements to have a profound effect on the constitutional design of participating states through a combination of entry incentives, monitoring mechanisms and enforcement regimes. But regional synergies are apparent elsewhere as well, although institutional forms presently are less developed. Examples range from the standards prescribed in the African Charter on Democracy, Elections and Governance of the African Union to the subtle role played by Malaysia in facilitating the peace agreement in relation to Mindanao in the Philippines.[4] The constitutional relevance of regionalism outside Europe is still based largely on impression, however. Much work remains to be done in assessing and comparing the implications of regional relations for global constitutional design.

The significance of the state

Despite the manifold consequences of globalisation for constitutional design, they by no means suggest severance of the tie between constitutions and their states. On the contrary, constitutional design is the product

---

[4] Speech of President Aquino during the signing of the GPH-MILF Framework Agreement on the Bangsamoro, October 15, 2012 (available at www.gov.ph/2012/10/15/speech-of-president-aquino-during-the-signing-of-the-gph-milf-framework-agreement-october-15-2012/).

of both sets of forces, in proportions that vary between states. In the event of a conflict between them, the state, at least for the moment, has the upper hand.

In the first place, the impact of globalisation is patchy. For reasons outlined in the previous section, states emerging from a conflict that has attracted international attention, developing states dependent on foreign aid and, perhaps, states in a close-knit regional relationship are exposed to its full force. Even these, however, may resist, in ways that suggest the continuing strength of attachment to their own autonomy and capacity for self-determination. Tunisia is a positive, recent example; Fiji, Zimbabwe and Hungary are more controversial others. And many states are not in these categories at all, retaining, in essence, a more extensive and effective measure of state sovereignty. These states are exposed to the full smorgasbord of international constitutional standards and options, but they choose without reliance on others and are more likely to be path dependent in relation to both process and substance. The much-admired Constitution of South Africa is the product of a process of this kind.

In any event, in present conditions, theoretical and practical considerations centre constitutional design in the state. In theory, constitutions derive their legitimacy from the people of the state, however defined. If anything, theory now is further reinforced by the expectation that the people will be actually and not just virtually engaged in constitution-making. In the interests of constitutional effectiveness, moreover, both the constitution-making process and the design choices made for the eventual constitution must be owned by the state, its leaders and its people. The process needs to secure legitimacy in their eyes. They need to be committed to the compromises that are inherent in any constitutional settlement. They are likely to be best placed to make the difficult decisions about legal continuity, institutional novelty and the deferral of contentious issues. Critically, they must both understand and accept the constitution by which public power is limited and pursuant to which they may be governed for some time to come. These desiderata are made all the more compelling by the weight of expectations often placed on constitutions in these times: to manage transition to democracy after a period of authoritarian rule; to transform unequal societies; to preserve peace between divided communities. The imperative of local ownership was acknowledged by the Secretary-General of the United Nations in 2009, in a guidance note that trod a difficult line between exhorting compliance with international norms and standards and recognising constitution-making as a 'sovereign national process'.[5]

Reflections

The extent of transnational influence on the design of state constitutions has consequences for constitutional theory and practice that are continuing to unfold.

First, there is now a question whether theories about a national people as the source of authority for a constitution should be adapted to accommodate international involvement. The question is prompted by various phenomena, some of which were canvassed earlier: the still relatively small number of constitutions effectively prescribed by international agreement; the significantly larger number of constitutions affected by international pressure of some kind; and the strengthening of international human rights norms to the point where constitutional compliance is claimed to have a bearing on admission to statehood.[6] It gains further traction from the historical reality that international influence on constitutional design is the norm, rather than the exception, in the experience of most states over time.[7] It would be premature to accept that there has been a paradigm shift in favour of what sometimes is described as an 'internationalised *pouvoir constituant*'.[8] Popular sovereignty retains important explanatory, as well as symbolic, power, whatever its flaws, and even the most egregious cases of international pressure on constitutional design preserve at least a façade of popular consent. At the very least, however, the recurrence of this question underscores the obvious point that national constitution-making is affected in various ways by transnational forces that challenge the traditional account.

---

[5] Guidance Note of the Secretary-General, *United Nations Assistance to Constitution-making processes*, April 2009 (available at www.unrol.org/files/Guidance_Note_United_Nations_Assistance_to_Constitution-making_Processes_FINAL.pdf).

[6] A. Peters, 'Dual Democracy' in J. Klabbers, A. Peters and G. Ulfstein, *The Constitutionalisation of International Law* (Oxford University Press, 2009), 275–76.

[7] C. Hahm and S. Kim, 'To Make "We the People": Constitutional Founding in Postwar Japan and South Korea' (2010) 8 *International Journal of Constitutional Law* 800.

[8] P. Dann and Z. Al-Ali, 'The Internationalized *Pouvoir Constituant* Constitution-Making under External Influence in Iraq, Sudan and East Timor' (2006) 10 *Max Planck Yearbook of United Nations Law* 423.

A second issue concerns the effectiveness of at least some new constitutions. Written constitutions in their current form are still a novelty in some states and may co-exist uneasily with customary norms and practices. Even where a new constitution is accepted in principle as fundamental law, recurring problems with compliance once a constitution comes into effect have caused constitution-making practice to incorporate implementation as a final, formal phase of constitutional design. Thus in Kenya, for example, the sixth schedule to the constitution of 2010 establishes both a commission and a parliamentary committee to oversee constitutional implementation. There is a question, on which further research would be useful, whether at least some impediments to effective implementation reflect a lack of national understanding and ownership that in turn is linked to levels of international assistance at the point of constitutional design. If so, there is a dilemma that needs to be resolved. International involvement in constitutional design usefully enables global knowledge to be shared. Form should not be secured at the expense of substance, however: unless global knowledge is accommodated to local context, the constitution is likely to fail.

A third consequence of the impact of globalisation on constitutional design is the erosion of boundaries between constitutional traditions that previously were sustained by spheres of constitutional influence, reinforced by differences in language and the differing demands of legal systems. Some cross-fertilisation has always occurred, but the ready availability of information and the eclecticism of international constitutional advisers have accelerated the process over the past twenty-five years. Thus, to take only two obvious examples, constitutional courts are becoming increasingly familiar institutions in common law legal systems[9] and *ex post facto* judicial review is now an established feature of constitutions in the francophone tradition, including, albeit cautiously, in the fifth French republic itself.[10] Transplants between significantly different constitutional environments increase the likelihood of unexpected effects. The appearance of convergence, to which they contribute, may mask underlying difference. The mix and match approach to

---

[9] The Constitutional Courts of South Africa and Zimbabwe are examples.

[10] E.g. Constitution of the Tunisian Republic 2014, Art. 120; Constitution of the Fifth French Republic, Art. 61.

constitutional design has changed, but not necessarily simplified, the challenge of comparative constitutional law.[11]

Operating constitutions

From design to operation in practice

There is a fine line between constitutional design and the operation of a constitution in practice. The early stages of constitutional implementation are a critical test of elite and popular support for a new constitution. Any constitution that lasts for a significant period of time evolves through formal constitutional amendment or institutional behaviour; dramatic examples sometimes attract the label of 'transitional constitutionalism'.[12] Not all constitutions are long-lived in any event, whatever the intentions of their makers.[13] A new constitution ushers in a new phase of constitutional design that may, but need not, involve major innovation. Most new constitutions incorporate substantial elements of earlier ones, in an application of path-dependency.

It once was fashionable to classify constitutions by reference to their effectiveness in practice. To this end, writing in the 1950s and observing the rise of communist systems of government, Loewenstein distinguished between 'normative', 'nominal' and 'semantic' constitutions.[14] For comparative purposes, it remains relevant to consider whether constitutions are taken seriously and generally observed, on the one hand, or whether they are widely disregarded, on the other. Definitive categorisation is now more difficult, however. Many public actors push the boundaries of written constitutions as far as they can, subject to whatever constraint mechanisms political and legal accountability offer. Many constitutions have at least some provisions that appear not to be observed at all while, conversely,

---

[11] C. Saunders, 'The Impact of Internationalisation on National Constitutions' in A. H. Y. Chen (ed.), *Constitutionalism in Asia in the Early 21st Century* (Cambridge University Press, 2014), 391.

[12] J. Yeh and W.-C. Chang, 'The Changing Landscapes of Modern Constitutionalism: Transitional Perspective' (2009) 4 *National Taiwan University Law Review* 145.

[13] Z. Elkins, Tom Ginsburg and James Melton, *The Endurance of Written Constitutions* (Cambridge University Press, 2009).

[14] K. Loewenstein, *Political Power and the Governmental Process* (University of Chicago Press, 1957).

even in states with a weak commitment to democracy and the rule of law, a written constitution is likely to have some effect, the extent of which may fluctuate over time.

There are variations between states in the expectations placed on constitutions, in any event, which should be taken into account in evaluating their effect. All organise the distribution of public power within the state and increasingly, in more recent constitutions, between the state and regional or international organisations. Many also play an explicitly symbolic role, as an emblem of the state, its history and its aspirations. In addition, however, some, of which the South African constitution is an important recent example, have the infinitely more ambitious goal of 'transforming' the private as well as the public sphere. Further, while all constitutions, by definition, have an integrative function, this is both more significant and more challenging in states in which the community is deeply divided along ethnic or other cultural lines.

The principal sphere of operation of national constitutions is circumscribed by the territory of a state. Increasingly, however, national borders are permeable, in ways that affect constitutions in practice. One set of examples involves the extended effect of national constitutions, beyond state borders or in application to non-citizens. These include whether constitutions allow, or even require, the enfranchisement of non-resident citizens and, if so, the implications of this practice for the concept of democratic representation; whether and to what extent resident non-citizens are entitled to constitutional rights; and whether and to what extent constitutional norms apply to the extraterritorial actions of public officials. State practice presently varies considerably in relation to each of these questions. Other examples comprise the wide range of external influences on the operation of national constitutions, which are examined in the next section.

Impact of globalisation

Transnational influences bear on the operation, as well as the design, of national constitutions. They stem from myriad sources broadly associated with globalisation, including the ease of communication, the mobility of people, the interdependence of national and regional economies, and the impossibility of resolving many problems that require attention in the public interest within the boundaries of a single state. In what follows they are considered in two dimensions: from the outside in and from the inside out.

External norms and standards that affect the operations of constitutions in practice emanate from international and regional orders of what might loosely be called government and from other transnational communities of interest of which the Commonwealth of Nations is only one of many examples. Archetypically, norms derived from these sources are in the nature of rights, which national institutions are expected to observe and in some cases positively to protect. Rights spill over into the operations of institutions, however, requiring democratic participation, independent courts, fair trials and open justice, to take only a few obvious examples. And a vast range of such obligations affect domestic action on matters that are not directly rights related, including environmental protection, free trade and counter-terrorism measures.

National actors are bound in international law by many of these norms and standards, as treaty obligations or by force of customary international law. Superficially, their domestic impact is weakened by the familiar difficulty of effectively enforcing international law, particularly in states that adhere to degrees of dualism. In practice, however, the significance of this factor is diminishing. Many international norms are incorporated into domestic law, by constitutions or legislation, if they do not already have direct effect. Regional arrangements demonstrate a range of techniques through which decisions on questions of regulation or administration that are taken outside a state can become effectively binding within it, as a matter of law or political persuasion.[15] As noted in connection with constitutional design, while institutionalised regionalism is less broadly and deeply established outside Europe, significant examples exist, affecting most regions. These can be expected both to multiply and to develop further. Even at the international level, innovative mechanisms to enhance compliance have demonstrated how the significance of impediments to enforcement can be diminished. Thus, some international human rights regimes, including the International Covenant on Civil and Political Rights ('ICCPR'), have their own committees to monitor compliance that also may deal with complaints of breach by individuals in relation to states that

---

[15] Notably, the European Union (see http://europa.eu/index_en.htm) and the Council of Europe (see http://hub.coe.int/), including the European Court of Human Rights (see www.echr.coe.int/Pages/home.aspx?p=home&tc),

have adhered to the relevant protocol.[16] In an example of a different kind, the World Trade Organization ('WTO') relies on a dispute settlement mechanism, underpinned by the authority of individual states to self-enforce rulings, to ensure a higher level of compliance with WTO rules.[17] The heightened significance of supra-national and international norms in domestic affairs has led at least one commentator to observe that national constitutions are now only part of a 'compound constitutional system', supplemented by international law.[18]

Even if the impact of international norms is placed to one side, participants in the constitutional process within the state are affected from the 'inside out' by transnational forces in a variety of ways. Almost every institution is at least a potential participant in one or more international networks through which knowledge is shared, mutual problems aired and moral support provided. Thus, for example, a Global Elections Organization ('GEO') provides an international forum for electoral practitioners, including election management bodies;[19] the Inter-Parliamentary Union convenes conferences of Speakers of Parliaments, inter alia;[20] and an International Coordinating Committee ('ICC') is an umbrella body for national human rights institutions, which also assists in protecting their status and functions, consistently with the internationally approved Paris Principles of 1993.[21] Other influences flow through less institutionalised channels: the ready availability of information about comparative practice; the international networks and pressure groups of civil society and the community at large; the conditionality of foreign assistance; and diplomatic and other forms of persuasion from neighbours, allies and critics.

Transnational influences on constitutional decision-makers have been studied most closely in relation to courts. In 2003, Anne-Marie Slaughter

---

[16] The relevant ICCPR body is the Human Rights Committee, which receives complaints pursuant to the First Optional Protocol, to which 115 states are now party (out of 168 parties to the ICCPR).

[17] P. Lamy, 'The Place of the WTO and its Law in the International Legal Order' (2006) 17 *European Journal of International Law* 969.

[18] A. Peters, 'The Globalization of State Constitutions' in J. Nijman and A. Nollkaemper (eds.), *New Perspectives on the Divide between National and International Law* (Oxford University Press, 2007), 251, 257.

[19] The sixth meeting of the GEO took place in Seoul in 2013: http://aceproject.org/today/special-events/GEO2013.

[20] The third conference took place in 2010: www.ipu.org/splz-e/speakers10.htm.

[21] The ICC is hosted by the Office of the United Nations High Commissioner for Human Rights: http://nhri.ohchr.org/EN/Pages/default.aspx.

drew attention to the degree of international interaction, both real and virtual, between members of the senior judiciary, presaging, in her view, the gradual emergence of a 'global community of courts', aware of their involvement in a common endeavour.[22] Part of the evidence on which she drew included the willingness of judges of many courts with a constitutional jurisdiction to refer to international and comparative legal experience in coming to their own decisions. This phenomenon subsequently attracted considerable attention, in the wake of the controversy over references to external sources of law by the Supreme Court of the United States.[23] It is a common practice in constitutional adjudication in a wide range of states and occurs, without express acknowledgement, in many others. In some courts, of which the Constitutional Courts of South Africa and South Korea are examples, it is systematised, through the provision of researchers with knowledge of other constitutional systems. It facilitates the transfer of ideas between bodies of constitutional jurisprudence in a process that tends to extend the influence of a small handful of prestigious courts, including the Constitutional Court of Germany and the Supreme Court of the United States. In this as in other contexts in which global forces impact on the operations of national constitutions, however, it is important not to overestimate their effect.

The significance of the state

Notwithstanding the realities of globalisation, most constitutions are the primary source of authority for the continuing exercise of public power within a state, by reference to the circumstances of the state. Political leaders, chosen through the mechanisms provided by the constitution, appeal to citizens for support by reference to issues that typically are framed as local concerns, whatever their actual provenance may be. At least in a relatively well-ordered state, the principal affiliation of voters is likely to be to the state of which they are part and in which they form a critical part of the accountability chain; and in less effective states, affiliations are likely to be sub-national, to region or tribe, rather than supranational. The primary interest of citizens is in services that are best

[22] A.-M. Slaughter, 'A Global Community of Courts' (2003) 44 *Harvard International Law Journal* 191.

[23] C. Saunders, 'Judicial Engagement with Comparative Law' in T. Ginsburg and R. Dixon (eds), *Comparative Constitutional Law* (Cheltenham: Edward Elgar, 2011), 571.

delivered by state or sub-state authorities, including health, education, housing, planning and personal security.

Contests over the meaning and effect of the constitution take place almost exclusively within the confines of the state. The outcome of elections is determined by state institutions and the resulting transfer of power is a local concern in relation to which international approval is only indistinctly relevant. The usual constitutional flashpoints, including inroads on rights, executive overreach, erosion of judicial independence and central encroachment on sub-national authority, typically are avoided or resolved through state institutions, by reference to the national constitution. The values in play may be widely accepted across the globe but are glossed by local understandings, practice and needs. Even constitutional failure as evidenced by, for example, unconstitutional abrogation, is likely to be regarded primarily as a local affair, as recent experiences in Fiji, Egypt and Thailand show.

National actors may be globally connected but their responsibility is to the state and its people, acting consistently with the constitution. The example of constitutional courts again serves to show how this works. Most judges with a role in constitutional interpretation are likely to be familiar with aspects of the constitutional jurisprudence of at least some other states. Many draw on it, whether expressly or not, in resolving questions before them. Whether this is controversial or not depends on local constitutional politics and culture. In any event, no constitutional judges regard comparative experience as authoritative; local sources, including, of course, those that apply international law, remain the primary touchstone for determining constitutional meaning and effect. And at least some references to comparative law do not finally apply it but distinguish it on the basis of local constitutional difference.

Generalisation notoriously is rash in comparative constitutional law. There are several categories of states in relation to which the claims in this part need qualification. One category, to which reference has been made already, is weak states: states that, for whatever reason, are unable effectively to serve their people and to attract their allegiance. In such states, constitutions are unlikely to be operative and transnational forces may be more influential, although still not a substitute for an effective state. A second comprises states in deeply integrated regional arrangements of which Europe is the primary example. Effective regional integration inevitably causes a different, more complex mix of national and transnational influences on the exercise of public power. It is no coincidence that most of the recent literature on constitutional pluralism and the internationalisation of constitutional law has emanated from Europe or from reflection on European conditions.[24] Even in these still relatively unusual circumstances, however, the continuing constitutional significance of the state is apparent. The application by the European Court of Human Rights of a principle of subsidiarity and a margin of appreciation encourages states to accept the decisions of a court over which they otherwise have limited institutional control. Judicial decisions have fostered a useful ambiguity about whether national or European courts have the final word in the event of conflict between national constitutions and European law.[25] This ambiguity extends to the rationale for the effect of EU law which, on at least one widely held view, depends on the authority constitutionally conferred by a member state rather than the logic of the treaties alone.[26]

Reflections

As in relation to constitutional design, the operation of constitutions is centred in the state but is affected in various ways by the forces of globalisation. Similarly also, however, the impact of globalisation varies between states and fluctuates over time. While the pace of globalisation suggests that its impact might be progressive, however patchy and gradual, this is not necessarily the case. As the example of the United Kingdom shows, the state occasionally reasserts itself, resisting deeper international engagement in favour of more local control, responsive to what are perceived as local norms.

Scholars differ over the implications of what sometimes is described as the internationalisation of constitutional law. For some, it involves a qualitative change in the nature and status of constitutions, including the emergence of a new hierarchical relationship with international law.[27] This line of thought is also likely to assume increasing universalism

---

[24] For a representative collection, see M. Avbelj and J. Komárek, *Constitutional Pluralism in the European Union and Beyond* (Oxford: Hart Publishing, 2012).

[25] For example, *Solange II (Re the Application of Wünsche Handelsgesellschaft)* [1987] 3 CMLR 225, 265 (*Bundesverfassungsgericht*); *Bosphorus v. Ireland* (2006) 42 EHRR 1.

[26] P. Craig and G. de Búrca, *EU Law: Text, Cases and Materials* (Oxford: Oxford University Press, 2011), 5th edn., ch. 9.

[27] A. Follesdal, 'The Principle of Subsidiarity as a Constitutional Principle in international law' (2013) 2 *Global Constitutionalism* 37, 62.

in norms of a constitutional kind, to anticipate the possible relevance of international approval of constitutions and to explore options for the constitutionalisation of international law and institutions. The still nascent proposal for the establishment of an International Constitutional Court, which was put to the General Assembly of the United Nations by the President of Tunisia in 2013, builds on this set of assumptions.[28]

For others, the state remains the primary focus of constitutions and constitutional law. Scholars in this vein acknowledge the increasing impact on constitutions of supra-national and international law, but are more likely to trace its roots to an exercise of state authority, consistently with state constitutions. They may assume the need for enhanced legitimacy of the international sphere, but are sceptical that it can be achieved through constitutionalisation in any familiar form, and emphasise, as an alternative, reliance on constitutional states as the building blocks of an international constitutional order. They are more likely to recognise significant diversity between constitutional systems and to assume that this will continue, albeit with variations in the patterns of similarity and difference over time.

While neither view is fully persuasive and the future genuinely is uncertain, the latter is closer to the realities of lived global experience in the second decade of the twenty-first century. If this is correct, however, it suggests a role for national constitutions that they are not necessarily equipped to meet. One of the consequences of the growing constitutional significance of international law has been the greatly enhanced authority of the executive branch, to which international relations generally falls. A challenge for the immediate future is to provide a more accountable constitutional framework for domestic decisions in relation to the international sphere without jeopardising the benefits that global engagement can bring.

Conclusion

This is a time of change for constitutions, affecting not only their design and operation in practice but raising the possibility of more profound

[28] President of the Republic of Tunisia, 'Project of the Establishment of an International Constitutional Court', 2013, 1–22.

consequences for their character and status over the longer term. Whatever the outcome, the interpenetration of constitutional and international law has implications for both. Constitutional law now demands an appreciation of international and relevant regional law, further complicating the task of constitutional comparison. Conversely, international law requires some understanding of constitutional principles and processes both to evaluate their relevance for international institutions and to minimise harm to the constitutional systems on which the international sphere relies.

Amongst the range of current challenges for the design and operation of constitutions, three merit particular reference by way of conclusion. The first concerns the relevance of international approval of national constitutions. Some of the more extreme claims for international approval can presently be dismissed as fanciful. Nevertheless, international involvement in the design of new constitutions is sufficiently widespread in practice to raise questions whether, on the one hand, the source of legitimacy for constitutions should be revisited or whether, on the other, international involvement should be better managed in some way. A second challenge concerns the state of constitutional theory in an age of rapid and sometimes indiscriminate migration of constitutional text, institutions, principles and processes. Do underlying theories migrate too and, if so, are they persuasive in new conditions? Are they supplemented or even supplanted by new theories, drawing on the history and contemporary conditions of the recipient state? Or do new, largely derivative constitutions provide a light textual framework, lacking theoretical depth? The answers to these questions are likely to vary, between constitutional systems and problem areas, but the issue is worth more attention than it has yet received. A third and final challenge is to ensure that the constitutional principles and practices that constrain state institutions operating within a state are adapted to apply to the same institutions when making decisions in relation to the international sphere. While some steps towards this end have been taken in particular constitutional systems, more comprehensive and deliberate action becomes more pressing as globalisation proceeds.

Further reading

L. Alexander (ed.), *Constitutionalism: Philosophical Foundations* (Oxford: Oxford University Press, 1998)

G. Frankenburg, 'Comparing Constitutions: Ideas, Ideals, and Ideology – Towards a Layered Narrative' (2006) 4 *International Journal of Constitutional Law* 439

B. Goderis and M. Versteeg, 'Transnational Constitutionalism' in D. Galligan and M. Versteeg (eds.), *Social and Political Foundations of Constitutions* (Cambridge: Cambridge University Press, 2013)

D. Grimm, 'The Achievement of Constitutionalism and its Prospects in a Changed World' in P. Dobner and M. Loughlin (eds.), *The Twilight of Written Constitutionalism* (Oxford: Oxford University Press, 2010)

C. Hahm, 'Conceptualising Korean Constitutionalism: Foreign Transplant or Indigenous Tradition' (2001) 1 *Journal of Korean Law* 151

J. Kokott, 'From Reception and Transplantation to Convergence of Constitutional Models in the Age of Globalization, with Special Reference to the German Basic Law' in C. Starke (ed.), *Constitutionalism, Universalism and Democracy: A Comparative Analysis* (Baden-Baden: Nomos Verlagsgesellschaft, 1999)

Sir John Laws, *The Common Law Constitution* (Cambridge University Press 2014)

M. Loughlin and N. Walker (eds), *The Paradox of Constitutionalism* (Oxford: Oxford University Press, 2007)

G. Neuman, 'Human Rights and Constitutional Rights: Harmony and Dissonance' (2003) 55 *Stanford Law Review* 1863

A. Peters, 'The Globalization of State Constitutions' in J. Nijman and A. Nollkaemper (eds.), *New Perspectives on the Divide between National and International Law* (Oxford: Oxford University Press, 2007), 251

C. Saunders, 'The Impact of Internationalisation on National Constitutions' in A. H. Y. Chen (ed.), *Constitutionalism in Asia in the Early 21st Century* (Cambridge: Cambridge University Press, 2014), 391

J. Yeh and W. Chang, 'The Emergence of Transnational Constitutionalism: Its Features, Challenges and Solutions' (2008) 27 *Penn State International Law Review* 89

Index

accountability, politics of, 13, 96–114
  accountability and British political
      tradition, 97–100
  accountability explosion, 108–112
  effectiveness of political accountability in
      Britain, 103–105
  elections, 103, 104
  forms of accountability, 13
  meaning/nature of accountability', 96–97
  ministerial accountability, 110–112
  other accountability mechanisms,
      104–105, 113–114
  Parliament, 105–108
  politics and law, 100–103
  two paradoxes, 112–114
    diffused accountability, loss of direct
        political accountability from, 113–114
    more accountability not always better
        government, 112–113
Adamson v. *Paddico (267) Ltd*, 143
African Charter on Democracy, Elections
      and Governance of the African
      Union, 261
Allan, Trevor
  state's authority founded on enforceable
      moral principles, 22
American Commonwealth, The (Bryce), 196
Animal Defenders, 161
Anns v Merton, 147
appointments, public, 108, 112
  vetting of major appointments by select
      committees, 108
Aristotle, 71
Aronson, Mark, 7
Attorney General v. *Jonathan Cape Ltd*, 25,
      32–34
Audit Commission, 222
Austin, John, 20
Australia
  Constitution, 73
  courts giving effect to constitution, 28
  exemplary damages, 148
  justiciability of constitution, 21

reshaping state powers, 7–8
separation of powers, 25
state and Crown, 9
AXA, 156

Bagehot, Walter, 11
  sovereign power as come-at-able, 98, 103
Bank of England, 109
Barro, Robert, 61, 62, 66
Behre, 241–243, 247, 248
Belmarsh, 130, 146
Bentham, Jeremy, 20
Bill of Rights, 49
Bill of Rights/Claim of Right (1689), 49, 116
Bingham, Tom, 66, 102
Blair, Tony, 8
  Prime Minister's question time, 105
Blunkett, David, 39
Bogdanor, Vernon, 8
Bondy, Varda, 250
Bracton, 44
Bradlaugh v. *Gossett*, 45
British Oxygen, 219
Bryce, James, 8, 206–207, 208, 211–214
  centrifugal and centripetal forces,
      199–200, 208
    Janus-faced nature of, 200–202
  constitutional law, role of, 202–205
  EU, and, 206
  Irish Home Rule, and, 196–199
Burgess, Michael, 197
Bush, George, 7
Bush, George W, 7

Caerphilly, 243–245, 247, 248
Cameron, David, 113
Canada
  Charter of Rights and Freedoms, 260
  constitution, 73
  constitutional references, 12, 25
  courts giving effect to constitution, 28
  exemplary damages, 148

Cart, 158–159
Center for Financial Stability, 60, 61
centrifugal and centripetal forces, 199–200
   Janus-faced nature of, 200–202
Cerar, Miro, 42
Charter of Fundamental Rights, EU, 232
Chaytor, 45
citizens as consumers of public goods, 3
Civil Service, 227
   Civil Service Code, 109
   parliamentary scrutiny, 112
Civil Service Commission, 109
Commission on a Bill of Rights, 210
Commissioner for Public Appointments, 108
Committee on Standards in Public Life,
   110, 227
common law constitutional rights, 78–80
Competition and Markets Authority, 231
Conservative-Liberal Democrat coalition, 3
constitutional law, role of, 202–205
constitutionalism, 70
   legal, 100
   political, 100
constitutions
   constitutional norms, 81
   exceptionalism of unwritten
      constitutions, 86–90
   global context, in. *See* designing and
      operating constitutions in global
      context
   hard and soft constitutionality, 80–82
   multidimensional. *See* legislative
      supremacy in a multidimensional
      constitution
contested nature and functions of public law,
   5–15
   government and the state, 5–9
   identity and worth of public law,
      14–15
   legitimacy of institutions, 12–13
   relationships between state institutions
      and officials, 11–12
   state and public law in world order, 9–10
context in which public law develops and
   operates, 1–5
contracting out. *See under* privatisation and
   public law
conventions, constitutional, 81–82
Countryside Alliance, 160
courts. *See* judiciary
Craig, Paul, 14–15
Creyke, R, 251, 253

Crossman, Richard, 11
   Crossman Diaries affair, 27, 32–34
Crown
   nature of, 8–9
   prerogatives, 9

Daintith, Terence, 238
Datafin, 185
Davies, A.C.L., 7
De Smith's Judicial Review, 237
deference. *See* judiciary
demographic changes in UK, 3
designing and operating constitutions in
      global context, 10, 256–273
   designing constitutions, 258–265
      impact of globalisation, 259–261
      reflections, 263–265
      scope of constitutional design, 258–259
      significance of the state, 261–263
   development of constitutions, 256–257
   operating constitutions, 265–272
      from design to operation in practice,
         265–266
      impact of globalisation, 266–269
      reflections, 271–272
      significance of the state, 269–271
   transnational influences on developing
      constitutions, 257–258
devolution, 2, 8
   'concordatry', 227–228
   convention of no UK interference in
      devolved affairs (Sewel Convention),
      84–85, 155
   ECHR, and, 117, 155, 210
   establishment of devolved governments,
      198
   European effect on, 206–210
   hard constitutional constraints, subject to,
      and, 83
   legislation making Scottish government
      'permanent' not a hard constraint, 83
   litigation over extent of devolved
      legislatures' powers, 11–12
   Memorandums of Understanding, 157,
      228
   Northern Ireland, 195
   Scotland, 155–156
      further powers promised, 198–199
   structure of, 155
   troubled state of the union, 227–228
   UK Parliament, implications for, 77–78
   Wales, 156–157

Devon County Council, exp RB, 180
Dicey, AV, 8, 62, 196
    convention and law, distinction
        between, 82
    English/Scottish union, 208
    equality ideal, 135
    historical teleology, 212
    Irish Home Rule, and, 196–199
    political constraints on legislative
        powers, 74
    punishment only by ordinary courts, 64
    rule of law, definition of, 135
    sovereignty of Parliament, 199, 209
    study of constitutional law, 20–21
discretion, 49, 57, 58, 64, 65
    agency, 221
    judicial. *See under* judiciary
    monarch's, 81
    officials'. *See under* state
distinctiveness of public law, 12, 14, 17–36
    commonality of values, 35
    fiscus, 25–26
    holding ministers to account through the
        courts, 22–23
    illustration of distinctions in practice,
        32–34
    judical review, development of, 30–31
    law and non-law in governmental
        matters, 20–25
    legal positivism, 20–22
    nature of public law, 18–19
    nature of the problem, 17–20
    public and private law, distinguishing, 14
    public and private parties, 19–20
    public bodies, different requirements
        applying to, justifiction for, 34
    public law and non-public law, 17–18,
        25–32
    public law and public non-law, 23–25
    special powers historically reserved to
        rules, 25–26
Donoughmore Committee on Ministers'
    Powers, 218
Dorset Yacht, 147
Dworkin, R, 168

Eba, 158
elections, 102
    bedrock of political accountability,
        as, 103
    decisive instruments of accountability,
        as, 103

decline in electoral participation, 104
    episodic nature of, 104
    party funding, 108
Electoral Commission, 108
    referendums, 109
Elliott, Donald, 251
Elliott, Mark, 10, 12
English Constitution, The (Bagehot), 98
English nationalism, 208
Equality and Human Rights Commission,
    123, 226
    review of Human Rights Act 1998, 129
ESRC study on impact of judicial review,
    241–248
European Central Bank, 232–233
European Coal and Steel Community, 207
European Commission, 229, 230, 232
European Convention on Human Rights
    (ECHR), 91, 101, 108, 117
    Article 8 (right to family life), 37–42, 127,
        184, 243
    preamble, 117
    rights under ECHR as hard legal
        constraints on states, 89
European Court of Human Rights (ECtHR)
    constitutive view of public law,
        promoting, 45
    margin of appreciation, 271
    nationalism, approach to, 51
    over-reaching by, 102
    subsidiarity principle, 271
European Parliament, 230, 233
European Union (EU)
    'Banking Union', 232
    devolution, effect on, 206–210
    EU law and political attacks on
        judiciary, 37
    EU law on domestic law, impact on, 4
    European citizenship, 209
    European Competition Network, 231–232
    'ever closer union', opposition to,
        207–208
    integration, 220
    James Bryce, and, 206
    juridical nature of, 44
    Member States as subject to EU law, 9
    national freedom of decision-making
        constrained, 10
    Open Method of Coordination, 230–231
    soft law, EU governance by, 228–233
    sovereignty, concept of, 209–210
    states' liability to private parties, 32

European Union (EU) (cont.)
  supremacy principle, 75, 100
    sovereignty and, 82, 85
  UK joining, 7, 10
  White Paper on European Governance, 229
Ewing, KD, 119

Factortame, 75, 82
Feldman, David, 12, 14
financial crisis
  Eurozone countries, 10
  impact of, 1–2
fiscus, 25–26
Flinders, M, 112
Foot, Michael, 99
France, 50, 194
  accession to European Charter for Regional or Minority Languages struck down, 52
  constitution, 256
  Crown and state, 9
  Declaration of the Rights of Man and the Citizen (1789), 116
  public law and non-public law, 28–29
  public law and private law, 27–28
  public law separate from ordinary courts, 47
  public law, broad view of, 50
  semi-presidentialism, 260
Freedland, M, 183
freedom of information. *See under* information and transparency
Fuller, Lon, 58, 61
  'inner morality of law', 57, 62
  legal methods not appropriate for all public administration, 63
  procedural aspects, 63
  'functionalist' public law theory, 165–170

Gaebler, T, 189
GCHQ, 223
Germany, 194
  Basic Law, 44
  Constitutional Court, 260, 269
  'soft power', 10
Global Elections Organization, 268
globalisation. *See* designing and operating constitutions in global context
  designing constitutions, and, 259–261
Goldsmith, Lord, 238

government
  central/local government in UK, substantial changes in, 2
  collective Cabinet responsibility, 33
  contracting out. *See under* privatisation and public law
  courts, conflict with, 45–46
  diferent legal requirements upon, public interest justifying, 34
  financial accounting, 25–26
  higher standards applying to, 143–148, 151–152
  holding ministers to account through the courts, 22–23
  judicial review, and. *See* judicial review
  law and non-law in governmental matters, 20–25
  misfeasance in public office, 148
  morality of government and of law, 13
  Parliament, and, 11
  privatisation. *See* privatisation and public law
  restructuring the state, 6–8
  role and functions of, 3
  routine official decision-making and judicial review, 239–241
  social justice imposed through government contracts, 19
  state, and, 5–9
  subject to legal norms, 13
Griffith, Professor John, 21

Hailsham, Lord, 11, 98, 99, 119
Harlow, C, 145
Hart, HLA, 43
Hayek, FA, 66, 167
Heath, Edward, 7, 8, 11
Hillingdon, 244
House of Commons Select Committees system strengthened, 2
Howarth, David, 12, 13, 14
human rights
  courts' absorption of human rights thinking, 53
  ECHR rights, 76–77
  Human Rights Act 1998. *See* Human Rights Act 1998
  legislation, 4
  positive rights, concept of, 48
  public sector equality duty, 32
  role of judiciary. *See under* judiciary

Human Rights Act 1998 (HRA), 76, 91, 101, 108, 110, 210
    constitutional significance of, ambiguity about, 123
    controversial nature of, 117–118
    Convention-compatible interpretation, requirement for, 124
    cultural change, effecting, 132, 146
    declarations of incompatibility, 126, 129, 130
        ignored on prisoner votes, 131
    greater judicial assertiveness, trend towards, 126–127
    impact of, 128–132
    introduction of, 117
    judiciary, role of, 122–123
    objections to constitutionalisation of rights, 122
    political disenchantment with, 131–132
    privatisation/contracting out. *See* privatisation and public law
    proportionality in Convention rights adjudication, 13
    proportionality test, application of, 124–127
    public law adjudication under, 124–128
    'publicness' and 'privateness', indicators of, 31–32

identity in public law, 51–52
Independent Parliamentary Standards Authority, 109
India
    courts giving effect to constitution, 28
    public law preventing amendments to constitution, 6
information and transparency, 108, 110, 226
    freedom of information, 2, 32, 108, 111, 112
Institute for Public Policy Research, 208
institutional expertise, 158–160
institutions. *See* state institutions
Intelligence and Security Committee, 109
interest rate policy transferred to Bank of England, 109
International Coordinating Committee, 268
International Covenant on Civil and Political Rights, 267
International Monetary Fund, 10
Inter-Parliamentary Union, 268
Introduction to the Study of the Law of the Constitution (Dicey), 20, 196
Irish Home Rule, 196–199

Jackson, 80, 92
James VI of Scotland and I of England, 8
Jennings, Sir Ivor, 119
Joint Committee on Human Rights, 123, 130, 131
Jones, 159–160
Judge Over Your Shoulder, The, 101, 238
judicial review, 236–254
    civil service view of, 45–46
    courts holding ministers to account, 22–23
    declarations, 30
    declaratory relief, and, 9
    deference. *See under* judiciary
    development of, 30–31
    ESRC study on impact on local government services, 241–248
    expansion of, 101
    interests of individuals and political sovereignty of state, tensions between, 26–27
    judges' perception of, 45
    legitimate expectation, 223
    quality of local government services, and, 241–245
    remedies, historical development of, 29–30
    routine official decision-making, and, 239–241
    rule of law supporting, 70
    rules, effectiveness of, 15
    variable intensity of review, 22
    what do claimants achieve, 248–253
        individual redress and public interest claims, 248–249
        procedural weaknesses, 250
        risk of Pyrrhic victories, 251–253
judiciary, 37
    activist judges, 70
    deference, 22, 42, 46
        challenging, 101
        human rights adjudication, 125, 126
    discretion, 138, 140–141, 142, 152
    domestic law as starting point for public law protections, 127–128
    ECtHR, and, 127
    functional considerations driving judicial decisions, 164–165
    human rights adjudication, role in, 122–123
    independence of, 259
    institutional expertise, respect for, 158–160
    international interaction between senior judiciary, 269

judiciary (cont.)
  judicial activism, 101
  Judicial Appointments Commission, role
    of, 109
  liberty, weaknesses in role of policing
    interference with, 120
  over-reaching by, 102
  parliamentary sovereignty, 84
  parliamentary sovereignty and
    fundamental rights, 92–93
  political attacks on, 37
  political bias, accusations of, 120
  political pressure, susceptibility to, 41–42
  proportionality test. *See* proportionality
  public law adjudication and Human
    Rights Act, 124–128
  resisting changes to law-making
    procedure, 37–42
  role of, 70, 100
justiciability
  meaning of, 22
  non-justiciability, 42

Kavanagh, A, 125
Kilbrandon Commission, 198
King, Anthony, 113
King, Jeff, 47, 240

Laski, HJ, 168
law and politics, 100–103
Laws, Sir John, 13, 35, 36
  state's authority founded on enforceable
    moral principles, 22
lawyers, public, 59
  centripetal forces, increasing, 12
  law as autonomous, 14
  politicians, and, 37
  public law and non-public law issues,
    advising on, 17–18
  public law and public non-law,
    24–25
  role of, 12, 13
  study of constitutional law,
    20–21
legal certainty, 58
  rule of law, and, 68
legal constitutionalism, 74
legal positivism, 20–22
  challenges to positivist approach to
    constitutional law, 21–22
  law as a normative system of a state, 20
legislation, role of, 65–66

legislative supremacy in a multidimensional
    constitution, 10, 90–94
  contemporary 'challenges' to legislative
    supremacy, 74–80
  common law constraints on legislative
    supremacy, 78–80
  devolution, 77–78
  implications of UK membership of EU,
    75–76
  status of ECHR rights in UK legal order,
    76–77
  hard and soft constitutionality, 80–82
  legislative-supremacy model and
    possibility of domestic-legal
    constraints, 90–94
  multidimensionality and exceptionalism
    of unwritten constitution, 86–90
liberty, 117
  liberty of subject, courts defending, 23
  loss of faith in efficacy of traditional
    approach, 121
  Parliament protecting/expanding, 119
  Parliamentary assault on, 130
  presumption in favour of, 119, 120
  traditional focus on, 118–119
  vulnerable to erosion, 119
local government
  decision-making, challenges to, 49
  ESRC study on impact of judicial review,
    241–248
  local government services, quality of,
    241–245
  substantial changes in, 2
Loewenstein, K, 265
Lord Chancellor, 4
Loughlin, Martin, 14
  'functionalist' public law theory, 165–170
  public law as one of three 'orders' of
    political conflict, 21–22
Loveland, ID, 240
Lumba, 142–143, 144, 148

Macmillan, Harold, 7, 8
Magna Carta (1215), 116
Major, John, 110
Malone, 120
Marbury v. *Madison* (1803), 21
margin of appreciation, 127, 271
market regulation, 2
May, Theresa, 37–42, 53
McCrudden, Christopher, 8, 12
McHarg, Aileen, 7, 13

McMillan, J, 251, 253
Memorandums of Understanding, 223
    devolution, and. *See under* devolution
migration, 3
Ministerial Code, 226
misfeasance in public office, 148
morality, 68
Morality of Law, The (Fuller), 62

Nash, 180
National Audit Office, 107
National Federation, 223
national security, 126
New London College, 225
New Public Management, 2, 220, 222
New Zealand
    constitution, 73, 256
    exemplary damages, 148
Next Steps agencies, 220
Nicklinson, 126, 127
Northern Ireland
    Belfast/Good Friday Agreement, 209–210,
        212
    devolution. *See under* devolution
    political changes, 197
    'Troubles', 198
Nozick, Robert, 5, 167

O'Reilly v. *Mackman*, 137
Office for Budget Responsibility, 109
officers/officials of state. *See* Civil Service;
        see under state
Oliver, Dawn, 35, 175
ombudsmen, 99, 103, 105, 145, 227
    introduction of, 98–99
    proliferation of ombudsmen-type redress
        schemes, 109
Osborne, D, 189

Page, Alan, 238
Paine, Thomas, 116
Paris Principles (1993), 268
Parliament
    accountability, 105–108
        ministerial, 110–112, 221
        new powers of Commons, 108–109
        partisan character of scrutiny,
            105–106
        scrutiny role, 2
    autonomy, 4
    Bill of Rights, and, 49
    changes to, 4

Commons' ordinances, 39
devolution, and. *See* devolution
external scrutiny, 4
fixed-term parliaments, 109
government, and, 11
House of Lords Appointments
    Commission, role of, 109
Joint Committee on Parliamentary
    Privilege, 45
legislative supremacy. *See* legislative
    supremacy in a multidimensional
    constitution
MPs conduct and remuneration, control
    of, 109
Parliament Acts 1911–49, 119
parliamentary privilege, struggle between
    Commons and courts over nature
    of, 45
Queen in Parliament, 4
recall of MPs, 112
responsibility to the people, 98
select committees. *See* select committees
sovereignty. *See* sovereignty,
    parliamentary
supremacy of, 37, 81, 84, 87, 100
Parliamentary Commission on Banking
    Standards, 107
Parliamentary Commissioner for
    Standards, 109
Partnerships in Care, 185
party competition, 48–49, 103
    failure of a party to win a majority,
        consequences of, 104
    support for political parties
        eroded, 104
party whip, 49
Petition of Right (1628), 116
petitions of right, 9
Phillips, Lord, 93
Plaid Cymru, 197
police, 109
    duty of care, 147
political constitutionalism, 74
political parties. *See* party competition
politicians
    Convention-compliant legislation, role
        in, 123
    decline in trust in, 3
    HRA, and, 131
    improper behaviour, 3, 4, 107
    lawyers, and, 37
politics and law, 100–103

politics of public law, 12, 13, 37–54
  descriptive politics of public law, 52–53
  integrating law and politics, 42–43
  law and public law, *Izuazu* example,
    37–42
  normative politics of public law, 53–54
  political dimensions, 46–52
    conflict over resources, 46–48
    identity, 51–52
    ideological struggle, 49–51
    party competition, 48–49
  politics, autonomous or constituted by
    law, 43–46
Poplar Housing, 186
positivism. *See* legal positivism
prerogative powers, 9
  government, and, 11
  judical review, and, 223
  Parliament encroaching on, 112
Prime Minister
  accountability, 109, 111
    question time, 105
  Cabinet, and, 11
  growth of powers of, 11
  judge of ministerial behaviour, as, 226
privatisation and public law, 7, 149–151,
    172–192, 221
  arguments for privatisation, 175
  commissioning state, 188–192
    impact of contracting out on
      government, 189–191
    impact of privatisation on government,
      188–189
  constitutional framework, 178
  contracting out, 176–177, 178–179
    defined, 173–174
    impact on government, 189–191
    review of contractor's decisions,
      184–187
    review of public body's decisions,
      183–184
  criticisms of privatisation, 175
  internal markets, compared to, 174
  merging public and private law, 19
  opposition to privatisation, reasons for,
    149–151
  private sector and privatisation, 2
  privatisation defined, 173–175
  procedural protections for contractors,
    181–182
  public law control during life of contract,
    183–188

  review of contractor's decisions,
    184–187
  review of public body's decisions,
    183–184
  public law control over privatisation and
    contracting out, 177–182
    possible challenges, 179–181
  public procurement, compared to, 174
  public/private divide, privatisation/
    contracting out, and, 175–177
procedural exclusivity. *See under* public law
  values in the common law
Prolife Alliance, 126
proportionality, 124–127, 160–161, 259
  comparative importance of right in scale
    of rights protected, 160
  deference, scope for, 161
  HRA, under, 13, 127
  Parliament's judgment, weight to be
    accorded to, 161
Prosser, Tony, 249
Public Accounts Committee, 107, 112,
public law
  autonomist conception of, 43–44
  changes in, 4–5
  constitutive conception of, 43–45
  contested nature and functions of. *See*
    contested nature and functions of
    public law
  context in which develops and operates,
    1–5
  dimensions of, 5
  distinctiveness of public law. *See*
    distinctiveness of public law
  identity and worth of, 5–15
  identity in, 51–52
  law and public law, *Izuazu* example,
    37–42
  litigation. *See* public law litigation,
    impact of
  nature of, 18–19
  non-public law, and, 25–32
  politics of. *See* politics of public law
  privatisation, and. *See* privatisation and
    public law
  public laws, and. *See* public law and public
    laws
  public non-law, and, 23–25
  rights and democracy in. *See* rights and
    democracy in UK public law
  rule of law. *See* rule of law in public law
  stability in, 66–69

state and public law in world order, 9–10
values in the common law. *See* public law
    values in the common law
public law and public laws, 14–15, 153–170
    different constitutional rules, 154–157
    different subject matter rules, 153–154
    differential application of public law
        doctrine, 157–165
        constitutional framework, 178–179
        functional considerations and doctrinal
            categories, 163–165
        functionalism and reductionism, 158
        importance of right/interest, 160–162
        institutional expertise, 158–160
        systemic functional differentiation, 163
    distinctive public law theory, 165–170
public law litigation, impact of, 15, 236–254
    judgments do not tell whole story,
        245–248
    judicial review and quality of local
        government services, 241–245
    judicial review, routine official decision-
        making and, 239–241
    what do claimants achieve, 248–253
        individual redress and public interest
            claims, 248–249
        procedural weaknesses, 250
        risk of Pyrrhic victories, 251–253
public law values in the common law, 7,
        134–152, *See also* public law
        litigation, impact of
    claims for a morally distinctive public law,
        143–148
    collateral challenge, 137, 140, 142
    diffusion of procedural exclusivity,
        142–143
    expansion of judicial review, 101,
        138–140
    government, higher standards applying
        to, 143–148, 151–152
    importance of interests outside HRA,
        161–162
    judiciary resisting changs to law-making
        procedure, 37–42
    'normative turn', development of,
        139–140, 146–147
    privatisation/contracting out. *See*
        privatisation and public law
    proportionality. *See* proportionality
public law and public non-law, courts role
        in, 23–25
public/private divide, 175–176

remedies, historical development of,
        29–30, 136–138
soft law, 223
strategic case for moral distinctiveness,
        149–151
values underlying procedural exclusivity,
        136–142
public opinion, politicians following, 3
public procurement, 181–182
    privatisation, compared to, 174
public sector equality duty, 32, 180–181
Public Sector Transparency Board, 108

Rawlings, Richard, 14, 145
Rawls, J, 168, 169
Raz, J, 168
referendums, 109
    Scotland. *See under* Scotland
Renton, Sir David, 99
resources, public, 46–48
Richardson, G, 240
rights and democracy in UK public law, 7,
        116–133, *See also* Human Rights Act
        1998
    declarations of individual rights and
        freedoms, 116–117
    impact of Human Rights Act 1998,
        128–132
    international/regional declarations of
        rights, proliferation of, 116–117
    liberty. *See* liberty
    public law adjudication and Human
        Rights Act, 124–128
    UK's traditional approach to rights
        protection/bill of rights debate,
        118–123
risk regulation, 224–225
Roth, 161
Rousseau, Jean Jacques, 116
rule of law in public law, 6, 56–72, 100, 259
    change, and, 67–69
    constructing a conception, 71–72
    contested concept, rule of law as, 58
    declaratory relief, 9
    democracy, and, 66
    essentially private law idea, rule of law as,
        58–59
    fresh start, 62–65
    ideological manipulation of rule of law
        ideal, as, 62
    judicial procedures, importance of, 62–63
    legal certainty, 58, 68

rule of law in public law (cont.)
  legislation, role of, 65–66
  measuring rule of law in ways hostile to
    regulation, 60–62
  morality, and, 68
  nature of rule of law, 57
  no more than rule by law, 69–71
  parliamentary privilege as exception to
    rule of law, 45
  predictability, value of, 66–67
  private law, and, 57
  public administration, and, 57–58
  pursuing constitutional grievances
    through ordinary law, 28
  rule of law, nature of, 60
  stability in public law, 66–69
  tribunals, 64
  unified ideal, 58

Salmond, Alex, 203
Saunders, Cheryl, 10
Schindler, 232
Schmitt, Carl, 43
Schuck, Peter, 251
Scotland
  continued membership of EU post-
    independence, 208–209
  devolution. *See under* devolution
  nationalist movement, 197
  referendum on independence, 198–199,
    214
  Supreme Court, and, 203
*Secretary of State for the Home Department
  ex parte Izuazu*, 37–42
*Secretary of State for the Home Department
  v. J*, 130
Security Services, 109, 112
select committees, 99, 103, 221
  election of chairs and members, 108–109
  nature and impact of, 106–107
  reforms creating more accountability,
    107–108
  scrutiny of ministers, 111
  weaknesses in, 107
separation of powers, 5, 22, 25
  no formal separation of powers in UK, 106
  strong version of, 47
Servite, 185
Slaughter, Anne-Marie, 268
social welfare, states' obligation to provide, 2
soft and hard constraints on legislative
  supremacy, 80–82

soft law, 14, 215–234
  bureaucratic rules, 216–218, 219–220
  contract-style techniques, 225
  EU governance, 228–233
  Executive, 226–227
  extended state, 216–220
  'Ofdogs', 221
  quasi-legislation, 218–219
  risk regulation, 224–225
  shake up time, 220–223
  'speeding on', 224–228
  tertiary rules, 222–223
  'Thatcher revolution', 220–222
  voluntarism, 219
'soft power', 10
South Africa
  constitution, 73, 266
  constitutional commissions, 260
  constitutional courts, 28, 269
  public resources, 48
sovereignty, parliamentary, 73, 80–81, 84,
    94–95, 98, 100
  common law rights and values, protection
    of, 90–91
  constraining effect of international law
    on, 85
  devolution not creating inhibition on, 77
  domestic legal constraints, 90–94
  EU membership, effect of, 100
  judiciary, and, 92–93
  multidimensionality and exceptionalism
    of unwritten constitution, 86–90
  principles of interpretation, application of,
    90–91
  Queen in Parliament, 4
  soft constraints on, 82, 84
  unable to be abandoned, 83
state
  architecture. *See* state architecture
  authority founded on enforceable moral
    principles, 22
  federal, 12
  global economy, and, 10
  goals of state action, 6
  government, and, 5–9
  international corporations and
    institutions, and, 10
  legislative supremacy. *See* legislative
    supremacy in a multidimensional
    constitution
  officers of state treated as private
    individuals, 9

officials, discretion of, 57, 58, 63,
    64–65, 217
officials, public law and, 18–19
public interest obligations of, 19
public law and state obligations,
    18–19
restructuring by government, 6–8
role and functions of, 3
rule of law governing conduct of officials,
    57–58
rules as instruments or policy, use by
    officials of, 216–218
rules, problems with mechanical
    application of, 63
shift from 'government' to 'governance' in
    modern state, 110
social justice imposed through
    government contracts, 19
treaties constraining freedom of
    choice, 10
state architecture, 8, 193–214
    Bryce and the EU, 206
    Bryce, Dicey and Irish Home Rule,
        196–199
    centrifugal and centripedal forces,
        199–200
    constitutional law, role of, 202–205
    devolution. *See* devolution
    federal states, 12
    global context. *See* designing and
        operating constitutions in global
        context
    Janus-faced nature of forces,
        200–202
    rise and fall of imperial federalism,
        195–196
    subsidiarity, devolution and federalism,
        211
    unitary state, UK as, 193–194
state institutions
    administrative institutions, 13
    judicial institutions, 13
    legitimacy of, 12–13
    officials, relationships with, 11–12
    political institutions, 12
    responsibilities, public law and, 27
    social institutions, existing as, 52
Statistics Authority, 109
Stockdale v. *Hansard*, 39, 45
Sumption, Lord, 102
Sunkin, Maurice, 15
Supreme Court, 5, 109, 203

Taggart, Michael, 145, 150
terrorism, 5
    foreign terror suspects, 129
    HRA, terrorism cases and, 130
    Northern Ireland, 121
    responding to, 4
Thatcher, Margaret, 2, 7, 8, 11, 121, 149, 154,
    225
Thoburn v. *Sunderland City Council*, 83
transparency. *See* information and
    transparency

Ullah, 127
UNISON, 182
United Kingdom (UK). *See also* English
    nationalism; Northern Ireland;
    Scotland; Wales
    accountability of government. *See*
        accountability, politics of
    colonial charters and constitutions
        limiting legislatures, 21
    constitution, 73, 81, 256
        common law constitutional rights,
            78–80
        constitutional conventions, 81–82
        constitutional norms, 81
        EU membership affecting, 207
        exceptionalism, 74
        multidimensional nature of, 85–86
        uncodified, 215
    constitutive conception of public law, and,
        44–45
    ECHR, and, 117, 121
        withdrawal from, 132
    ECtHR, and, 117
    legislative supremacy. *See* legislative
        supremacy in a multidimensional
        constitution
    Parliament. *See* Parliament
    political constitutionalism, 74
    Prime Minister. *See* Prime Minister
    strong government, attachment to, 97–98
    UK bill of rights, proposal for, 132, 210
United Nations, 257, 261, 262
    International Constitutional Court,
        proposal for, 272
United States, 194
    Bill of Rights (1791), 116
    constitution, 50, 73, 86, 90, 256
    courts giving effect to constitution, 28
    Crown and state, 9
    Declaration of Independence (1776), 116

United States (cont.)
expenditure/activity of federal
institutions restricted, 7
individual rights, 116
Marbury v. *Madison*, 21
public law, narrow view of, 50
'soft power', 10
Supreme Court, 269

Waldron, Jeremy, 6
Wales
devolution. *See under* devolution
nationalist movement, 197
Walker, N, 213
war, civilians displaced by, 3

Weaver, 186
Wednesbury, 124, 147, 175
welfare state
restructuring by Margaret Thatcher, 7
social welfare, states' obligation to
provide, 2
whistleblowers, 108
WM, 161–162
Wolfensohn, James, 60
World Bank, 10, 60
World Trade Organization, 268
Wright, Tony, 13

YL, 183, 186, 187
Young, Hugo, 98

The Charity Thieves

A Novel

by

Robert Cubitt